ARTHUR PENN

INTERVIEWS

CONVERSATIONS WITH FILMMAKERS SERIES
PETER BRUNETTE, GENERAL EDITOR

Courtesy Associated Press

ARTHUR PENN

INTERVIEWS

EDITED BY MICHAEL CHAIKEN
AND PAUL CRONIN

UNIVERSITY PRESS OF MISSISSIPPI / JACKSON

www.upress.state.ms.us

The University Press of Mississippi is a member of the Association of American University Presses.

Library of Congress Cataloging-in-Publication Data

Penn, Arthur, 1922–
   Arthur Penn : interviews / edited by Michael Chaiken and Paul Cronin.
     p. cm. — (Conversations with filmmakers series)
   Includes index.
   ISBN 978-1-60473-104-0 (cloth : alk. paper)—ISBN 978-1-60473-105-7 (pbk. : alk. paper)
   1. Penn, Arthur, 1922–—Interviews. 2. Motion picture producers and directors—United States—Interviews I. Chaiken, Michael. II. Cronin, Paul. III. Title.
   PN1998.3.P4525A3   2008
   791.43023'3092—dc22
   [B]   2008012010

British Library Cataloging-in-Publication Data available

CONTENTS

INTRODUCTION

THE INTERVIEWS in this collection span a forty-five year period in the working life of Arthur Penn, an American film director whose changing fortunes rival those of the greatest characters in one of his own films.

Born in Philadelphia in 1922, Penn grew up through the Depression, spending his childhood divided between the city of his birth and, after his parents' divorce in 1925, New York. The dislocation of Penn's home life, coupled with the stigma of being a child of divorce, would have a profound and lasting effect on his psychological and emotional development. The interviews collected in this book are an attempt to form a chronological portrait of this development, something that reveals as much about Penn the man and his principles as it does about Penn the film director. As evidenced by his numerous digressions into politics and deep concern with the society around him, any serious study of Penn's films also calls for a reflection on the troubled times in which they were made. Moving among comedy, tragedy, realism, and absurdity (often within the same story), his best work can be said to preserve an entire era under glass, while his least noteworthy films—still always interesting—speak more to the state of the industry in which they were produced than to any deficiencies of their director.

Throughout his adolescence Penn lived with his father Harry, a Lithuanian immigrant who worked as a watchmaker, and his brother Irving, five years his senior. Penn admired his father's acumen for business and prodigious talents as an engraver, though he could never quite muster in himself the same dedication to the watchmaker's craft. These early years in Philadelphia coincided with Harry's final illness, the result of which, Penn told Richard Schickel in 1990, was a fragmented relationship. "I never knew much about my father. He was a withdrawn man and I was a withdrawn adolescent. We didn't make enough contact to amount to a hill of beans. I regret that deeply." A developing interest in theater and stagecraft would have him looking to his older brother for direction. Attending the highly regarded Philadelphia Museum School of Industrial Art, Irving would go on to become one of the most important and influential photographers of the twentieth century, making clear to all that the extraordinary visual sensibility possessed by Harry's two sons was a hereditary gift. As a teenager Arthur had similar artistic aspirations but lacked his brother's studious and disciplined nature. It was the bombing of Pearl Harbor during his senior year in high school which ultimately led him away from the sedentary life of a watchmaker.

Penn's enlistment in the army after graduation moved him from New York (where he had returned to live with his mother) to Fort Jackson, South Carolina. Once there he formed a small theater troupe of enlisted men to help pass the time between the long hours of basic training. Spending his days on leave in neighboring Columbia, Penn met director Fred Coe who introduced him to the community theater group he was running. Coe exposed Penn to the stern, practical demands of running a theater troupe, skills which would serve him well in the months ahead.

Stationed in Europe, Penn saw action in the Ardennes and the Battle of the Bulge. When the war ended in Europe he remained in service, expecting to be sent to the Pacific to prepare for the invasion of Japan. Instead Penn remained a citizen soldier in Germany becoming involved with an army entertainment unit, the Soldier Show Company, before being relocated to Paris. It was there that Penn would work with Joshua Logan on the staging of a number of successful plays, notably *Golden Boy*, which toured throughout occupied Europe. With virtually no prior experience Penn had become a theater director of some acclaim, one whose future, if uncertain, seemed filled with promise.

Like so many in the years immediately following the war, Penn took advantage of the benefits of the G.I. Bill when, on his brother's recommendation, he enrolled at Black Mountain College in North Carolina. Black Mountain, a short-lived experiment in communal education, one whose non-hierarchical administrative structure encouraged collaboration among students and faculty, was fertile ground for Penn to develop his skills as a director. By the late 1940s Black Mountain's faculty included some of the most prominent artists and thinkers of mid-century America including Robert Motherwell, Charles Olson, Walter Gropius, and German *émigrés* Josef and Anni Albers. For Penn it was an opportunity to study classical literature and poetry under the mentorship of writer and sculptor Mary Caroline Richards while at the same time, in aleatory fashion, teach drama classes. Drawing on his experiences in the Soldier Show Company, Penn directed a production of Erik Satie's surrealist comedy *The Ruse of Medusa* with music by John Cage, choreography by Merce Cunningham, set design by Willem de Kooning (all teaching at Black Mountain) and featuring Buckminster Fuller who was at the college working on his geodesic dome.

Penn later completed his education at the University of Florence where he studied Italian and Renaissance poetry before finding a job as a floor manager for NBC television, dividing his time between New York and California, working with Milton Berle, Eddie Cantor, Dean Martin, and Jerry Lewis on the popular *Colgate Comedy Hour*. Fred Coe, now a prominent producer at NBC, hired Penn to direct several episodes of the highly original and groundbreaking live television program *First Person Singular*. The live television experience, which Penn credits as being his first exposure to the possibilities of the camera, was to serve as finishing school for a generation of film directors (Frankenheimer and Lumet among them) who rose to prominence in the early sixties. At the same time, from the start of his life in film Penn maintained a second career in Broadway theater, counting Lillian Hellman's *Toys in the Attic* and William Gibson's *Two for the Seesaw* among his early successes.

Penn entered Hollywood at a time when the studio system was in ruins, still recovering from the historic 1948 Supreme Court ruling that deemed studio control of movie theaters and distribution channels a violation of antitrust laws. It was in this troubled period, at the height of the Hollywood blacklist, that his first film, *The Left Handed Gun* (1957), starring Paul Newman and adapted from a play by Gore Vidal, was released in America. Playing on the bottom of double bills the film received little notice and quickly vanished from theaters, finding resonance a short time later with a handful of European critics who understood the film for what it was: a brilliantly crafted, existential, western—one of the first of its kind. "When I read the reviews in France I couldn't believe my eyes because in America no one even saw the film, and certainly no one wrote more than three lines about it," said Penn in his 1963 *Cahiers* interview. Through its sparse, grim retelling of the Billy the Kid story, his debut would contain many of his major themes: man's conflicted sense of self, the primacy of the father and son relationship, the rigorous demands of society, the desire for greater personal freedom, the impassivity of nature, the quest for truth, the edifying falsehoods of myth.

Stunted by the commercial failure of his debut film, the release of his second feature *The Miracle Worker* (1962), which Penn had directed previously on stage and for television, would garner him great notoriety and influence. Yet despite the film's artistic and commercial success, Penn's attitude to the American film industry—and the intransigent technicians it employed—was already deeply hostile by the time of this collection's first interview in 1963. To the point of churlishness he suggests quite simply that "Hollywood just isn't real," adding—with unfortunate prescience—"As far as I can see the place is killing itself. Pretty soon it'll be churning out only big blockbusters and TV series. That's all, no more actual films. Eventually the corporations turning out forty or fifty films a year will make only four or five." As many of these interviews will reveal, few American directors can be as blunt and hoary as Penn (most of all when it comes to assessing the value of his own work), but if his comments carry the patina of scorn and envy they also have the subsistence of truth, particularly when characterizing the seismic shift that took place within Hollywood once corporations began annexing the studios. More than thirty years later Penn was still excoriating the system, telling Beier and Müller in 1994 that "Every medium goes through a period of fools, which is where we are now."

In the early sixties the critical and box office success of *The Miracle Worker* in America gave Penn unique privilege and high rank among other major film directors of the time. Yet his outspoken detestation of the mechanizations of the Hollywood system, coupled with his moral outrage at America's foreign policy in the wake of World War II, put him squarely at odds with an industry with little use for psychic outlaws. At his best, particularly when dealing squarely with the predicament of the independent artist forced into abeyance to the demands of commerce, the interviews herein are both self-critical and judgmental, as when he tells the editors of *Cahiers* in 1965 that filmmaking in Hollywood is "by committee" and that the more a film costs is directly related to the number of minds involved. As such, "with each additional mind the power of a film is diluted, not strengthened." Penn correctly predicted that the "real developments" in American cinema would come out of the 16mm counter-cinema, though he seemingly never entertained the notion of taking that route himself, instead persevering through the series of injustices which befell him as a studio director.

His unceremonious removal as director on *The Train* (1963), a growing admiration for European *auteur* cinema (Truffaut, Godard), the critical drubbing of one of his most personal films, *Mickey One* (1965), and post-production of *The Chase* (1966) co-opted by its producer Sam Spiegel without his knowledge or consent had made Penn, by the mid-sixties, the ultimate Hollywood outsider (both figuratively and literally: he spent most of his professional filmmaking career in New York and Stockbridge, Massachusetts). Yet it was

Penn—whose criticisms of the Hollywood system were as bitter and pointed as any ever lobbed against it—who helped to revive the moribund studio system with the blockbuster success of what is perhaps his masterpiece, *Bonnie and Clyde* (1967).

Perhaps no single film in the history of American cinema had struck so deep a psychic chord with audiences and critics alike. Penn's mythic retelling of the Bonnie and Clyde saga disarmed nearly everyone who saw it in its miasma of youthful beauty, berserk violence, sex, and slapstick comedy. American critics were baffled, not being able to make up their minds if the film was an unmitigated disaster or an unrivaled masterpiece. A generation coming of age in the sixties, however, needed little deliberation. Disgusted by the values of their parents' generation and the worsening crisis in Vietnam, with martial law quickly becoming a viable recourse for quelling political dissent at home and abroad, with the clarion call of revolution being sounded in Latin America, Africa, and Eastern Europe, young people around the world immediately saw *Bonnie and Clyde* for what it was: a thinly veiled mirroring of their times, one whose prophetic, tragic message would find its embodiment in the growing civil unrest of the era. "Youngsters today feel powerless in the face of this dehumanized world which is becoming more and more reliant on technology. We don't actually understand youth culture which is the same thing as being afraid of it. It doesn't scare me though," Penn told Yvonne Baby of *Le Monde* in 1968.

Remarkable in its ability to conjure past, present, and future in its thematic pertinence and Mod-ish stylization of the Depression era, *Bonnie and Clyde* grew to become a phenomenon not just in the United States but worldwide, giving Penn a notoriety he was not completely prepared for, but one the studios were quick to capitalize on, particularly in regards to the youth market the film helped them locate. As the progenitor of a bold New American Cinema which, up until that point, had been a movement very much on the fringes of commercial moviemaking, *Bonnie and Clyde* was followed shortly after by Dennis Hopper's anti-authoritarian generational manifesto *Easy Rider* (1969) and would soon have the studios taking risks on smaller budgeted, personally crafted films by an up-and-coming generation of film-schooled directors, Coppola, Scorsese, and Lucas among them. The film also inadvertently opened the floodgates to an endless stream of shock violent images that has permeated so much of mainstream cinema ever since. If the violence in *Bonnie and Clyde* is rooted in a particularly American pathology, the meretricious violence of the film's descendants would offer all the visceral impact with little of the moral, real world consequences expressed by Penn and his screenwriters.

While Penn's early interviews set the general tone for much of what follows, it is the post-*Bonnie and Clyde* conversations that form the heart of this
collection and, in many respects, are the most revealing. Penn's address at
Dartmouth College in May 1968, published here for the first time, marks a
distinct break from the earlier pieces. He begins his remarks to students with
a curious admission for someone who, at the time, was at the fount of power
for a film director working within the studio system: "Let me begin by trying to describe myself. When it comes to American film, I am an outsider."
Dashing the hopes of any number of would-be directors and producers in
the audience, Penn touches upon the rampant nepotism within the American film industry where "nephews and sons-in-law" are easily introduced
into its "highly familial but clearly structured system without disturbing it,"
before concluding his address with a confessional, the significance of which
goes well beyond filmmaking, straight to the center of that watershed moment in the spring and summer of 1968 when the Occident, in the throws
of apoplexy, could no longer rely on the adages of the past. "Hollywood
would probably prefer we didn't ask certain questions, but I believe the point
we have reached in film is no different from the crossroads that our entire
culture has reached." Penn qualifies this statement by suggesting this is "a
personal crisis that each man deals with in his own way." Dartmouth lays
bare the dilemma that Penn would try manfully to reconcile in his own work
over the next decade: how an artist working inside the commercial film industry might reach a popular mass audience without having to condescend
to the "structured clichés" blandly accepted as the "norm" in Hollywood. "A
norm," Penn declared to Dartmouth students, "that on the very first day I
stepped onto a film set I found myself in opposition to."

As an engaged artist and thinker—and an autodidact who described himself to Michel Ciment in 1982 as someone who "never stops learning"—the
lessons of 1968 weighed so heavily on Penn that by the early seventies he
was faced with a debilitating crisis of conscience. The assassinations of Martin Luther King Jr. and Robert Kennedy, the sweeping victory of Richard
Nixon in the 1968 presidential election, and the daily horror and brutality
of the Vietnam War were a shattering denouement to the utopian idealism
of the sixties, one that had many on the Left in search of reckoning of these
cataclysmic events. Penn would follow *Bonnie and Clyde* with two comedic
tragedies, *Alice's Restaurant* (1969) and *Little Big Man* (1970), before taking a
five-year hiatus from feature filmmaking altogether.

Since Penn was stigmatized as being a director obsessed with violence, *Alice's
Restaurant* and *Little Big Man* have a more pronounced humanist sensibility
than any of his earlier films. While the righteous outlaws Bonnie Parker and

Clyde Barrow were being championed by the radical fringe of the New Left, Penn looked to a group of pacifist, draft-dodging hippies for the inspiration for *Alice's Restaurant*. The film's pre-electric Dylan vibe, performances by Dust Bowl era progeny Lee Hays, Arlo Guthrie, and Pete Seeger, and quaint Stockbridge settings all give *Alice's Restaurant* a decidedly rustic feel in comparison to the garish pop explosiveness of *Bonnie and Clyde*. In their quest to establish a new community divorced from bourgeois morality, with a desanctified church serving as their communal home, Penn portrays the lifestyle of his fugitives from modernity with a deep and specific sympathy but also with reserved, critical distance. The church, a *tabula rasa* for Arlo and his friends, becomes for Penn a symbol of personal struggle and conflict that ultimately leads to disillusionment with the Aquarian ethos. "What I'm trying to say," Penn tells Aghed and Cohn of *Positif*, "is that their lives have basically stayed the same, that the choices they made have meant things that are even more difficult for them today. That's really what I wanted this film to express."

Little Big Man, based on Thomas Berger's novel, is an epic reimagining of the settling of the American West where the roots of American imperialism are explained metaphorically through the saga of Jack Crabb, the lone survivor of the Battle of Little Big Horn. A witness to history, Crabb's tale of Native American genocide is at once an allegory of the Vietnam War and a requiem for the old, worn myths of the American West. In 1971 Penn told *L'Express* that he took his inspiration from John Ford films such as *Cheyenne Autumn* with its sympathetic depiction of the "Indians' bloody march" and the "miserable life they went on to lead." Offering that "American cinema has continually parodied and ridiculed native Indians, depicting them as savage beasts, in order to justify the fact that we wiped them out," Penn concludes that a mythic and heroic account of the settling of the West "might ease some people's consciences but I'm having none of it."

The perennial outsider, vanquished by his critics, then heroically hitting back with a masterstroke: this is what characterizes Penn's first decade in film. When he returned to directing it was with all the hardened cynicism of a battle weary soldier. *Night Moves* (1975) turns the Philip Marlowe–styled detective picture on its head, following truth-seeker Harry Moseby, played by Gene Hackman, on a labyrinthine whodunit that leads him on his own dark night of the soul. An allegory of its times, a portrait of a man succumbing to the *ennui* around him, *Night Moves* offered bleak hope for filmgoers in the post-Watergate era. A mystery that grows in proportion to the moral weakness of its main interlocutor, the film ends in vertigo: a maimed Moseby, endlessly circling the waters on an unmanned boat, totally lost at sea. "Harry Moseby's inability to understand his own problems, to discover his own identity, leads to his inability to recognize that the problem—the case he has been hired to solve—doesn't actually concern him," Penn explained to Jean-Pierre Coursodon in 1977.

By the late seventies Penn's growing sense of futility in trying to fight Hollywood led him back to the New York theater where he would direct George C. Scott in *Sly Fox* before reuniting with Anne Bancroft in 1977 for the Broadway bio-play *Golda*. His films *The Missouri Breaks* (1976) (which Penn dismissively tells Clouzot was directed with all the vigor of "passionless sex"), *Target* (1985), and *Dead of Winter* (1987) were, by Penn's own admission, acts of conscription. Despite Penn's misgivings, *The Missouri Breaks* stands out as a darkly comic, ur-Western, replete with some staggeringly funny and subversive moments whose highlights include a playfully absurd performance from Brando as bounty hunter Robert E. Lee Clayton. Much to the horror of United Artists—which spent a fortune casting Jack Nicholson and Marlon Brando in the lead roles—the film was anathema to mass audiences thanks to its laconic style and thwarting of genre conventions. It became Penn's parting salvo to Hollywood, the deal killer between him and the studios.

Penn's last major success with critics and audiences was *Four Friends* (1982). An autobiographical account of screenwriter Steve Tesich's immigration to the United States from Yugoslavia in the late fifties, the film is an elegy to the subsequent decade, though one far different from *Alice's Restaurant*. Praised at the time of its release for its sensitive portrayal of working-class youth coming of age against the backdrop of the civil strife of that era, the film follows the intersecting lives of four childhood friends as they navigate their way through personal relationships and the accompanying pains of young adulthood. Considered by some as one of the best films ever made to document the immigrant experience in America, *Four Friends* remains the most optimistic of Penn's films, a mature statement about the American Dream where individuality is not self-evident but self-realizing: an achievement hard won, inductive, attainable.

Penn managed to direct a handful of small, personal films which saw limited theatrical release in the eighties and nineties, including the cult film *Penn & Teller Get Killed* (1989) with illusionists Penn and Teller, and *Inside* (1996), a compelling drama about the horrors of apartheid. He would also return to direct for television in the ensuing years—where his son Matthew had become a successful producer and director—for the popular crime drama *Law & Order*, the family drama *The Portrait* (1993) with Gregory Peck and Lauren Bacall, and an episode of his friend Sidney Lumet's television series *100 Centre Street*.

While many of the interviews in this book delve deeply into the social and political implications of Penn's work, there are numerous statements to be found in these pages concerning the craft of which he is a master: film directing. While many interviews published today eschew technical details in favor of analytic explanations of story and character, Penn is refreshing in being willing and able to explain the practical decisions he has made throughout his working life. Examples abound in the pages that follow. In terms of story structure, for example, to René Prédal he explains that "as long as I'm not sure exactly what I want to do with the final scene of a film, I'm not able to give the story a precise structure." It's no surprise that the lengthy question and answer session he gave at the American Film Institute, recorded during production on *Little Big Man* and aimed squarely at students of film-making in Los Angeles, yields fascinating insights into the problem-solving a director has to exercise at every turn on the film set and in the editing room. The script of *Bonnie and Clyde*, for example, notes Penn, "didn't specifically call for tracking shots. I just decided we would use lateral and horizontal moves for a while and then, as the film goes along, start moving more nervously and abruptly as the jump cuts become more conspicuous."

Importantly, Penn's many years in theater—what at Dartmouth he called his "true *métier*"—and longstanding relationship with Lee Strasberg's Actors Studio (where he would serve as president for eight years in the nineties) instilled in him at an early age a deep sensitivity and appreciation of the actor's craft, a theme that stretches throughout this interview collection. His perceptive awareness of the medium of cinema, his painterly and balanced style of *mise-en-scène*—built firmly around the physicality of his actors—never eclipses or diminishes the nuanced and emotive performances that are a hall-mark of his films. "What happened was that throughout the course of several years I became more and more involved with the acting process and less and less involved with the mechanics," Richard Schickel recorded in 1990, when discussing with Penn his early years in television. "I began to accept as a given that I could do the mechanics in my sleep, which in point of fact turned out to be relatively true, even when I moved over to film." Inevitably Penn has clarified to interviewers his understanding of fundamental differ-ences between film and theater, as he did in Robert Hughes's 1970 documen-tary, filmed during production on *Little Big Man*: "What people say in a scene is often the least important of its many aspects. For me this came as a great surprise, having come out of theater where every idea and nuance of psycho-logical stance and viewpoint was demonstrated through what people said, how they said it, and what language they chose to say it. Suddenly I got into movies where I found that what was happening on screen was contradicting what the actors said. This dynamic just set me trembling, it really knocked me out."

Never one to succumb to the totalizing, director-is-all philosophy of the *auteur* theory, in several interviews Penn credits Dede Allen—his editor from *Bonnie and Clyde* through to *The Missouri Breaks*—with helping him to find the pace and rhythm of his films. He also pays homage to cinematographer Ghislain Cloquet in a 1982 interview with Michel Ciment for *Positif*. A collaborator of Robert Bresson, Chris Marker, and Marguerite Duras, Cloquet would shoot both *Mickey One* and *Four Friends*. Penn greatly admired Cloquet for his economical and precise way of working. In reflection of Cloquet's method Penn suggested that "American cinema could well do with being a little impoverished, something the rest of the world has to deal with all the time." When it comes to writers, Penn speaks in equally respectful terms, noting in this book's final interview that when it came to his writer colleagues in the early days of television, "These guys were excellent writers who knew more than I did. I certainly wasn't teaching them anything but at times it was good for me to ask certain questions and have them elucidate certain things." In regards to his friend and collaborator Marlon Brando, Penn is particularly eloquent. Quick to dispel accusations that he is difficult to work with, Penn tells of Brando's incredible fidelity as an actor and vigorously defends him (see the Claire Clouzot interview in *Ecran*) against the numerous, unjustified attacks on him by the mainstream press. Working with Brando, Penn told Richard Schickel, was "a privilege, like going to school with one of the greats."

The intent of this collection is to help nourish scholarship and interest in Arthur Penn's work. We hope this volume is both revelatory and readable in its attempt to offer something new to his admirers and to those coming to the films for the first time. Though the last book-length critical study of Penn in English was published in 1969 (Robin Wood's *Arthur Penn*), there exist several important interviews with Penn published in English over the years. As well as a great many pieces published in journals and magazines since the early sixties there are a handful of more substantial interviews worth exploring in detail, including those found in Joseph Gelmis's *The Film Director as Superstar* (Secker & Warburg, 1971), Eric Sherman's *The Director's Event* (Signet, 1972), Gorham Kindem's *The Live Television Generation of Hollywood Film Directors* (McFarland, 1994), Tom Luddy and David Thomson's piece in *Projections 4* (Faber & Faber, 1995), and Edward Humes's *Over Here: How the G.I. Bill Transformed the American Dream* (Harcourt, 2006). Interesting too are three books about Penn's most famous film: *The Bonnie & Clyde Book* (Simon and Schuster, 1972) contains the transcript of Penn's press conference following the film's premiere in Montreal in 1967 as well as an English translation of the André S. Labarthe and Jean-Louis Commolli December 1967 interview for *Cahiers du cinéma* (reprinted in *Evergreen Review*, June 1968), while John G. Cawelti's *Focus on Bonnie and Clyde* (Prentice Hall, 1973) includes a selection of reviews written when the first was first released. More recently Lester D. Friedman's *Arthur Penn's Bonnie & Clyde* (Cambridge, 1999) includes pieces by Penn and screenwriter David Newman about their experiences making the film, as well as the reviews by Bosley Crowther and Pauline Kael that Penn discusses in the interviews that follow. (Friedman is also the author of a British Film Institute monograph about the film.) Joel Zuker's *Arthur Penn: A Guide to References and Resources* (G. K. Hall & Co., 1980) remains a useful survey and collection of citations. The two best critical accounts of Penn's influence, particularly in regards to the New American Cinema, are Peter Biskind's *Easy Riders, Raging Bulls: How the Sex-Drugs-and-Rock 'n' Roll Generation Saved Hollywood* (Simon and Schuster, 1999) and Robert Kolker's *Cinema of Loneliness: Penn, Stone, Kubrick, Scorsese, Spielberg, Altman* (Oxford, 2000).

In an attempt to bring to light new material to English speakers, none of the interviews cited above are included in this volume, for any diligent researcher will have no trouble locating them. Instead *Arthur Penn: Interviews* is comprised entirely of new translations from French sources (plus one Italian) and a number of transcripts of difficult-to-find or unpublished interviews originally conducted in English. The book ends with our own interview with Penn, conducted at his apartment in New York throughout 2007. The wide range of pieces collected here means there is inevitably some repetition (and contradiction) in the pages that follow, though we believe it has also resulted in a unique overview of Penn's lengthy career.

The American Film Institute piece is drawn from two seminars given in Los Angeles in 1970 (30 January and 7 October). *Rising Out of the Ashes*, from the archives of Philip Porcella, is published for the first time (the title is our own). Richard Schickel's piece is an edited version of an interview recorded in 1990 and used in his 1995 documentary. "Is There Anything Film Can't Do?" is a version of Lars-Olav Beier and Robert Müller's interview, originally published in German in their 1998 book about Penn (Dieter Bertz Verlag). The original recordings being lost, a first-draft translation of the 1977 piece from *Cinéma* was done by the original interviewer, Jean-Pierre Coursodon. In all cases the interviews presented here have been carefully edited from original recordings or verbatim transcripts, language and grammar have been cleaned up, and the ideas under discussion clarified.

The editors gratefully acknowledge the assistance of Jean-Pierre Coursodon, Sam DiIorio, Remi Guillochon, Barbara Krieger, Gerald O'Grady, Presley Parks, Doris Perlman, Philip Porcella, Gillian Walker, and especially Arthur Penn.

This collection is dedicated to the memory of William F. Van Wert.

MC
PC

CHRONOLOGY

1922	27 September, born in Philadelphia to Harry (a watchmaker of Russian decent) and Sonia (*née* Greenberg, a nurse). His brother, the photographer Irving Penn, is born in 1917.
1925	Harry and Sonia divorce. Moves in with his mother and brother.
1936	Returns to Philadelphia to live with his father. Attends Olney High School where he works in the school theater. Penn also works as a director at the Neighborhood Playhouse and at the local radio station.
1941	Death of Harry Penn.
1943	Moves to New York and enlists in the U.S. Army Infantry. While at Fort Jackson, South Carolina, he meets Fred Coe at the Civic Theater in Columbia.
1944	Called to the front as a infantryman. Sees action in the Ardennes.
1945	Works with Captain Joshua Logan and the theater troop Soldiers Show Company in Paris. Meets Paddy Chayevsky. He is demobilized in Wiesbaden where he runs the theater company.
1946	Returns to the United States.
1947	Studies philosophy and psychology at Black Mountain College, North Carolina, where he also teaches an acting class.
1949	Studies at the Universities of Perugia and Florence.
1951	Starts as floor manager at NBC on variety shows and news. Assistant director at *Colgate Comedy Hour* (NBC) in New York and California. Trains floor managers in Los Angeles. Studies with Michael Chekhov.
1953	Writes three television plays. Fred Coe invites Penn to New York where he works as a director on *Gulf Playhouse: First Person*

(NBC) on scripts by, among others, Paddy Chayevsky. He also directs for *Philco Television Playhouse* (NBC).

1955   Directs the play *Blue Denim* by James Leo Herlihy, in Westport, Connecticut. Marries Peggy Maurer, with whom he has two children, Matthew and Molly.

1957   Directs several television dramas for *Playhouse 90* (CBS), including William Gibson's *The Miracle Worker*.

1958   *The Left Handed Gun* starring Paul Newman. Directs William Gibson's play *Two for the Seesaw* on Broadway, produced by Fred Coe and starring Henry Fonda and Anne Bancroft. Establishes Florin, a production company.

1959   Directs Gibson's *The Miracle Worker* on Broadway which runs for nearly two years. The play is produced by Fred Coe and stars Anne Bancroft and Patty Duke.

1960   Directs three Broadway shows: *Toys in the Attic* by Lillian Hellman and starring Jason Robards, which runs for over a year, *An Evening with Mike Nichols and Elaine May*, and *All the Way Home* by Tad Mosel, based on the novel *A Death in the Family* by James Agee, and produced by Fred Coe. Consultant for Senator John F. Kennedy during the 1960 presidential television debates.

1962   Directs film version of *The Miracle Worker* with Anne Bancroft and Patty Duke. His Broadway production of *In the Counting House*, written by Leslie Weiner, closes after four performances.

1963   Directs Jack Richardson's play *Lorenzo* on Broadway, which closes after four performances.

1964   Starts work on *The Train* but is fired early on into production and replaced by John Frankenheimer. Directs the Broadway musical *Golden Boy*, starring Sammy Davis Jr., based on the play by Clifford Odets, which runs for nearly a year and a half.

1965   Directs and produces *Mickey One* starring Warren Beatty.

1966   *The Chase*, scripted by Lillian Hellman, starring Marlon Brando. Directs Frederick Knott's play *Wait until Dark* on Broadway, produced by Fred Coe and starring Lee Remick and Robert Duvall.

1967   Directs *Flesh and Blood* for NBC. Releases *Bonnie and Clyde* starring Warren Beatty, Faye Dunaway, and Gene Hackman.

1969   Co-writes and directs *Alice's Restaurant*.

1970   *Little Big Man*, starring Dustin Hoffman.

1973   *The Highest*, segment of the 1972 Olympic Games film *Visions of Eight*.

1976	*The Missouri Breaks* starring Marlon Brando and Jack Nicholson. Directs *Sly Fox* on Broadway, by Larry Gelbart, based on Ben Jonson's *Volpone*. The play, starring George C. Scott and Trish Van DeVere, runs for over a year.
1977	Directs William Gibson's play *Golda* on Broadway, starring Anne Bancroft.
1981	Directs and produces *Four Friends*.
1982	Directs William Gibson's play *Monday after the Miracle* on Broadway, which closes after seven performances.
1985	*Target* starring Gene Hackman.
1987	Directs *Dead of Winter*.
1989	Directs and produces *Penn & Teller Get Killed*.
1993	*The Portrait* starring Gregory Peck and Lauren Bacall.
1995	Short film for the compilation project *Lumière et compagnie*.
1996	Feature film *Inside*, shot in South Africa.
2001	Directs an episode of *100 Centre Street* for television.
2002	Directs Turgenev's *Fortune's Fool* on Broadway, starring Alan Bates and Frank Langella.
2004	Revival of *Sly Fox* on Broadway, starring Richard Dreyfuss and Eric Stoltz.

FILMOGRAPHY

1958
THE LEFT HANDED GUN
Warner Bros. Pictures
Producer: Fred Coe
Director: **Arthur Penn**
Screenplay: Leslie Stevens (based on the play *The Death of Billy the Kid* by Gore Vidal)
Cinematography: J. Peverell Marley
Editing: Folmar Blangsted
Music: Alexander Courage
Featured Cast: Paul Newman (Billy The Kid), Lita Milan (Celsa), John Dehner (Pat Garrett), Hurd Hatfield (Moultrie), James Congdon (Charlie Boudre), James Best (Tom Folliard)
102 minutes

1962
THE MIRACLE WORKER
United Artists
Producer: Fred Coe (Playfilm Productions)
Director: **Arthur Penn**
Screenplay: William Gibson (based on the play *The Miracle Worker* by William Gibson, adapted from Helen Keller's autobiography *The Story of My Life*)
Cinematography: Ernest Caparrós
Editing: Aram Avakian
Music: Laurence Rosenthal
Featured Cast: Anne Bancroft (Annie Sullivan), Victor Jory (Captain Arthur Keller), Inga Swenson (Kate Keller), Andrew Prine (James Keller), Patty Duke

(Helen Keller), Kathleen Comegys (Aunt Ev)
106 minutes

1965
MICKEY ONE
Columbia Pictures
Producers: John Avildsen, **Arthur Penn**, Harrison Starr
Director: **Arthur Penn**
Screenplay: Alan M. Surgal
Cinematography: Ghislain Cloquet
Editing: Aram Avakian
Music: Stan Getz, Eddie Sauter
Featured Cast: Warren Beatty (Mickey One), Alexandra Stewart (Jenny),
Hurd Hatfield (Castle), Franchot Tone (Rudy Lopp), Teddy Hart (Berson),
Kamatari Fujiwara (The Artist)
93 minutes

1966
THE CHASE
Columbia Pictures
Producers: Sam Spiegel
Director: **Arthur Penn**
Screenplay: Lillian Hellman (based on the play *The Chase* by Horton Foote)
Cinematography: Joseph La Shelle, Robert Surtees
Editing: Gene Milford
Music: John Barry
Featured Cast: Marlon Brando (Sheriff Calder), Jane Fonda (Anna Reeves),
Robert Redford (Charlie "Bubber" Reeves), Robert Duvall (Edwin Stewart),
Angie Dickinson (Ruby Calder), James Fox (Jason "Jake" Rogers), Janice
Rule (Emily Stewart), Miriam Hopkins (Mrs. Reeves), Richard Bradford
(Damon Fuller)
133 minutes

1967
BONNIE AND CLYDE
Warner Bros./Seven Arts
Producers: Warren Beatty
Director: **Arthur Penn**
Screenplay: David Newman, Robert Benton, Robert Towne (uncredited)
Cinematography: Burnett Guffey

Editing: Dede Allen
Music: Flatt & Scruggs, Charles E. Strouse, Charles Henderson
Featured Cast: Warren Beatty (Clyde Barrow), Faye Dunaway
(Bonnie Parker), Michael J. Pollard C. W. Moss), Gene Hackman
(Buck Barrow), Estelle Parsons (Blanche), Denver Pyle (Frank Hamer),
Dub Taylor (Ivan Moss), Evans Evans (Velma Davis), Gene Wilder
(Eugene Grizzard)
111 minutes

1969
ALICE'S RESTAURANT
United Artists
Producers: Hillard Elkins, Harold Leventhal, Joe Manduke
Director: **Arthur Penn**
Screenplay: Venable Herndon, Arthur Penn (inspired by the song
"The Alice's Restaurant Massacre" by Arlo Guthrie)
Cinematography: Michael Nebbia
Editing: Dede Allen
Music: Arlo Guthrie, Garry Sherman, Joni Mitchell
Featured Cast: Arlo Guthrie, Patricia Quinn (Alice Brock), James Broderick
(Ray Brock), Pete Seeger, Lee Hays, Geoff Outlaw (Roger Crowther),
Tina Chen (Mari-Chan), Kathleen Dabney (Karin)
111 minutes

1970
LITTLE BIG MAN
National General Pictures
Producers: Gene Lasko, Stuart Miller, **Arthur Penn**
Director: **Arthur Penn**
Screenplay: Calder Willingham (based on the novel *Little Big Man* by
Thomas Berger)
Cinematography: Harry Stradling, Jr.
Editing: Dede Allen
Music: John Hammond, John Strauss
Featured Cast: Dustin Hoffman (Jack Crabb), Faye Dunaway (Mrs. Louise
Pendrake), Chief Dan George (Old Lodge Skins), Richard Mulligan (General
George Armstrong Custer), Jeff Corey (Wild Bill Hickok), Robert Little Star
(Little Horse), Cal Bellini (Younger Bear), Martin Balsam (Mr. Merriweather),
Aimée Eccles (Sunshine)
139 minutes

1975
NIGHT MOVES
Warner Bros.
Producers: Gene Lasko, Robert M. Sherman
Director: **Arthur Penn**
Screenplay: Alan Sharp (based on his novel *Night Moves*)
Cinematography: Bruce Surtees
Editing: Dede Allen, Stephen A. Rotter
Music: Michael Small
Featured Cast: Gene Hackman (Harry Moseby), Jennifer Warren (Paula), Susan Clark (Ellen Moseby), James Woods (Quentin), Melanie Griffith (Delly Grastner), Ed Binns (Joey Ziegler), Kenneth Mars (Nick), Janet Ward (Arlene Iverson), Harris Yulin (Marty Heller)
100 minutes

1976
THE MISSOURI BREAKS
United Artists
Producers: Elliott Kastner, Marion Rosenberg, Robert M. Sherman
Director: **Arthur Penn**
Screenplay: Thomas McGuane
Cinematography: Michael Butler
Editing: Dede Allen, Jerry Greenberg, Stephen A. Rotter
Music: John Williams
Featured Cast: Marlon Brando (Lee Clayton), Jack Nicholson (Tom Logan), Randy Quaid (Little Tod), Kathleen Lloyd (Jane Braxton), Harry Dean Stanton (Calvin), Frederic Forrest (Cary), John McLiam (David Braxton), John P. Ryan (Si), Sam Gilman (Hank Rate), Steve Franken (The Lonesome Kid), Richard Bradford (Pete Marker)
126 minutes

1981
FOUR FRIENDS
Filmways Pictures
Producers: Stephen F. Kesten, Gene Lasko, Julia Miles, **Arthur Penn**, Michael Tolan
Director: **Arthur Penn**
Screenplay: Steve Tesich
Cinematography: Ghislain Cloquet
Editing: Marc Laub, Barry Malkin

Music: Elizabeth Swados, Carolyn Dutton
Featured Cast: Craig Wasson (Danilo), Jodi Thelen (Georgia), Michael
Huddleston (David), Jim Metzler (Tom), Scott Hardt (Young Danilo),
Elizabeth Lawrence (Mrs. Prozor), Miklos Simon (Mr. Prozor)
114 minutes

1985
TARGET
CBS Entertainment/Warner Bros.
Producers: David Brown, Richard D. Zanuck
Director: **Arthur Penn**
Screenplay: Howard Berk, Don Petersen
Cinematography: Jean Tournier
Editing: Richard P. Cirincione, Stephen A. Rotter
Music: Michael Small
Featuring: Gene Hackman (Walter Lloyd), Matt Dillon (Chris Lloyd),
Gayle Hunnicutt (Donna Lloyd), Randy Moore (Tour Director),
Ilona Grubel (Carla), Tomas Hnevsa (Henke), Jean-Pol Dubois (Glasses)
117 minutes

1987
DEAD OF WINTER
Metro-Goldwyn-Mayer
Producers: John Bloomgarden, Michael MacDonald, Marc Shmuger
Director: **Arthur Penn**
Screenplay: Marc Shmuger, Mark Malone
Cinematography: Jan Weincke
Editing: Rich Shaine
Music: Norman Hollyn, Patrick Mullins, Richard Einhorn
Featured Cast: Mary Steenburgen (Julie Rose), Roddy McDowall
(Mr. Murray), Jan Rubes (Dr. Joseph Lewis), William Russ (Rob Sweeney),
Ken Pogue (Officer Mullavy), Wayne Robson (Officer Huntley)
100 mins

1989
PENN & TELLER GET KILLED
Lorimar, Warner Brothers
Producers: Timothy Marx, Arthur Penn
Director: **Arthur Penn**
Screenplay: Penn Jillette, Teller

Cinematography: Jan Weincke
Editing: Jeffrey Wolf
Music: Paul Chihara
Featured Cast: Penn Jillette, Teller, Caitlin Clarke (Carlotta),
David Patrick Kelly (The Fan), Leonardo Cimino (Ernesto),
Celia McGuire (Officer McNamara)
89 minutes

ARTHUR PENN

INTERVIEWS

A Meeting with Arthur Penn

ANDRÉ S. LABARTHE / 1963

L: *What gave you the idea to make* The Left Handed Gun?

P: I saw a television play about Billy the Kid by Gore Vidal that Robert Mulligan directed, but it's quite different from the film. Leslie Stevens and I took a different angle on *The Left Handed Gun*. We wanted to make a film not about *the* West but about *a* West, about our version of the West, something quite different from other films, even with the small budget we had. *The Left Handed Gun* wasn't expensive to make because, for example, the Mexican village had been built twenty years before for *Juarez* and was just sitting idle on the studio backlot. It was falling apart, though, and we had to stick pieces of cardboard over the ravages of time. The day after we finished shooting the whole thing completely fell to pieces. I was happy that we were able to use a lot of props which made the set look authentic.

L: *What's interesting about the film is the way it depicts violence.*

P: We tried to reference the myth of how cheap life is in Westerns, how a man can pull the trigger of his pistol, kill someone, and just walk away. No one stood around to mop up the blood or pick up the pieces.

L: *What is your perception of the characters in the film? We saw Billy depicted as being gay.*

P: That was something I came up with. We started out with various ideas, beginning with the myth of Billy the Kid. To us this was actually a very complex moment in time when people started to question their own identities.

From *Cahiers du Cinéma* (February 1963). © *Cahiers du Cinéma*. Translated by Paul Cronin and Remi Guillochon.

The funny thing about Billy is that while he was still alive he was depicted as a hero in several comics coming out of New York. We really liked the idea that people who didn't know anything about Billy were nonetheless telling stories about him.

Here is a young man, profoundly troubled by the murder of the old man who has become a father to him. It doesn't really matter who the man is. What matters is that Billy feels very close to him and wants to avenge his death. This meant we had to construct a story that brought together these two ideas of myth and latent homosexuality. We had a great scene where Hatfield walks into a bar like a jilted lover and says, "He can't go on killing like this. He must be stopped." What he's trying to say is, "I can't have him ignore me for much longer." I thought the scene of Hatfield's betrayal was moving but at the same time quite bizarre. The difficulty we had was to construct a story building up to this scene which is the most important in the film. Unfortunately it never made it into the finished version. Most of it was cut by Warner Bros. from the American and European versions.

L: *The film makes sense, all the same.*
P: In Paris they understood the film immediately. When I read the reviews in France I couldn't believe my eyes because in America no one even saw the film and certainly no one wrote more than three lines about it. At that point I realized I couldn't work in Hollywood any more. I just couldn't stay a moment longer, so I went back to New York and to my theater work. Three years later my brother's assistant sent me reviews of the film from various European newspapers. It was a miracle. They'd really understood it! We don't have any real critics in America today. Or maybe one: James Agee, but that's it. Unlike most of the other critics he actually loves cinema. Reviews from Europe are more intelligent because the critics there really do appreciate film.

L: *What was the budget for* The Miracle Worker?
P: $1,250,000. But when United Artists bought the rights to the play, they paid out $400,000, plus $150,000 for the script, which meant we actually spent only $700,000 on filming it, which isn't a lot of money for a film shot in New York.

L: *Was it difficult to make?*
P: Very much so. The real people behind the story were still alive which meant there were inevitable restrictions and I had to be rather cautious. Some of the characters, the father and brother for example, weren't well fleshed out on the page. They were just too obscure, not rounded enough. I

also discovered that the adaptation from the stage play was too literal. There was just too much talking.

L: *Did you read Helen Keller's correspondence?*
P: Of course, her letters are extraordinary. You know that only four years before the beginning of the story [Anne Bancroft's character] Annie Sullivan couldn't read and write? I always thought she was the most interesting character, more so than Helen's family and entourage. There was just much more to explore when it came to Annie so we set about trying to understand her. We wanted to show how her brother's death made her feel so guilty that she felt she owed God a life. In essence it's the story of a woman in need of resurrection.

L: *How long is the fight between Helen and Annie?*
P: It's pretty long—nine minutes—but we didn't shoot it in a single take. We used three cameras, and I could have used even more. There's another scene in the film, when Helen is in the house with the black child she's jealous of, which is a single take of seven minutes.

L: *What does the film mean to you?*
P: I always felt Annie is the real hero. There isn't really a villain except perhaps "nature" on which we can blame Helen's problems. This is the reason why the father seems so believable. All the characters are out of control. In *The Left Handed Gun* Billy was a normal guy who goes crazy but with *The Miracle Worker* it's the other way around. We tried to highlight this transition. It had to be dramatic so we concentrated on the idea of a physical struggle between the two women. My reservations notwithstanding, after having worked for nearly a year on the film, I'm very happy with it even if I didn't have complete control.

L: *What do you think of all those young American directors who sign long contracts with Hollywood studios?*
P: Even short term contracts in Hollywood stink. Hollywood just isn't real. If you go straight from theater into making a huge film you're wasting your time. There isn't the opportunity to get the experience you need. Young directors end up making conventional films because they've had to follow the lead of Hollywood technicians. As far as I can see the place is killing itself. Pretty soon it'll be churning out only big blockbusters and TV series. That's all, no more actual films. Eventually the corporations turning out forty or fifty films a year will make only four or five. The way these companies work is changing. Today they'll give money to whoever wants to make a film,

wherever they want to make it. But they don't care what the film is about or who's in it.

From a political point of view we've just come out of a really tough period in American history. Even though the McCarthy era is now over we've only just started making films and writing plays again with political points of view. There was such unhappiness in America at the time, both ideologically speaking and also in terms of the films being produced. Corporations were afraid and there were such crass films being made that had nothing to do with real life or real people. It was the death of the studios, and that's why today we're seeing a return to a smaller and perhaps looser kind of filmmaking.

L: *What about Kazan?*

P: He's a special case, a theater director from New York. He's made some films over the years and he's certainly very talented, but he's not a film director first and foremost. I don't feel he really knows how to use the medium of film. We actually share a common experience: before he filmed it, Kazan directed *A Tree Grows in Brooklyn* on Broadway. The point is that it's not very interesting to make a film version of your own play and I suspect this is why *The Miracle Worker* isn't the greatest piece of filmmaking. When you work for two years on a play you inevitably lose the element of spontaneity. I think this is what happened to Kazan. On the other hand *The Sea of Grass* is good and *East of Eden* is very good. *On the Waterfront* falls somewhere between the two. As for *A Face in the Crowd* I think it was a very good idea for a film but he didn't quite push it as far as he should have. It just seems to be lacking something. Maybe he was a little frightened.

L: *Cukor and Minnelli?*

P: Cukor and Minnelli are typical Hollywood products. Despite this they definitely have their own style and own way of doing things. Their films look good even if they're not terribly substantial. Both of them come from the New York theater scene and have something indefinable about them. It's an almost Parisian sensibility. Though they're not hugely talented there's something endearing—and fashionable—about them. But I don't consider them great filmmakers. Take Minnelli for example, who adapted a William Gibson novel called *The Cobweb*. I don't know any other film that has been so poorly adapted from such strong original material. When he makes musicals he really gets into his stride and they're quite wonderful. The same goes for Cukor. He's the quintessential romantic filmmaker.

L: *Do you feel he has a talent for depicting female characters?*

P: I don't know. It's certainly a pretty silly thing to say about someone, even if it's true which I don't think it is in this case. There are romantic characters throughout all his work. You're very kind to say that about him. Everyone is so beautiful in his films.

L: *What do you think of the new films coming out of New York?*
P: I don't think much of them. The only movement I really like is the one that Truffaut and Godard are part of. I also like Resnais, though I didn't really understand *Last Year at Marienbad.*

L: *What are you working on at the moment?*
P: Two films, in various stages of production. The first is a light-hearted story, a black comedy in which I plan to use every technical trick in the book. I want to show the capricious nature of modern life. It's about the problems of a man who lives far from the city, away from telephones and missiles. There'll be no plot whatsoever. Whatever happens, happens. The actors won't know when they're being filmed.

The second film is about the Mob which as you know will often buy off a young singer or actor and help him until he's successful, at which point it's payback time. It's a serious story with a comic twist that revolves around this idea that we all owe something to someone but don't know who or what or how we're going to pay them back.

Arthur Penn: *Mickey One*

ADRIANO APRÀ, JEAN-ANDRÉ
FIESCHI, AXEL MADSEN, AND
MAURIZIO PONZI/1965

Q: *You've done quite a lot of theater since* The Left Handed Gun.

A: The film wasn't well received in the United States. I'd had enough and didn't want to make another film. No one was interested in working with me anyway, and thanks to a playwright friend of mind, William Gibson, I got some theater work. First I directed *Two for the Seesaw*, then *The Miracle Worker*. And I just wrote a musical called *Golden Boy* with Sammy Davis Jr.

Q: *How do you go about directing actors in the theater?*

A: What I try to do is start from an everyday level. What do they eat? What are they going to wear? Theater is a convention. It's artificial in that everything has to be laid out, but real life doesn't work like that. I want everything to look natural, but the theater lies. It just doesn't respect reality the way film does. The paradox is that in order to give the impression of reality, theater is forced to say certain things. In order to articulate thoughts, words are needed. In other words, for the audience to be able to understand the thoughts of the actors on stage, the director needs to create something artificial. But on film the truth appears just the way it does in real life.

Unlike theater, film has several levels of understanding. Shakespeare's plays have such exquisite and expressive language, so full of ideas that move from illusion to illusion, that it's possible to uncover layer after layer. But

From *Cahiers du Cinéma* (October 1965). © *Cahiers du Cinéma*. Translated by Paul Cronin and Remi Guillochon.

with naturalistic theater it's very difficult to articulate this kind of thing. For example a scene on stage might read as follows: "Do you want a drink, my dear?" "Yes please." "Do you want to go to the bathroom?" "The bathroom's over there." This kind of dialogue doesn't have a deeper meaning, but in film it does. Godard is a master at this, and Fellini too. *La Strada* is so textured that it becomes a kind of "divine comedy." The various levels of understanding in *8½* interconnect with one another and serve a structural purpose. All of this is done with great craft which is the sign of true art. It's the sort of thing you might see without really appreciating its significance. This is difficult to do with theater and certainly isn't easy when it comes to Hollywood cinema.

When I see a good film there's a feeling of greatness, as if the film is enveloping me and filling my conscience—as well as the audience's—with real meaning. I might immediately grasp the significance of the film, or perhaps only much later.

Q: *If your work in the theater aspires to realism, your film work—especially* Mickey One—*seems to aspire to unreality.*
A: With film it's really the opposite problem. Cinema is very different from what I've just been saying. Showing reality on film isn't very difficult. All you need to do is set the camera up in front of what's happening. At the same time I feel that cinema is pretty much able to capture the realm of the unconscious at a psychological or unreal level. In other words on an abstract level, where things might not be so obvious to us.

Q: *Do you try to find connections between the concrete and the abstract? When* Billy *fires at the moon in* The Left Handed Gun *we move from the imaginary to the real.*
A: It's important to try and connect the unreal to the real, to consider them as being interchangeable. At the moment, for example, I'm working on a Western with a story that's inspired by Greek mythology. It's like when people take mescaline and are transported from reality into a dream world. My point is that the relationship between the real and abstract has to be powerfully organic. The abstraction has to be rooted in reality rather than being superfluous. That's the first thing I look for when I read a script.

With *Mickey One* I tried to make a film that had no relation to television or theater. I think it's a very modern film, a truly American film, unlike most others. It's the story of a stand-up comedian, played by Warren Beatty, who owes a debt but doesn't know to whom. This problem of living such a cautious life might be a particularly American problem.

Q: *What do you mean by "modern"?*

A: Well, my work deals with those issues that concern me, like the social and political involvement of the United States with the rest of the world. I'm interested in events that are directly related to the problems raised by the fact that this country has been forced into a leadership role, one we are wholly unprepared for. There is a great disparity between our way of thinking and the way everyone else on this planet thinks. We're quite isolated as a country. The long-term effects of McCarthyism on the American people also trouble me because our way of life has become very cautious and circumspect. This makes it dangerous even to want to express ideas. The film gave me the chance to work in a completely different way, which I found to be a useful and radically new experience.

Q: *Your work has an almost childlike quality.*

A: Yes, certainly. I'm drawing on my own experiences as a child. When I was three years old my parents divorced and I stopped believing in the adult world. For me, grown-ups just weren't real, they only became so upon death. The only real people around were my friends and my brother. It was only after my father died that I began to understand him. Then several friends of mine were killed in the war. . . . I've always retained that childlike quality in my work. I think François Truffaut is similar in this respect, which is one of the things I like about his films. Having said that, I don't think Truffaut could survive in a place like America, at least not in Hollywood. You couldn't make a film like *Jules and Jim* within the studio system. We just don't have actors who would be willing to work with directors like the ones you have in France. Jeanne Moreau is a wonderful and dedicated actress who really believes in the people she works with. We don't have anyone like that here. Being a star in Hollywood is big business and I don't know of anyone who would give all that up to get involved with a film just for the love of it. The economics of the system doesn't cater to this. American cinema is limited, at least as it stands at the moment. Technically speaking, the industry is a well-oiled machine. In the hands of masters like Hitchcock and Hawks film has become a true art form, but I have little faith in Hollywood's ability to produce truly modern and personal films.

Filmmaking "by committee" is a fine art in Hollywood. A film is never made by a single mind but by several at the same time. The more a film costs, the more minds are involved. These guys aren't dummies. But inevitably with each additional mind the power of a film is diluted, not strengthened. The real developments in American cinema today will probably emerge from 16mm filmmaking, though even in Hollywood we're seeing young directors appearing. They say that Sidney Pollock is talented although I haven't seen any of his films.

Film has to be free spirited. A director has to have his own ideas and needs to be the *auteur* of his films. But it isn't easy to come to a studio, stand in front of a committee, and get your own ideas across. A pitch like this has to be done in a way that gets the idea across to more than just one person, which means that very ordinary language is required. As a result the project's real "personality" is often left at the front door.

Q: *What is the best way of directing Warren Beatty?*
A: He needs a kind of controlled freedom. To give a good performance he needs to understand exactly what the director is doing. Warren's always testing me, he never lets up. We'd finish a take and he'd ask me how it was. "Very good," I'd say. "No," he'd insist. "It was terrible! Let's do it again." Brando is the same way. They didn't know each other until I introduced them last month.

Q: *And what about* The Chase, *your new film.*
A: Between us, it's not really my film. Sam Spiegel produced it. I'd never directed such a significant project before and it gave me the opportunity to work on a big scale. My only previous experience working in Hollywood was when I made *The Left Handed Gun* in 1958, but it wasn't a good one. Today, with *The Chase*, I wondered if I might have been able to handle the mechanisms of the studio system and actually enjoy myself this time. I discovered that I'm not enough of a tyrant to work in Hollywood. I found it very difficult to collaborate with people who have worked in such a particular way for such a long time. I couldn't hope to change their ways of doing things. I'm just not selfish or authoritative enough.

I don't feel the future of film rests in *cinéma-vérité*. I'd rather move in the opposite direction, toward more controlled and established images—like traditional Greek theater—that are direct and totally pared down. And I'm drawn toward a kind of classical violence that's born out of the battles fought between individuals who know each other, unlike the kinds of people James Bond kills, those anonymous faces working for anonymous organizations.

Violent Times

YVONNE BABY / 1 9 6 8

B: *How did you come to direct* Bonnie and Clyde?

P: Warren Beatty—the star and producer of *Bonnie and Clyde*—bought the rights to the film and two young journalists, Robert Benton and David Newman, wrote the original story. I wanted to make a film with a strong narrative drive. I remember seeing photos of Bonnie and Clyde as a child and wanted to revisit one of the myths of my youth.

You have to understand that the economic depression of the 1930s in the United States also represented a spiritual depression. The whole country was in a profound crisis. People lost their self-esteem, including Bonnie and Clyde, who handled this in their own way, by committing a series of brazen crimes. Back then the banks kept hold of the mortgages of houses that had been sold off and the Depression was so widespread that small tenant farmers lost their entire livelihoods. People everywhere were going bankrupt. The banks symbolized the economic crisis which is why people resented them.

During this period Bonnie and Clyde decided to stand up and take control of their lives. When they set out to rob these banks they became, despite their crimes, "heroes of the people." Maybe this was naïve but it was an innocent era. Once they had killed someone, other victims followed and they were caught up in such a vicious circle that their way of looking at the world was inextricably altered. You have to realize that back then these kinds of crimes weren't so shocking to people. The forces of law were resented by people worried about their homes being repossessed. They saw Bonnie and Clyde as knights in shining armor, which makes the film a romance, a ballad with a very simple story. Perhaps too simple.

From *Le Monde* (26 January 1968). Reprinted by permission of *Le Monde*. Translated by Paul Cronin and Remi Guillochon.

B: *And very violent.*

P: I wanted to show that this was a violent era in our history, that during the Depression this kind of episode was really quite ordinary. What Bonnie and Clyde did—and I say this with a touch of irony—was no big deal when seen in the context of this period of unemployment, death, and famine. When they see the film today, people might think that what Bonnie and Clyde did was really awful but these days we are continuously exposed to worse horrors. Not here, but elsewhere around the world. That's why I find all this talk of violence so hypocritical. I should add that there's an implicit connection between the film and the Vietnam war, and that filming Clyde's death reminded me of President Kennedy's assassination.

B: *Do you think, as someone phrased it, that your film "risks being interpreted by some youngsters as a glorification, almost an apology, for crime"?*

P: Everyone has read the Anglo-Saxon and French stories and ballads that are brimming with violence. For example I couldn't tell you how many murders there are in *Romeo and Juliet* but I know there are a lot. Are you telling me that Shakespeare's plays exert a bad influence on young people?

I don't think art makes people do certain things. Art merely mirrors the era in which we live. Youngsters today feel powerless in the face of this dehumanized world which is becoming more and more reliant on technology. We don't actually understand youth culture, which is the same thing as being afraid of it. It doesn't scare me, though. I think young people are more attuned to these marauding threats than the rest of us. They seem to be able to avoid catastrophes in ways that are more imaginative, poetic, and spiritual than the rest of us. The people who are worried about how books and films like *Bonnie and Clyde* might influence youngsters are the kind of people who are happy to talk about nuclear weapons and regard war as a natural extension of politics. They're the sort of people who want to put an end to certain threats by making even worse threats.

B: *The film has had quite an impact on the fashion world in the United States and now in Europe.*

P: That was purely coincidental. You can never impose a fad on people. Hollywood spends millions trying to do that without success. If *Bonnie and Clyde* has influenced fashion it's not because of the film but simply because we're ready for this kind of look. I'm astonished that this aspect of the film has been so influential. When we were filming we had absolutely no idea this would be the case, but I'm very happy about it. I'd much rather the younger generation express themselves through fashion than through war.

B: *What are you working on now?*

P: I'd like to adapt a novel by Thomas Berger that's set between 1845 and 1874–75 when the white settlers were fighting the Native Americans. Because a war was never officially declared, the Indians never quite knew what hit them. They drew up treaties that the whites constantly reneged on. It was a terrible chapter in America history, one I'm looking at from a comic perspective. It'll be a violent film, but then you have to search high and low for a period of American history that isn't violent. I think our notion of morality changed during the war with the Native Americans and I suspect this is the same morality we carry with us today.

Bonnie and Clyde Is like a War Film

PATRICK BUREAU/1968

Between June and August 1963, Arthur Penn, director of *The Left Handed Gun* and *The Miracle Worker*, was in Paris working on his first studio film, *The Train*, starring Burt Lancaster and Paul Scofield. After three days of shooting Lancaster showed Penn the door, claiming the director was incompetent. In fact Lancaster knew full well what Penn had been planning: a blockbuster, but a reflective and—more importantly—an antiwar one. Scofield's officer's cap was to feature just as much as Lancaster's Maquis beret. Disappointed and bewildered, Penn learned the hard way that directors still didn't have much clout.

"In Hollywood, stars know that without them a film doesn't exist. Money and power are what keep them going. As a result many of them are undirectable. Elia Kazan has given up working with stars. In France, Jeanne Moreau is the kind of unpretentious and modest star we don't have over here. Godard's *Breathless* and Truffaut's *The Four Hundred Blows* and *Jules and Jim* have radically and definitively changed our idea of what film can be, even at the level of editing."

On his return to New York, Arthur Penn directed a hit play on Broadway, *Golden Boy* with Sammy Davis Jr., then made a small film, *Mickey One* with Warren Beatty and Alexandra Stewart. It was photographed by Ghislain Cloquet. Then he made a big budget film for Columbia, *The Chase*, with Marlon Brando.

"Things were relatively calm during filming. It was only afterwards, when I was obliged to go to New York to direct a play, that producer Sam Spiegel

From *Les lettres françaises* (31 January 1968). Translated by Paul Cronin and Remi Guillochon.

took the film to London where he edited it himself. There was nothing I could do about it."

Penn would like to continue moving between theater and film. Both are important to him.

"Good cinema plays an important part of our daily lives. For me, there are moments when life literally explodes. Films are the best medium to convey that. Every Greek tragedy has moments like this, and it's what I aimed for in *The Left Handed Gun* and *The Miracle Worker*, where I exaggerated the breakfast scene so much that it didn't look real any more."

The European critics are unanimous: Arthur Penn is perhaps the most important filmmaker of his generation, a view not shared by American critics.

"In France you take an interest in film directors but in America no one gives a damn. Everyone knows who I am right now because *Bonnie and Clyde* is the highest grossing film in Sweden and England, as well as America. I've made only five films, but I consider this the best one yet. It's better written and better made."

Not many films have been preceded by the fanfare that has accompanied *Bonnie and Clyde*, which happens to come at a moment of profound crisis. Penn talks about the impact the film has made on the public.

"Apart from Mailer, Styron, and Bellow, and the poems of Corso and Ginsberg, there's nothing going on in the world of American letters. The artistic community is against the war in Vietnam but the most pressing question at the moment is how best to express this. In *The Confessions of Nat Turner* William Styron wrote about a slave revolt but this isn't very helpful to us at the moment. Most people are ashamed of what's going on in Vietnam. Everyone's demonstrating but no one is making films. Ah yes! John Wayne is shooting his pro-war *The Green Berets*. We have to do something, we have no right to remain silent. I'd like to make a film on this subject based on a story I would come up with, but it's not easy.

"For years in America we've stumbled from one war into another. It's neverending. American history is full of the violence that everyone's talking about, and this permanent state of war we're in makes this point even more evident. Every so-called civilized country has gone through the same process. In America, the settling of the West and the war against the Indians was absolutely savage. I think we've come to terms with this by establishing a very moralistic culture. It's not violence that frightens us, it's the moralists. If this violence is one of the things I feel deep down, it's because this is a peculiarly American problem. My next film will be a Western, a history of the native Indians and what happened to them a century ago. All the Indians, gangsters, and murderers are quite colorful, aren't they? I want people to feel disgust, to experience horror when they see all this death around them, just as I do. I'd like to think that it's all quite absurd, that we're much more sensible than this.

"I saw Pontecorvo's *The Battle of Algiers* in New York. It's a great film and shows that when faced with war we're capable of doing terrible things. *Bonnie and Clyde* is like a war film. It's set in same era as *The Grapes of Wrath*, during the brutal Depression of 1932 that had far-reaching effects on the entire country. It's a painful period when many Americans lost everything. Southwest Texas, where we shot the film, was very badly affected. In *Bonnie and Clyde* society has inflicted economic, social, and moral humiliation upon the individual. So what do Bonnie and Clyde do? They wage war against this onslaught in order to find their identities. They represent the popular front of individual liberation. I wouldn't want to psychoanalyze the entire United States but there is certainly a sociological aspect to the Depression. I want to show how these two people emerged from this environment. I'm not saying they're right or wrong, I just wanted to tell their story from start to finish, when the police caught up with them and shot them dead with a hail of bullets.

"I wanted the film to develop on different levels, from a social point of view and even a political one, and I wanted this to be done through its macabre humor. There's real irony when a democratic society moves against two people. I think the film's success—especially with young Americans—stems from the fact that they see it as a return to anarchy, or more importantly, as being antiwar."

Bonnie and Clyde is all of these things and more. Perhaps it's not really a film about violence, rather a wonderful and tender love story. It's certainly already become a legendary tale, and Arthur Penn has already headed back to Broadway and his next film about Indians.

See you soon, Mr. Penn.

Arthur Penn in Paris

RENAUD WALTER / 1968

W: *Is* The Left Handed Gun *your best known film?*
P: My reputation was made in France. The film wasn't a success in the United States, though it did have some allies here. Until then we'd all been used to traditional Westerns with John Wayne. Paul Newman was unknown at the time and American audiences found the film difficult to understand. It wasn't until 1957 that a more personal kind of cinema started appearing.

W: *Was* The Miracle Worker *more of a success?*
P: I'd directed the play and after making *The Left Handed Gun* was so disappointed with American cinema that I didn't want to make another film. But a friend asked me to direct *The Miracle Worker* which turned out to be a completely different experience because we made it in New York.

W: *You said in an interview for* Cahiers du Cinéma *that you don't like* The Chase.
P: I like it but I didn't like the way it was made. I was interested in the ideas behind the film but it could have been edited better. It was too long and slow, and somewhat lethargic.

W: *Why did you begin* Bonnie and Clyde *with Faye Dunaway naked?*
P: To show that Bonnie is available, waiting for someone to fall for her and take her out of there. It was a quick and elliptical way of showing this without having to go on about it later. The basic idea is that she's all alone, wondering what will become of her and how terrible life is. She goes to the window and sees Clyde. It serves as a good romantic introduction to the story.

From *Cinéma* (April 1968). Translated by Paul Cronin and Remi Guillochon.

W: *There is one scene you cut, the one in the bathroom.*
P: Yes, the short scene between Bonnie and C. W. Moss. Bonnie puts on a necklace and sings "We're in the Money," the song from *Gold Diggers of 1933.* C. W. is in the bathtub and Bonnie is smoking a cigarette. As she walks past the tub she throws her cigarette in and he jumps up. It was meant to be a joke, but afterwards comes the love scene in the bedroom and the two scenes just didn't work together. It was a tough scene to start with and ended up being quite ridiculous so we cut it. It was a shame, though I never really considered it as part of the film. It was just something that came to me. I thought it might be amusing for him to take a bath in front of Bonnie as if he were her little boy.

W: *Was it improvised?*
P: Yes. We also improvised the love scene on the bed with Warren and Faye.

W: *How many takes did you do of that scene?*
P: We did it once all the way through with two cameras then got all the pick-ups. Every now and then one camera slipped into the other's frame. Then we shot the scene a second time. It was embarrassing for Warren and Faye at first but once the crew left the set we began filming and it was easier for them to improvise.

W: *What about the question of homosexuality between Clyde and C. W. Moss?*
P: That was in the original script but it didn't interest me. I asked the writers not to develop the idea and they didn't. Instead C. W. is shown as being completely innocent as though he were a little kid, which is a very different idea altogether. I would imagine that had this been a *ménage à trois* situation, which is actually a very complicated and sophisticated relationship, they would never have robbed any banks. It's too psychologically difficult. These are simple people.

W: *But in* The Left Handed Gun . . .
P: Sure, there's something between Hatfield and the three boys but not in *Bonnie and Clyde.* There is nothing voluntarily homosexual, but do we ever really know? There's always something complicated about a friendship forged in the face of death. You can see this in the army where there's nothing really homosexual about your friendships with your buddies. It's not homosexuality in a physical sense even if it's really the most intimate bond two people of the same sex can share.

W: *Like when C. W. plays chess with Buck and Clyde, and Bonnie is saying to Clyde, "Hurry up and come with me"?*

P: It's more that Clyde's love for his gang and his life with these men means more to him than his love for Bonnie. Of course behind all of this there is also the embarrassing problem of his impotence, which is why he would rather hang out with the boys.

W: *You seem to like simple characters. For example neither Billy the Kid nor Clyde can read.*

P: I don't know why but I think exploring a period is more interesting through the eyes of ordinary people. Truly exceptional people don't belong to any particular era.

W: *There is no real communication between the characters in* Bonnie and Clyde.

P: This is true. Clyde and Bonnie each have their way of searching for their own identity. The characters are trying to define themselves through their actions, which makes them somewhat introspective.

W: *Did the scene of Blanche being blinded remind you of* The Miracle Worker?

P: In all honesty, it didn't. She simply lost her sight because of her bullet wound.

W: *Is there any symbolic meaning to things like the fragile doll that Bonnie has at the end of the film or the missing lens in Clyde's glasses?*

P: Yes, perhaps they are symbolic, but this isn't something I pushed. It was just a funny and personal way of making something happen on screen. Losing a lens from a pair of glasses happens to everyone. I thought it was a good way of showing how alive Clyde was just before his death.

W: *How do you explain C. W. Moss's actions at the end of the film when he looks through the window but doesn't do anything to save them?*

P: What I had in mind was for him to put his faith and beliefs to the test. He's genuinely naïve and looked upon Bonnie and Clyde as gods. He really believed that no one could ever catch the two of them, and so by looking through the window it's almost as if he wants to witness a miracle. When he sees them leaving he's thinking, "Ah! I was right! I knew they could do it." His father takes advantage of this naivety when he sets up the ambush. It's a kind of simple-minded religious experience for him.

W: *C. W. Moss is not unlike Hatfield in* The Left Handed Gun, *the reporter who also witnesses the death of his hero. In all your films there are witnesses who go on to create myths.*

P: That's true, but Hatfield is quite different. He wanted to make someone famous, and what happened was that one day Billy the Kid simply stopped resembling the image that Hatfield perpetuated, and Hatfield couldn't take it so he said to himself, "One of these images has to go." That's why he arranges Billy's death. C. W. Moss is very different. He wants to test his faith in Bonnie and Clyde.

W: *In* The Left Handed Gun, The Miracle Worker, *and* Bonnie and Clyde *the same theme emerges, that of moving from reality to legend, like the beautiful sequence when Bonnie reads her poem.*
P: I've always been interested in this idea of looking beyond the legend. It's not only living legends that interest me but also those from our recent past. Just look at how many novels and plays are based on legends.

W: *Bonnie and Clyde are isolated in that they don't belong to any particular social group. Why was this?*
P: That's really how it was. They were outsiders in their own community and, I believe, after several bank holdups became the first gangsters to become famous throughout the whole country. What's interesting is that they were really only small-time. They never stole huge amounts of money. In fact, at the time their fame infuriated the Mafia because the Mob was accused of various crimes that Bonnie and Clyde had committed. It seems that at one point even the Mafia wanted to get rid of them. That would be a great film. Maybe we should make it.

W: *Are there any elements of documentary in the film?*
P: No. We took inspiration from everywhere but not from documentaries. I was going for a more romantic look, which is why we made it in color. We wanted to make a very modern film about the past.

W: *Hobos suggest a very specific period of American history.*
P: That's true. Hobos are connected to the economic situation at the time. Understanding the economic crisis of the era is the best way to explain Bonnie and Clyde. We also looked at lots of photos from the era, for example migrants on the road. Do you remember the scene at the camp when they're shot at and wounded?

W: *Was that scene based on a photograph?*
P: No, it's an homage to John Ford's *The Grapes of Wrath.*

W: *Tell us about the scene when Bonnie and Clyde are killed.*
P: I wanted to manipulate time and space in the scene. I wanted it to slow down as the blood started to flow. We had four cameras, each one shooting

a different speed. We did four takes using different speeds, different lenses, and different angles. We ended up with so much good footage that we could have made an entire film of the massacre alone.

W: *The film is very much a tragedy.*
P: I hope so. It was a tragic age.

W: *Where was the film most popular?*
P: Young people in Britain and America have responded positively because it speaks to them about their own lives. The film is political in that it deals with the Depression, that moment when young people felt excluded from a society that was destroying itself economically. Bonnie and Clyde decided to do something and make a change. They were experiencing an identity crisis, something that today's young generation well understands. Contemporary America is engaged in quite absurd activity, both politically and socially, but instead of reacting violently to make its voice heard the younger generation is responding passively. These are the people who have made *Bonnie and Clyde* a success. After seeing the film, sometimes three or four times, they leave the theater and realize that what's happening in the streets isn't very different. It was extraordinary to walk into movie theaters and find them full of young people.

W: *Our sympathies lie with the baddies in* Bonnie and Clyde.
P: In such a catastrophic economic situation like that of the thirties, with starving people losing their homes, seeing two young people like Bonnie and Clyde doing these kinds of things makes us feel sympathetic despite the violence. The film doesn't pass judgment on what they did, it only shows what happened at a certain moment in time when these two young people took initiative.

W: *In France some people have accused the film of being an incitement to violence.*
P: I don't think *Bonnie and Clyde* is that violent. I took my twelve-year-old son to see it and he thought it was boring. Violence itself doesn't interest me. It's easy to blame cinema for the violence around us. I've seen lots of horror films but they've never made me go out and kill someone. Why not blame literature, our parents, even ourselves? People condemn films but perhaps it's cinema that condemns society.

W: *Was the film censored?*
P: No. There was no age restriction on the film in America. The Hays Office doesn't exist any more and the censors aren't stupid. Today's censor is a

charming man who isn't a censor in the true sense of the word. Nudity is a problem but language and ideas aren't.

W: *What do you think of Hollywood?*
P: It's changed a lot. The new studio heads are young, they're all in their thirties, which makes a big difference. You can go see them and say you want to make a film about Bonnie and Clyde and they'll say yes. Back in the day when the old guard wasn't in tune with modern life, they really didn't have a clue. Their values came from another era and they moralized to excess. The young people who run Hollywood today are very intelligent but the studios have become no more than places to collect equipment. We made *Bonnie and Clyde* in Texas and recently American films have been shot all over the world. Hollywood doesn't really exist anymore.

W: *I understand you like films of the French* nouvelle vague?
P: Yes, I'm very taken with Godard and Truffaut who have totally changed the direction of cinema, especially when it comes to editing. In the United States directors have also been influenced by Japanese films, like Kurosawa and Mizoguchi. Their films are remarkable.

W: *Did you use nonprofessional actors in* Bonnie and Clyde?
P: A woman was watching us film in Dallas and I thought she looked like Faye Dunaway so I asked her to play Bonnie's mother. And the farmer in the scene at the beginning isn't a professional actor. The actor who plays Eugene, Gene Wilder, had never been in a film before, though he's worked in the theater. Eugene's girl is played by John Frankenheimer's wife.

W: *Where did you find Michael J. Pollard?*
P: He's had small parts in a few films like *The Russians Are Coming! The Russians Are Coming!* though he didn't have any lines. In the airport scene when the crowd is rushing he's there with a runny nose. Someone tells him to blow his nose. Blink and you'd miss it. When I saw him I said to myself, "This guy is C. W. Moss." I found out he and Warren worked on a play together in New York and are good friends. It was a lucky coincidence. He's wonderful and very original.

W: *You often work with the same actors. Are you trying to establish your own group?*
P: No. What happens is that when you work more than once with someone you start to learn their style. Warren Beatty and I understand each other instinctively. If you think an actor is good, it's a pleasure to work with him.

W: *It's the first time we've seen American actors working in such a naturalistic way, like in Kazan's films.*

P: I consider Kazan to be the greatest director of actors. He taught everyone. He has a particular way of working: half improvisation and half planned. A situation is defined with its own limits but within that situation the actor is free to do what he wants. I like this way of directing, it makes things seem more natural on camera. Each take has a different meaning and each situation is slightly altered by bringing in a new element. It's impossible to recreate the same scene twice. You can't say to an actor, "Do exactly what you just did" because then the actor is forced to pay close attention to his acting, which is what I don't want to happen. I watch over the actor but he still does whatever he wants to do.

W: *Do you prefer filming or editing?*

P: I like them both. Editing is one thing, filming another. You have to change personality when you move from one to the other. You need a lot of energy when shooting. You have to get close to the actors, play their games, and choose the camera angles. It's really wonderful. When you're editing you have to be very critical of the footage at hand. "I shot this and it's bad. Get rid of it." During editing we're faced with the mistakes we made during filming.

W: *Do you prefer theater or film?*

P: Film. Technically speaking it's quite incredible what the film director is able to do.

W: *Do you think* Bonnie and Clyde *could ever be adapted for the theater?*

P: Yes, it would make a great opera and if I knew how to sing I'd want to be in it. In fact someone's considering putting it on Broadway. It wouldn't be like *West Side Story*, more like Kurt Weill. We'd see death in its most violent forms. A black comedy.

W: *What do you make of all the publicity surrounding the film?*

P: It's luck. A lot of people think we're making money off of the publicity but we don't have anything to do with it. I'm not sure what I can do to stop people from wearing those hats on the streets. The success of the film was quite unexpected.

W: *Your next film is a Western?*

P: Yes, kind of. I want to make a film about the American Indians between 1840 and 1874. I'm not that concerned about it being successful so long as I'm able to tell the truth. The American Indians have been portrayed as bloodthirsty savages determined to stop the white man from living peacefully when, in fact, the opposite is true. The whites took land from the Native Americans. It's a sad chapter in our history and I want to portray it truthfully. It'll be fiction, not a documentary, and with adventure films like this it's possible to underscore political issues in didactic ways. I start shooting in a year.

Arthur Penn at Dartmouth College

D A R T M O U T H   C O L L E G E / 1 9 6 8

Let me begin by trying to describe myself. When it comes to American film, I am an outsider.

I never envisioned myself as being a film person. I rarely went to the movies as a child, and when I experienced a rather terrifying horror film at the age of about seven, I don't think I went back until I was well advanced into puberty. I always thought of the theater as being my true *métier*. It was only by accident that I found myself making a film because along came live television which I had brief experience with, after which I was invited to make a film at Warner Bros.

I was completely bewildered at what I encountered while working for that studio, and I think that what bewildered me about the film world back then continues to bewilder me. I was startled to discover that the people in Hollywood referred to motion pictures as an "industry" and to the films as "product." That this was how they looked upon what we were turning out was a staggering insight to me.

Of course there's no mystery to any of this. Throughout the development of this new industry—one full of complex technology—there began to be established certain norms, something that had a twofold purpose. One was to improve the technical quality of the glossy Hollywood product being made. Sound and image were of the highest level. The other was to find a place for all the nephews and sons-in-law. With a process so meticulously evolved, relatives and cousins could be introduced into this highly familial but clearly structured system without disturbing it.

From May 20, 1968. Previously unpublished. Printed by permission of Dartmouth College.

This was the Hollywood that prevailed until the incursion of television, which invaded the domain that Hollywood had occupied with such privilege and without competition. And Hollywood, of course, was terrified. At the same time, in the period shortly after the war in Europe, films of extraordinary quality were beginning to be produced and imported into the United States.

What happened was that Hollywood retracted. It withdrew. Instead of trying to make a new kind of film, it just reduced the quantity of what it had been making all along. It wasn't until the Hollywood film was somewhat overwhelmed by European cinema that it came to a kind of crossroads, which is where we find ourselves today. Our highly technological film industry is now confronted with either continuing as it has done in the past, or returning to a kind of pre-industrialized state with craft guilds where each man is allowed to make his own kind of film. This is the dilemma that constantly confronts not only the studios but also the American filmmaker.

Oddly enough—or perhaps not so oddly—the American film is the only national cinema that is not at least in part subsidized. In this country film is profoundly, shockingly expensive. This means that experimentation and freedom is not as readily available to the American filmmaker as it might be in other countries. The issue confronting motion picture companies at this point is whether or not they are willing, in a certain sense, to subsidize a kind of anarchy which will ultimately unseat the power structure that has existed for so many years.

The point is that technical norms have depersonalized film in this country to the degree that they have removed from American films those things we associate with European cinema. I'm speaking about the highly personal editing of Godard. The lengthy and introspective films of Antonioni. The flamboyant brilliance of Fellini. These things are not possible within the existing Hollywood norm.

And I'm not talking about only technological norms. I don't mean only those films designed for predetermined audiences full of structured clichés and visual concepts so interchangeable that all personal elements have been removed. I mean norm as a state of mind, a norm that continues to haunt us to this very hour in American filmmaking. A norm that on the very first day I stepped onto a film set I found myself in opposition to. With the very strong unionization in this country we are simply unable to do what Truffaut and Godard do, which is grab a camera and go out with three or four friends and make a film. Anyone of us, in our most secret fantasies, dream of doing just that. Today European directors find themselves crying out against both the spirit of imitation of American film and the intrusion of our film industry upon the filmmaking of their countries.

Chains of distribution in European countries have been bought in part or in whole by American companies. The cries of pain are more and more audible. Previously the Europeans couldn't understand why we don't just go and make what we want to make. They had no comprehension of the fact that our notion of a film has to be committed to paper and that this paper has to be filtered through a series of descending intelligences until finally we arrive at a point where someone will write a check for a film that his son or daughter will want to see.

We can sit here and excoriate Hollywood all night. It's an easy whipping boy. But let me finish by saying that today we are at a crossroads. The impulse to swing exists and perhaps a different kind of film will emerge. It's a personal crisis that each man deals with in his own way. Hollywood would probably prefer we didn't ask certain questions, but I believe the point we have reached in film is no different from the crossroads that our entire culture has reached.

The question as to whether or not we will be mobilized into a kind of impersonal unity—or whether we will permit ourselves the privilege of disparate, individual choices—is a profound one in all forms of art.

The American Film Institute Seminar with Arthur Penn

AMERICAN FILM INSTITUTE/1970

Q: *Most of the industry spokesmen who have come to speak here have been very encouraging in principle but rather discouraging in fact. They assure us that the industry is changing, but what they really mean is that the market is changing and different kinds of films need to be produced. But there hasn't been much they can point to that might be seen as an opening for young filmmakers.*

A: I think that's absolutely accurate. Anybody who characterizes making motion pictures as an industry is the kind of person who'll suggest that you undertake some apprenticeship to the point where the powers-that-be develop sufficient confidence in your submissiveness and willingness to be a part of the structure, at which point they'll finally take a chance and put some money down on your head. I think the audiences that go to films today frighten the studios considerably. What they want is that you bring your youth—your membership in that mystical generation—with you to the job. But don't bring so much that you invade their sensibilities. This is essentially the line you'll constantly be confronted with, one of individual conscience, that all of us face in varying degrees.

The question is, to borrow a phrase, how much of the so-called film industry is genuinely the only game in town? Does one definitely have to work within the system? Is the establishment the only way to go? My sense is that increasingly it's not the way to go. Without copping a plea, before this moment there really was no other way. For want of individual boldness on the

The American Film Institute Seminar with Arthur Penn, held January 30, 1970, and October 7, 1970. © 1970 American Film Institute.

part of the guys who made the films, and because making films is so expensive, one found oneself necessarily going to the studios. This has been the state of play up to now. But it would be my warmest contention that each of us—me included—would do well to search our own conscience and discover whether or not membership in this relatively elite society—one that has built into it a considerable amount of wealth and technical well-being—is necessarily the way films should be made. It is my most earnest belief that it isn't the way they should be made. One does not have to go through the studios. Each day we're seeing increasing evidence of the self-destruction of those institutions to the point where they are beginning to disappear, not because of any external forces but through a series of internal decisions. They have invalidated themselves. The studio system is a kind of self-consuming beast.

Q: *Could you give us an example of some of the problems you have encountered at the studios?*
A: Well, it's a loaded deck to begin with. You come in with either a script or an idea to which they respond. At that point they say to you, "How much will it cost?" You're then expected to provide something of a budget. Now, I don't know how to make up a budget for a film. I can't provide such a thing because budgets vary enormously depending on which studio you make the picture for and what their overheads are. The question is: how much of their obese presence will you allow to be laid onto you?

So what you do instead is enter into their game by saying, "I can't tell you how much the film will cost but I think I can tell you the number of days it'll take to make." They then say, "OK, so how many days?" You break it down and say, "Ninety days," which is how long it took to shoot *Little Big Man.* They then take those ninety days and through some mystical process begin to break it down into dollars. They come up with a sizable amount, but one that doesn't contain any margin for error whatsoever. One of the things about filmmaking—if we can call it an art—is that because money is such a vital component of the process, at least as it is practiced in Hollywood, if you get to the set and have a bad idea and execute something poorly, you don't have the opportunity within that ninety-day schedule to do it again. So what I do instead is that on those days in particular, instead of choosing a single particular way of doing a given scene, I work on it from a multiplicity of viewpoints. Consequently I end up with a considerable amount of film with varying angles and degrees of closeness, which means I can alter its rhythm when it finally finds its place in the film. Since the ninety-day schedule doesn't allow a real margin of error, inevitably that figure is really only a guess, a statement of intent rather than anything to be held to. But immediately the studio says "Yes" and the wheels of production start to grind, the onus of guilt and all the responsibility shifts onto the filmmaking unit. The crew is all unionized, so what may originally have been conceived of as ninety days with a six-man crew becomes something else again with a one hundred and seventy–man crew.

Some producers characterize the director as someone who says one thing but delivers something else. Of course this is not wholly accurate. In fact it's wholly inaccurate. What might be much closer to the truth is that you enter into a mutual contract where you put up with each other's inadequacies, and never forget that the inadequacies of the studio are very considerable indeed. It's worth mentioning here that with the demise of so many studios one is confronted by an incontrovertible fact: the studio executives have what would most properly be characterized as having a "negative identity." They don't make the films. In fact, they genuinely exist to stand in the way of films. They police them and oppose them by coming out to Montana and saying, "Why are you shooting so much? How come you're exposing so much film?"

Q: *Does this affect the ownership point system?*
A: Do people understand how that works? What often happens is a director will reduce his salary so as to participate in ownership of the film. But this ownership of the film is predicated on the original ninety-day budget, which you know on day one you won't be able to hold to. So you are essentially giving up ownership in your film. I think for each $10,000 you go over budget you lose one percentage point and very quickly your ownership of your film. This myth that the so-called creative people in Hollywood are in partnership with the studios is, to a large degree, inaccurate.

Q: *What is the nature of interference from the studios?*
A: It's not so much interference, more a genuine kind of malaise and melancholy in the hearts of the executives. After the screening of one film of mine you could cut the air with a knife. One of the executives said, "We had no idea it was going to be so personal." Another guy rather wittily said, "I wish I'd known it was going to be that kind of film. I would have brought my kid to tell me what it's about." Essentially this was the level of dialogue that afternoon. So with a light heart I skipped out of there with the print under my arm and jumped off a bridge.

In my experience it's been like this with almost every film. When we finished *Bonnie and Clyde*, the film was characterized rather elegantly by one of the leading Warner executives as "a piece of shit." It went downhill from there. It wasn't until the picture had an identity and life of its own that they acknowledged it was a legitimate child of the Warner Bros. operation. A few days after finishing *The Left Handed Gun* I was invited to see an assembly. I was then uninvited to ever attend such a thing again. That was my total contact with the material after I'd shot it. Later, United Artists were very anxious that Elizabeth Taylor play the lead in *The Miracle Worker* because she had expressed considerable interest in the role. We had all worked together as a group on Broadway, on *Two for the Seasaw*, which had then been purchased from under us and made into a very bad film, so we decided we weren't going to let that happen again. We wanted Anne Bancroft to do the film of *The Miracle Worker*. We greeted United Artists with this fact after they'd purchased the rights to the play and they were deeply chagrined. After months of negotiation we hadn't given in, but consequently the project was regarded as a risky film by the studio and the cash given to us very tight. When indeed we did exceed this modest budget—$1,300,000, with $200,000 of that to purchase the play in the first place—by even a slight margin, the excess came out of our salaries. Fred Coe, Anne, Bill Gibson, and I all ended with half salary. Now, the salaries were not bad to begin with, but we ended up with $37,500 each. This is a film that one would think has been a successful and money-making picture. But it's only in the past few months that we've gotten back the remainder of our salaries. So I would say these are clearly rather stringent conditions under which to work.

The man is hanging over your shoulder, and if you want to get this or that shot then you're going to pay for it yourself. It gets to hurt when you realize you can get a better shot but you're going to have to lay out all the bread for it yourself.

Q: *How does the relationship between the people with the money and the creative people work?*
A: If the man who is putting up the money for your film is putting up money only for your film, it's a very different relationship to a corporation that is putting up money for twenty pictures. There's an interdependency among all the films a studio makes, which means what they're doing is hedging their bets. The prime consequence of this is a kind of middle-think where the acceptable tone of everything they choose to finance is gray. The sense of something anomalous, revolutionary, unusual, perverted, or out-of-hand just isn't built into the self-censoring structure which tends to take out the highs and lows.

I suggest that the best way to make films would be for the investor to participate—to a degree—in the filmmaking process. This will make it his film as much as it is the director's. Having someone who says, "If this picture bombs then I can always lay it off on this picture or make a deal with the distributor later on" has generated a lack of genuine effective paternalism on the part of the producing organizations. They are not the true fathers of their films.

Q: *How would you distribute films under this kind of structure?*
A: I don't know. This is only a guess but I think the whole business is going to change. Perhaps the studios will become solely financing and distributing organizations. The less studio infrastructure there is to maintain, the less burdensome they are to the film itself. Although you won't get the one-to-one relationship that I fantasize about, at least you won't have the daily anxiety of these enormous studios imposing such large overheads onto your film. When that happens the film inevitably has to accommodate itself to a broad spectrum of taste, and by so doing anything that might offend people, or that might individuate or particularize it, is removed.

On the other hand I think that what's going to happen is that theater owners will wake up to the fact that with the demise of so many studios there will be a scarcity of films, and to some extent they are going to move into the position of financing films themselves. One of the choices available to those directors who are able to achieve that sublime state of being, able to make a film for two or three hundred thousand dollars, is to have the distributor invest in the film. It may be one of the more burdensome things you have to put up with, but it's not nearly as burdensome as working with a major studio. And if the distributors don't like the finished film, they won't distribute it.

Q: *How would you propose that the studios be run?*
A: I don't believe studios have a genuine function and see no reason for them to exist today. In the old days the idea was that the studios were turning out quality product every year, fifty or sixty films every year at a given studio. They had their own means of distribution and were completely self-contained units. That's no longer the case for any studio here in town. What we're seeing is that the studios are ceasing to have a genuine function. If they weren't so well placed in terms of real estate they would have been consumed a long time ago. Century City is what really saved Twentieth Century Fox.

Q: *There have not been many top quality directors working on small budget films for small audiences.*
A: Yet there's no question this is the way to go. The key is to make films for less money. Much less money. Up until recently it's been extremely difficult,

if not impossible, for directors who enjoy any kind of reputation to work on small budget films. The point is that what is considered a minimum crew depends on who is making the film. It's perfectly possible to make a film independent of any of the unions, but for a director with a reputation—for those of us tempted to move in this direction—the fear that confronts all of us is that our films won't be projected by the union projectionists. The consequence is that one might invest several hundred thousand dollars in a film and have no way of distributing it. This issue has actually become considerably disarmed as a possible fate because in recent years union support has been purchased for a fixed sum after production has finished, or agreements have been worked out with the union that involve as few as three union members.

Q: *Could you see yourself working like this?*
A: Yes. I would like to persuade myself that I'm going to try and confront these kinds of alternatives as a way of making films, though I'm not sure I have the guts to do it. Although they may not agree, I think what the studios are interested in is your individuality and anomalous character, and they will pay lip service—including to some small degree subsidizing the American Film Institute—in order to try and bring you into their structure. But I would counsel that you resist this as hard as you can. Explore the ways to make films that don't involve the majors. I believe that we are at a time of massive change in filmmaking, and it lies with you—and those of my generation who have the guts—to bust it open. I think Francis Ford Coppola is trying it, I think a few guys back East are trying it. Those winds of change are more important than those who are entrenched in real estate out here.

What I also believe is that the criteria for verisimilitude which is obtained in American films—not least of which is pride in the high degree of technology—is essentially an inhibiting factor. When one looks at so many of the European films at the same level they do not compare. I'm not saying favorably or unfavorably, but they just aren't comparable. They have a different character, a rougher human character to them.

Q: *For example?*
A: I would say almost all the work of the *nouvelle vague*. Certainly what Godard has done, though not so much Truffaut, who is more of a meticulous technician. Chabrol, Bertolucci, even some of Bergman's films. To pass with merely an acceptable level of technique and craft is almost unheard of on a Hollywood soundstage. There are simply too many men with too many functions whose existence depends on their ability to have an effect on a given shot or moment. You cannot phase them out. I know it sounds absurd,

and as the director you should be able to tell them to stop, but it's almost impossible for them not to put up a light, and before you know it there are six people involved in the light that you didn't even want in the first place. But they show up on the set in the morning and are very earnest about being there. Consequently, you have to feed and transport them, and if the film is on location, house them too. What happened in Calgary where we were shooting *Little Big Man* was that we ended up with something like forty-three drivers to transport a crew of two hundred. This meant that lunch hour was a sight not to be believed. We fed our teamsters and the crew, and it was not uncommon that during our bigger battle sequences we had a thousand people for lunch.

Q: Mickey One *was heralded at the time as a landmark of New American Cinema. Could you tell us how the film came about?*
A: I could probably make a good case for the studios by telling you what happened. I made an arrangement with Columbia Pictures at the time because I was "hot." The deal was that I would make two films, whatever I wanted, and they would give me a million dollars per film. *Mickey One* was the first of those. They didn't have the right to refuse anything and I even had the right to deny them the privilege of reading the script, although that was fundamentally impossible because one of the clauses in my contract said they had to be able to evaluate the script and determine if it was possible to make the film for a million dollars. In other words I couldn't start a film that would end up with them spending five or six million dollars. So they did read the script of *Mickey One* and they hated it. But they went ahead with it anyway.

   It's is an extremely meaningful film to me even though it suffers from an unfortunate obscurity. I thought it was all crystal clear for audiences, but some of the things I thought I was saying with the film apparently weren't there, something that was distressing after the fact. One of the things that happened is that personally I went into a deep tailspin as a result of what was apparently a befuddling experience for most of the people who saw *Mickey One*. What's interesting is that the clarity of the film is there because it seems to have increasing meaning for a new generation of filmmakers and viewers. It seems that what I did was somehow assume these future generations were already there. Now, I don't want to suggest that I really anticipated anything or was ahead of my time. After all, there was a considerable amount of ineptitude involved too. I wasn't fully aware of what I was doing and wasn't always working totally consciously. I blew it in a couple of places where I think I could have made the whole thing more lucid without altering its central structure—its cyclical form—and themes. The end result was that by mutual agreement Columbia and I didn't make the second picture under that agreement. We made *The Chase*, which cost $8 million, but not another $1 million picture.

Q: *Is there a particular way you work with actors?*
A: I am of the American Method school of acting and directing. What I search for are controlled accidents. By that I mean we set up the scene quite clearly but then try to introduce qualities that might perhaps throw the actors off and catch them in an unguarded moment. This might cause them to make what might be regarded as a mistake, but I consider it to be quite illuminating. It's all about getting inside the well-prepared actor.

Alice's Restaurant is full of this because Arlo really can't act. I would set up the situation and tell him how to play it, and he'd tell me he couldn't play it that way. So I'd say, "Well, do what you do." And it would often be very different from what I would have in mind, but it would be invested with his personality and would often disarm the other actors. It produced a kind of electric response from Pat Quinn and Jimmy Broderick. The other actors were wonderful stimulants to Arlo and pretty soon he found himself able to believe in these make-believe situations. Another example is the woman who plays Bonnie's mother in *Bonnie and Clyde*. She is not an actress, she's a local schoolteacher who was watching us shoot one day. We were struck by her resemblance to Faye so we asked if she would play the part. She was so uninvolved that it absolutely threw Warren into the task of trying to engage her so he could elicit some kind of unprepared response from her.

Dustin Hoffman does this kind of thing constantly. One of the social activities at CBS Films is to go to the dailies of *Little Big Man*, though we do this not so much to watch the scenes but to study the close-ups on the actors and listen to what Dusty is saying off-camera. He does this constantly. He's always asking other actors to do it to him, not to play the scene but to try and break him up, unseat him. He wants to be caught unaware.

Q: *How do you respond to what critics write about your work, particularly Pauline Kael's piece on Bonnie and Clyde?*
A: I was outraged by it, frankly. It was one of the worst pieces of reportage inside a great piece of criticism I've ever read. She suggested that whoever made this film was pretty good but that I was not very good. Now, I don't know who else made this film. She adored it, she thought it a first-rate piece of work, but she had the sense that the script had sprung full-blown from nowhere and that we had somehow gotten it onto the screen through the marvelous presence of Warren Beatty and Faye Dunaway and a terrific cam-

eraman and superb filmmaker and got it into the theaters. Well, that's a lot of crap. And it's also irresponsible. She called my office to check out certain things and there were many things she could have informed herself about had she been disposed to doing so.

It seems to me there was some genuine underlying condition that caused her to write that way. I've never met the lady and I do think she is clearly one of the leading analytic minds about film in the country. But when *Mickey One* was screened at the New York Film Festival, I had a rather heated encounter with [*New York Times* critic] Bosley Crowther. As a result of having heard something derogatory Pauline Kael had said about *Mickey One*, I said she seemed to be a lady on the make. She had come to New York and was going to try and make her name. That probably got back to her. What also happened was that Kael called up from San Francisco right after we finished *The Chase* and asked, "How is the film going? I thought *The Left Handed Gun* was a first-rate piece of work and I liked *The Miracle Worker* a lot. I hope this is going to be good, but I must say I've been disappointed with so many people." She talked about Tony Richardson who made *Tom Jones* which she thought was just terrific and then made *The Loved One* which was a piece of crap. So I said, "I just don't know." When that piece about *Bonnie and Clyde* came out in *The New Yorker* I must confess that one of my first thoughts was that it smacked of a lady spurned. I had somehow failed her. One of the things that Pauline Kael's reviews have as a strong undertone is a kind of female sexuality. Calling her book *I Lost It at the Movies* suggests something to me.

Q: With *Bonnie and Clyde how did you plan the coverage needed to create the feeling of violence in the screen? How do you divide up all the pieces of action in the scenes, for example the one where the police surround the house just after the brother and his wife join them for the first time? It's made up of so many different shots. How do you put them together in your own mind and decide what's necessary to create the scene?*
A: I see it all together in my mind to begin with when we get to where we're going to shoot. In this case it was at the end of a driveway with a garage. The actors were upstairs in the house, which meant they would have to get downstairs, into the garage and out that driveway. What happens then—and this may be a better answer to your question—is that I take the whole thing apart.

One concern in breaking it down like this is that the energy of the basic concept remains. On cutting from shot to shot, energy has a tendency to dissipate, and all you are really doing is drawing attention to the changes of angle. By cutting there is nothing added except a greater sense of geography, which means one can now see here where previously one could only see there. Of course there are certain things one wants to be close to, like when they explode out of the garage with the car. That has a real kinetic force to it. If you're too far back you lose that sense of explosion. We wanted the experience to be one of just rocking you back in your seat as much as the police must have been rocked back by this thing hurtling out of the house.

Of course there is also a human element in every scene. What do we want to know about the people, particularly the principal people, in terms of that event and how they react to it? For example a very decisive moment takes place in that scene when we see Blanche as an absolute hysteric. Up until then she's been a pain in the ass but here she becomes an absolute raw hysteric. And the problem of how you deal with an hysteric when you're part of a gang—and a criminal gang at that—becomes an organic element of the story thereafter.

Let me say something about coverage. I shoot an awful lot of film. I like to do the master shot then cover it from all angles. Shooting over-the-shoulders, individuals, medium close-ups all gives me an awful lot of material to work with. All you have to deal with is the lab bill. We were shooting a scene and I realized there was a moment where the dramatic tension was going soft. I felt that if I didn't get some kind of coverage I wouldn't be able to control the speed and rhythm of the scene, so I shot it with an individual of Warren, an individual of Faye, and a tight close-up on each. This gave me the opportunity to alter the tempo. It's always important to have a safety valve, something that can get you out of a situation. On a given day you arrive on the set with a certain rhythm in mind, one you feel is right for the first scene of the film. But the thing is that you rarely shoot in sequence, and if you don't provide yourself with material that can enable you to expand or condense time and change the rhythm, you'll be obligated to cut the film to the rhythm you felt that particular day. The point is that the atmosphere on a particular day on the set might not necessarily be right for the scene once it's placed in continuity in the finished film. Of course the other reason why I shoot a lot of film is that I like actors. I enjoy pushing them as far as they can go.

Q: *Are you conscious that you're maintaining the geography of the scene in our minds at all times?*
A: Yes, particularly in a scene like this, otherwise you're going to have Bonnie and Clyde and the cops all moving in the same direction. These are not fixed rules by any means, but they can be useful, believe me. I'm making a film at the moment where we're shooting Custer's last stand. Before Custer and his men are surrounded, he is chasing some Indians up a hill. He gets all

the way up to the top of this hill and then here come six thousand more Indians, and he's caught in this enormous pincer movement. It's a hard thing to show. I wanted that one moment when Custer, as it says in the script, gets to the top of the hill and sees every Indian in the world. We only had four hundred extras so we kept moving them around. They chased him, then they were ahead of him, then they were behind him, then they went around him. So screen direction becomes extremely important in terms of making the best use of what you have to work with at a given time.

Q: *You didn't storyboard that?*
A: No, I don't storyboard. I don't know why. I guess it dates back to my days in live television where there was no possibility of storyboarding and everything was shot right on the spot—on the air as we say—at the moment we were transmitting. I think storyboarding is pretty lousy. I prefer to be open to what the actors do, how they interact to the given situation. So many surprising things happen on set and I have the feeling that storyboarding might tend to close your mind to the accidental.

Q: *Most of the tracking shots in* Bonnie and Clyde *are in the first section of the film. Was that intentional on your part or did the script call for this?*
A: The script didn't specifically call for tracking shots. I just decided we would use lateral and horizontal moves for a while and then, as the film goes along, start moving more nervously and abruptly as the jump cuts become more conspicuous.

Q: *When Clyde robs the bank you cut to a long shot of the town. Is that for geographical reasons?*
A: There are a multiplicity of reasons. First of all there's the question of what the street is like before the robbery and what it's going to be like afterwards. It's a relatively empty street in an empty town. It's the first long shot we've seen of the town, with only one person standing on a corner. It adds an ingredient of drama, the question of "Is that guy going to stop them? Is he going to catch Bonnie and Clyde?"

Q: *The opening shots of the film beautifully set up Bonnie's relationship with Clyde. We learn what she sees in Clyde and what she wants from him. But I am not sure I know as precisely what Clyde sees in Bonnie.*
A: The next scene explains this, where he sees her as a completely sympathetic partner, a non-demanding partner who has similar aspirations to the romantic as he does. The next scene is where he starts to divine her fantasy life. When they are walking down the street together, before Clyde robs

the bank, Bonnie's sixth sense tells her there is romance, escape, excitement around this guy. It just wasn't within my capabilities to get all of that into the first location. The nervousness was intentional. I really wanted them both to be so high-strung and high-pitched that they would do anything.

Q: *When she says, "Stay there, I'll be right down," he stays there instead of running, even though he has been caught breaking into the automobile.*
A: No, he hasn't. He's been caught looking at an automobile. He hasn't broken into it, he hasn't touched it really. He's intrigued when he sees her standing naked in the window. He feels there's a purity there, and I was trying to suggest that even before he appears Bonnie is a girl with a real hunger in her. She wants to be a movie star and have her name in the paper. A girl who would stand up in the window like that is a girl who is willing to do a lot to become famous. And there's a big part of Clyde which we discover a little more subtly—it's not quite so narcissistic as it is in Bonnie—concerning this drive he has to become a public personage. It's something alive in both of them.

Q: *Did you have a permanent fix on the characters before you started shooting? I ask because you have described a process where you keep yourself open, where you are never caught in an idea or a concept you cannot change depending on the situation. How much improvisation—not in terms of dialogue but in terms of character—do you allow?*
A: A good deal of it is intuition. During specific discussions with the actors I'm able to explain my understanding of the character, what the intention of the character is in a given scene and what the line of intention might be in the Stanislavsky sense. It's important to suggest to an actor that they are operating within a structured situation, but at the same time that they can turn loose anything which occurs to them, so long as I—the director—make the final decision about what is appropriate or inappropriate.

With *Bonnie and Clyde* there were many things that happened between Warren and Faye I wasn't anticipating, for example the match-business just before he robs the bank. When it happened I said, "Gee, that's beautiful. Let's get that on film." When those kinds of things happen they become extremely meaningful. In that scene Clyde's line of action might be to make everyone think he is somebody more than just a boy walking along the street with a newspaper under his arm. As the scene unravels he becomes more and more involved in this until finally she says to him, "Prove it." There is actually a lot of dialogue missing there. When he takes the pistol out she says, "You've got one all right, but you don't know how to use it." Well, on paper lines like that seem good. Actually, when you play the scene they seem good, but when you finally see it up there sixty feet wide it's really corny. So we cut a few lines but left the action and behavior. We just took the verbalization of it out.

Q: *What about later in that sequence when they introduce themselves to each other? Was that in the script?*

A: It was a tough dramatic problem. I thought of a lot of ways of doing it and none of them really suited me. I thought it was a terrific piece of writing on the page but behaviorally it was kind of a cheat, so I thought about withholding it until the worst, most inappropriate moment. I thought it should interrupt the most complicated and important piece of action and that Clyde should introduce himself before he is aware of what he's really doing. In the original script it was in the same place but it said something like, "He comes out. They look around for an automobile and she says, 'I'm Bonnie Parker,' and he says, 'I'm Clyde Barrow,' and they jump into the nearest car." So the lines were meant to come somewhere between the time when he's gone in to rob the grocery store and when he comes out with the money in his hand and they drive off.

Q: *How closely did you work on the Benton and Newman screenplay while developing the film?*

A: Pretty closely. The script was in good shape when I first read it. What they had down cold was the behavior, the kind of Southern interaction between Blanche and Buck, between Buck and Bonnie. A lot of that is intact in the film. But I restructured the interior section of the film quite considerably. The family reunion, I remember, occurred quite a bit earlier than it does in the finished film. The kidnapping of Velma and Eugene also occurred at a different time. The issue was about the sense of escalation of the foreshadowing of death in the story, that somehow this desirable public life they are enjoying is also bringing them closer to death. We altered the sequence of scenes to escalate upward from that chatty little kidnapping scene, which ends with him telling them he is an undertaker, to the scene with Bonnie's mother.

In the family reunion scene Warren was concerned that he didn't have enough to play. I thought he had enough to work with but a writer named Robert Towne—who is a close friend of Warren and was with us in Texas—came up with what I thought was a superb turn. Bonnie's mother turns to her and says, "You live three miles from me and you won't last long." It was meant to convey the puritanical Baptist idea of "You danced a lot and now you've got to pay the piper." Clyde is trying to charm the pants off her and she says, "That's not gonna work." It was Robert's line and it helped enormously. It helped Warren play the scene, and it certainly helped Faye and the mother.

Q: *What was the point of that scene? You play with jump-cuts and slow motion too.*

A: I went for a grainy look and some shots in slow motion to suggest that Bonnie is trying to grab hold of the past but it's slipping through her fingers. It's just not possible to recapture any longer. She and Clyde have reached the point of no return. In a matter of hours this scene is going to drift out of her life and into her memory so I decided to use the film as a representation of that emotion. The location was chosen because of the sand and the rusty color. It was the only time in the film we ever get away from the green and slightly urban look of the small towns. We shot it through gauze on location but optically balanced some shots afterwards.

Q: *The original script ends with Bonnie and Clyde dying but we never actually see them killed. It's only hinted at. I was wondering why you changed it.*

A: The way the film originally ended was with the deputies gathered in the bushes waiting for them. We cut between Bonnie and Clyde who are getting closer and the deputies waiting. There was kind of raw comic dialogue, things like "Man, it's cold. I wish I was home with my wife." "I wish I was home with your wife too," that kind of country talk. Then Bonnie and Clyde arrive and at the moment the shooting starts comes a black-out.

Now, these are people I read about in the newspaper in the early thirties, practically the first identifiable personalities I remember as a kid. I felt we couldn't end the story like that. I thought we had to turn them into legends, move from reality into a new degree of experience. In a certain sense it's the same reason why we didn't do it in black and white. It was to say that this is not a document of what happened. It leaps forward in time and brings it up to the present, which is where the idea of changing rhythms in the final scene came from. I wanted the scene to say "We're moving out of this kind of time and this kind of place into another experience." The ending was so clear to me when I read that script. In fact it was the only thing which was clear.

Q: *How many cameras and how many takes did you do for the last scene?*

A: We shot as a gang of four cameras running at different speeds: a master, then on Warren and then on Faye. Later on we got them into a two-shot. One of the cameras was moving at an enormously high speed so it would run out of film quickly. By the time we got up to speed one camera was almost out of film. The actors were wired, every one of those bullet hits is a squib. We didn't have to rehearse because you can feel them go off. They're in a metal dish and have a little powder and blood in them. It took us half a day to prepare the actors. We got one shot in the morning and one shot in the afternoon.

Q: *What did you tell the actors to do in the final scene, just before they are shot?*
A: As I remember, I gave Warren something very simple. I took for a fact that Clyde is a country boy who did a certain amount of hunting, and when you see a bunch of birds like that something has caused them to spook. To me he's saying to himself, "It's not kosher here. Whatever is going on in those bushes isn't right."

Q: *Was the Judas scene, that strange shot tracking through the town, conceived by you or the writers?*
A: Originally it was a two- or three-page sequence where Sheriff Hammer and C. W.'s father meet in the ice-cream parlor. There was dialogue of them preparing the situation, but you really don't need it. I remember I lifted the dialogue out of the scene before we even shot it. It's almost abstract, a classic betrayal scene. I evolved it as a straight pan shot. Actually it would be a nifty thing for us to study some day because there are actually something like five cuts in that pan. They are hard to see and I didn't believe it when Dede Allen told me she'd done it. She made the whole thing shorter which helped the shot enormously.

Q: *The details are there. The father walks out with ice-cream and that night you see C. W eating it. The next day we are back in the town. You shoot from the back-seat of the car through the front window and there is the ice-cream parlor again.*
A: That was all intentional because we wanted to make it clear it was the same town. We wanted you to say, "Oh my God, it's going to happen on the street!" And then you have the shot of C. W. looking at them from across the street with an almost sort of They-Can-Walk-On-Water look on his face. He's thinking, "They did it! They got away. They proved my faith in them!"

Q: *Are there any particular ways to direct violent scenes?*
A: I think you have to make the decision before the fact whether or not you're really going to play the violence or whether you're going to do a ritu-alized version of the violence. You see the ritualized versions at the Japanese Kabuki theater or Kurosawa's films. If you really want a kind of verisimilitude,

I think you have to go beyond the objective into the subjective. You have to explode into the unconscious of the people watching, and to do that I think you have to blow the frame apart with the most significant cuts. You have to give the audience more than they expect, something of such kinetic explosiveness that they say, "I can't really be seeing that. This is an unfamiliar image to me, and I can't stand it." This goes back to Eisenstein, the scene on the steps in *Battleship Potemkin*. When he finally cuts to the man with his glasses and the blood on his face it's so unbearable. It's a spectacular piece of montage. There's a dead steal from it in a certain sense in *Bonnie and Clyde* with the guy on the running board. I wanted audiences not to believe that they'd just seen a man shot in the face through a window.

Q: *Is there a way of setting up violent scenes?*
A: If anything, the thing here is to divert the audience, to lure it away from the possibility of violence. I think it's more effective this way.

Q: *The moment at the end of the film when they look at each other, just before the machine guns start, is one of total recognition of what is about to happen. How did you get us to the point that we actually care about these two pretty awful people?*
A: I think a balance is struck somewhere early on in the film and they cease to be awful people. I wouldn't stand by this historically for a minute, but dramatically speaking it's right to say that there is a certain validity to whatever it is they're doing. They certainly start out as a couple of punks but slowly we begin to endow them with characteristics. They watch a man return to his home which has been foreclosed by the bank and with the mindlessness of that act weighing upon him, without premeditation, Clyde finds himself telling this man "We rob banks." He's saying they have found an identity for themselves, which is to be on this farmer's side rather than on the bank's. What slowly happens is that their story takes on mythic proportions and pretty soon they find themselves faintly heroic figures. I think audiences resist this for a while but after a while begin to fall in with them. Somehow beyond all the reality of what it is we've been confronted with comes this escalation into a kind of fairytale, into a kind of fable upon which we begin to hope for certain things. Once you start doing that, we've got you. You're hooked.

Q: *I was wondering if you encourage your actors to come and watch the daily rushes.*
A: Yes. Everybody connected with the picture can come to the dailies. Watching dailies is a depressing experience because there is no way in which you're not learning to deal with the fragmentation of the film shoot, and

fragmentation kills. I find that when you don't allow the actors to see the dailies, a kind of anxiety seems to develop around them. They start asking people who did see them how they look and what they did wrong. If an actor is going to be depressed about his performance, let him watch the dailies himself. Let it be self-generated. But of course it can also be a useful experience. The actor can discover repetitive mannerisms that he may not be conscious of and may want to steer away from in the future. I also think you can make things quite clear to an actor from their having seen dailies which would not otherwise be clear. What you do see every once in a while is an actor just take off and do something golden, and then everybody comes out of the dailies licking their chops.

Q: *How was it working with Warren Beatty?*
A: Warren isn't the easiest guy to work with. He's a very insistent and extremely intelligent guy who'll make you defend what you say until either you make it very clear to him or completely abandon your position. In the case of *Mickey One* we were working on a fairly obscure piece of material and I got to the point of saying, "Warren, shut up and do it my way. I can't discuss it with you anymore." What that did was deprive us of a certain kind of interchange, something we later enjoyed enormously on *Bonnie and Clyde* where Warren would say to me, "I'm going to question you and quarrel with you any time I want to. And you can tell me to go and shut up or quarrel back with me. But you always finally have the right to say, 'Look, I said everything I have to say about it. I'm directing the picture and you're acting in it, so do it my way.' But I want to be able to talk to you about it." So that was the way we worked on that film, and it worked just fine. We had some very raw exchanges and often the crew would think that we were fighting but in point of fact we were really just engaging and trying to kind of irritate each other. It was, "No, God dammit! I don't want to see that cold, dead, handsome face show up on the screen one more damn time. I'm sick of it. It's not enough just to deliver that good looking body. Go to work!" A lot of Warren's best acting comes out of that state of mind.

Q: *Did you have a rehearsal period on* Bonnie and Clyde?
A: No, we rehearsed it as they were preparing the dollytrack. For the first scene, for example, I let Faye go upstairs and left Warren downstairs and they just started to play the scene with each other. Then they came downstairs and the movement along the sidewalk developed. I had the idea that I wanted to do a long tracking shot but I wasn't absolutely fixed on it and would have done something else if it had occurred and I liked it. Essentially

they could either stand in front of her house and talk, which seemed to me not very interesting, or walk along the street. I kept pointing out the nuances in the scene, like the waitress thing which was very important to me. Warren was right on it. Faye, I think, had an even campier idea of how to play Bonnie at this point and she wanted to turn it on even more when he said, "I'll bet you're a movie star."

The day we got to the town to shoot it turned out they were ginning cotton. All the cotton in the area had ended up in this town to be ginned, so you hear that sort of chooka, chooka, chooka all through the opening of the scene. That had to be incorporated somehow into the awareness of the actors and it accounts for a certain kind of disconnectedness which they have when they talk to each other. What Faye is looking at off-screen is that ginning operation.

Q: *Did you even have a script reading before shooting?*
A: Yes, but it was highly informal and it was in my motel room. There is no money for script readings on most pictures. We would sit around and talk but often we got our best rehearsal in the motel the night before we shot a given scene.

Q: *Do you give the actors explicit instructions?*
A: No, I watch what they do and then suggest it might be more interesting this or that way and tell them not to overlook this or that fact. But I try not to tell them how to do it, ever. Very occasionally I will give the actor a line reading but prefer setting a problem in motion which will result in what I want rather than telling them how to achieve the final result.

Q: *In the past you have spoken about why you feel* The Miracle Worker *is not such a good film.*
A: Yes. I over-articulated and over-dramatized—and consequently de-cinematized—a large portion of that film. When we did it on stage, we had to use dialogue to establish the basic dilemma confronting Annie Sullivan, which is that she is a child who cannot be reached. Of course this is visible to everybody from the moment the curtain goes up, just as it's visible to anybody when the film starts. It was important that we had scenes where it's clear Annie was not just addressing herself to this physically handicapped child but was also addressing herself to the reverberations of that physically handicapped child as they were experienced by the child's parents, most particularly by the father. There were major scenes between Annie and Captain Keller in which they argue it out nose-to-nose. Finally he'd say, "All right, you can take her to the carriage house. But two weeks only, Miss Sullivan.

Two weeks and then she comes back to us." Well, "two weeks" is a theatrical device. It's something which says to the audience, "You're not going to be in this theater all night." "Two weeks" means time will run out on Annie Sullivan and Helen in that carriage house. I realize now that in the film this scene could have been done much more effectively if I'd just let the camera sit on Helen, then on Annie, then on Helen, then on Annie, cut to the Captain, cut to Annie. We could have got rid of vast amounts of dialogue just by confronting the sheer enormity of what lay ahead of Annie Sullivan in terms of her work with Helen. But I didn't. I was comfortable with what I'd done on the stage and it had worked for me there, so I did it in the film. And in that regard I was hoisted by my own petard.

Q: *Are you able to choose which cameramen you want to work with?*
A: I fantasize about the kinds of relationships European directors and cinematographers have. You hear about some of these great love affairs. I had only one experience like this, on *Mickey One* with French cameraman Ghislain Cloquet. It was just marvelous. He really understood the script and could envision images which supported the story. He was fast, there was no nonsense, no posturing. You have to recognize that in Europe it's a very different kind of relationship. There the cinematographer and the director work together on a film. Here a director is part of the management and the cinematographer is head of the crew, the chief technician on set. If a technician has something to say he goes to the cinematographer and asks the cameraman to ask me something, so one doesn't get the feeling of working with real colleagues. There is a sense of "The director wants this. How do we retain our standards and still give him what he wants?"

Q: *Why were you fired from* The Train?
A: The script had been around for two years or so. It had gone to every studio and I was looking for a really strong action picture. William Morris sent me a whole bunch of scripts and I chose *The Train* because I saw that I could impose an interesting story onto it. They asked me who I wanted and I said, "It should be one of the big butch Hollywood stars." So we put a call in to Burt Lancaster right then and there. He asked me, "Is this a script you really like?" I said, "Yes." "Okay send it to me." A week later he called me and said, "You've got a deal." So that was it. We went to United Artists and put a package together. Now, even at this point there were a lot of things I didn't know. I didn't know that Burt owed United Artists a million and a half dollars from [his production company] Hecht-Hill-Lancaster which was going to be written off on this picture. In other words he was going to close out his debt to the studio in the amount of a million and a half dollars. This was in addition

to receiving a quite considerable salary. They were in to him for something like two and a half million bucks.

It's worth looking at Lancaster's career at this point. This is my interpretation and he's got every right in the world to deny this and say I'm full of crap. He had gone off and done *The Leopard* which is a film I hadn't seen at that point but it was a book I admired and it was something I think Burt was very proud of. It was enormously well received in Europe, it had opened at the Cannes Festival where it won a prize and Burt won great accolades. I had only met with him once before this in Hollywood before I went to Paris to prepare *The Train*. The next time we met was in Paris and he was really ebullient. Everything was gold. It couldn't have been nicer. Then *The Leopard* opened in this country and got blasted. I think Burt linked me in his mind with that group of arty directors like Visconti and those kind of European directors, at least more than he did with those kind of solid, reliable action directors like Frankenheimer. When that moment of panic hit, it hit pretty badly. I didn't know it at the time. It actually hit him before he came to France, where I already had started shooting. Then Burt showed up and we went to work. We worked two days, that's all. First day we had a very amiable lunch, then worked on a scene. I remember we were working on a scene in the cab of an engine with Michel Simon, who doesn't speak any English. I was shooting rather a lot and I heard Burt saying, "Oh Christ, not another angle, come on!" And I'd say, "Yes, one more." And then I remember saying something to him like, "Look, this next take, I don't want to know what you're doing or what you're thinking, but I wish you'd have a private thought, something you wouldn't like to tell me. I don't care what it is." And there's kind of a very fishy look from Burt. Anyway, we wrapped for the day and I saw some dailies and went home and this friend of mine who was writing the picture called up and said, "Hey, I just left Lancaster and you're off the movie." And I said, "That's impossible. I created this movie, I can't be off. I made it happen." I was stunned. Then the head of United Artists came to Paris and said, "Any discussion is academic." That was the end of that.

Q: *Did you ever see the finished film?*
A: I saw it only recently on TV and I thought it was okay, though it missed the point entirely. Frankenheimer threw out our script which had a very different emphasis to it. He made an action movie and we wanted to make a movie about the commerce of war. That was really the center of it. There was an art dealer, played by Claude Dauphin, who was the major character of the whole piece and who was completely written out of the Frankenheimer version.

Something that's very important for you guys to bear in mind is that when you make a deal with actors to be in your film you're not making a deal with them to be in your film, but making a deal with them to be in United Artists' film or Warner Bros.' film or Columbia's film. In the not too distant past the contract used to read "Warner Bros., who herein after shall be known as the author. . . ." I'd got Jeanne Moreau and Paul Scofield to come be in this nonsense action film because I kept telling them, "Look, I know it's just this now but I'm going to do that with it." They signed on as friends, anxious to work on a picture with this kind of complexity, and when that was no longer true they were trapped in a rather awful situation. Both tried to get out but couldn't. It taught us all a lesson.

Q: *Do you worry about success?*
A: Yes. It's a constant dilemma, one that you can't really avoid, I suppose. But there comes a moment—it happens overnight—when you find yourself living in a manner not only to which you're not accustomed but which you don't deserve. I don't mean to be moralistic or socialistic about it but it just seems improper. I don't have the mechanism just to go out and give everything away, even if something inside tells me I should probably do just that.

Q: *What's your next project after* Little Big Man?
A: I don't have one.

Q: *Do you like the security of knowing there is another thing in the pipeline?*
A: I used to but now not so much. I used to do work compulsively. There was a time when I would go nuts in the theater. I had five shows running at once on Broadway. They couldn't stop me. I would finish one, it would open, and we'd start the next one. I got that way a little bit in the movies.

Q: *Do you have your own production company?*
A: Tatira-Hiller. Tatira is Warren and Hiller is me. Having your own production company is one of the greatest myths in the world. It's one of the things that the studios discovered long ago they can give you without actually giving you anything. You have the sense of being autonomous and your own boss, yet in reality you have none of that. When it gets down to the nitty-gritty, if somebody puts up the bread for something, it's their project.

Let me finish by telling you a story about the scene in *Bonnie and Clyde* when they ride out of town to their deaths. It goes back to what we were talking about at the start of our discussion. Back in the day you went to work at the studios as a director. You were called the "director" and your job was to shoot the movie and tell the actors what to do. But in point of fact the movie was really in the hands of the technicians. They were the fifty-two-weeks-a-year men who turned out films for the studio. The point is that there are procedures and standards and norms which have been solidified. If a cloud goes over a shot—as it did in that scene in *Bonnie and Clyde*—then it's not going to cut with the next shot. I said, "Let's go" and one of the guys said, "Cloud coming." I said, "Well, for Christ's sake, let's shoot with the cloud coming." And he looks around and says, "Right, he wants to shoot with the cloud coming. . . ." I remember I was about to buckle but Warren said, "Shoot it, shoot it. Now!" He screamed and we started to roll and he took off in his car after Faye on the other side of the street. It was Warren who gave me that last kick in the ass to get over wanting to be a nice guy with the technicians. The amount of resistance! This "We've Never Done It Like This Before" way of working. Directors in America have to deal with this notion of "We have thirty years experience of doing it. We do it better than anybody in the world." And that, in one sense, is absolutely true. But they also do it more impersonally than anybody in the world. The amount of negativism on set when I say that I want to do a particular kind of tracking shot! "You can't do that! Absolutely no way!"

By the time we did *Bonnie and Clyde* it had become more common to use more than one camera. But on my first picture there were a couple of times where I wanted to use more than one camera, it just seemed absolutely logical to me. We would do a big action sequence and then go back in to cover it. So one time I said, "Here is the main camera, here is the A-camera. Let's put another camera over here." The cameraman said, "I can't do it. I'm lighting for this camera." And I said, "Well, okay, you're lighting for this camera, but look, stocks are a lot faster now and the cameras and lenses are really good. Why don't we put a second camera here?" He said, "No." So finally I said, "Look, you've got to do it." So he said, "Okay, I'll do it." But he made up a slate which read "Not responsible for this camera." He knew it was going to be seen in the projection room and he was certain that an executive was going to have a sufficiently discriminating eye to be able to detect whether or not this was the camera he'd lit for, which was absolutely not the case at all. As a matter of fact the stuff was a lot better on that camera than it was on the one he'd lit for.

This all goes back to the studio heads who are for the most part quite ignorant. They watch the dailies even though they don't really know what the dailies relate to. They barely remember the script they originally read because they made the deal a year ago. They're sitting in this screening room at Warner Bros. and three minutes of film comes on from this picture and three minutes of film comes in from that picture. What happens, of course, is that some executive jumps up and says, "Aha! A cloud! Who's the camera-man on that picture? Get him out of here!" This is all because in his mind it's an anomaly. It didn't happen yesterday and it hasn't happened for the last three weeks and none of the other shots have clouds in them, so it mustn't be any good.

I know I'm laboring the point and I'm also doing it in comic-book terms, but in point of fact there's a very important idea behind this, which is this: trying to break the rules in Hollywood is an important goal. Your mission should be to put your personal stamp on the film.

Arthur Penn, 1922– : Themes and Variants

ROBERT HUGHES/1970

Early days

I was sort of phobic about films. Those horror shows scared me to death. I went under the seat and didn't come out for ten years. It was a great place to go and play hooky from the world, but it was weird that I really got belted by film. *Citizen Kane* just staggered me. I walked out of that the way you walk out of any major life experience. I wandered the streets for hours thinking about what had happened to me.

Much later I was writing and directing a little bit for television and then got the chance to come East and work with Fred Coe on what became the *Philco Playhouse*, the big live, dramatic show of Sunday nights in the fifties. I think television has become our medium of commerce, which is not what it was in the early days. There wasn't a big enough audience for the sponsors to be that interested in it and consequently there was very little interference. Nobody really ever came in and said, "Do that kind of play and don't do that kind of play." We were pretty much allowed to do what we wanted. As the popularity of the medium increased, the content of the medium altered. And at a certain point—I don't think we were terribly conscious of it—we realized we had run out of the freedom and eloquence to say what it was we wanted to say with television. Suddenly there was a man from the agency in the booth, and then there were two men from the agency in the booth, and pretty soon there were people shaking their heads about scripts before we even started rehearsing them. Finally they assigned a kind of censor, and

Transcript from Robert Hughes's documentary *Arthur Penn, 1922– : Themes and Variants*, Thirteen/WNET, 1970. Printed by permission of Rebecca Hughes.

before we knew it bang went the medium. And each of us in his own way drifted away from it.

Some went into film very early, like Del Mann. Some went into the theater, which is the path I took, although in point of fact I actually did my first film before I did my first play, but I was thinking theater at the time. I had a string of hits that really was indecent. I had five hits in a row, one right after another. It was insane. At one point I had five hits running at once on Broadway. It was just incredible.

Visuals

I read about my visual sense but wasn't particularly aware I had a visual sense until around *Bonnie and Clyde*, although I can look back on things in *The Miracle Worker* that I like a lot, for example that grainy section of flashbacks.

What people say in a scene is often the least important of its many aspects. For me this came as a great surprise, having come out of theater where every idea and nuance of psychological stance and viewpoint was demonstrated through what people said, how they said it, and what language they chose to say it. Suddenly I got into movies where I found that what was happening on screen was contradicting what the actors said. This dynamic just set me trembling, it really knocked me out, because then we could focus on a guy who says, "Good morning," but really means, "I want to kill you." His face could tell you one thing and his voice would be telling another. It's such a different experience to the theater.

The Left Handed Gun

The only extant accredited photograph of Billy the Kid is of him standing holding a rifle. Either the plate was flipped—the plate is inverted—so that the rifle is in his left hand, or it wasn't and Billy was in fact left handed. I chose to call him "the left handed gun."

With Paul Newman and the other kids we did a lot of frivolous prankster stuff, something we'd never seen in Westerns before. It's insane that young people in Westerns aren't portrayed as being cantankerous, giddy kids who do all kinds of crazy personal things with sexual overtones. That was a particularly gratifying part of *The Left Handed Gun* because it was fun to get Paul and these two guys loose and giddy and reckless. Although I never defined it as a psychological gesture, we did find behavioral ways to achieve this kind of liberty and freedom that is rather difficult for an actor to come by, particularly on a movie set where you shoot piece by piece.

In a peculiar way it became a personal film for me. I began to invest it with my own feelings, and many of my own psychological formulations are in the film. I identified very closely with Billy. What I was doing was working intellectually and viscerally, both out of my experience with the drama and also from a plain gut experience about what felt right to me. I can't explain it, but I just know that Billy is going to come out of that saloon and grab that broom and be in a kind of ecstatic grief rather than a repentant grief. There are other things that were more intellectual. We distinctly set up parental figures in the blacksmith and his wife who Billy would be forced to violate. These were reflections of his search for a father figure. Once one has been acquired there is a kind of violation of this familial integrity. That seems to me to be fundamental to the character of Billy the Kid.

The Left Handed Gun was made under the auspices of the old studio system. I ran into "That's the way we do it" rather frequently. Having just come from television which was a medium that we made up as we went along—because nobody had ever been there before—making a film in this way was really a congested experience for me. It seemed very closed and not the best use of the medium. I remember we were shooting on the Warner Bros. back lot and another crew came by and asked Pev Marley, the cameraman, "How's it going?" "Gee, I don't know," he said, "I've got one of those television guys." The whole crew laughed. They knew what he meant: I've got one of these nuts who's asking for impossible stuff. I remember at that moment I was asking him to shoot into the sun, something that was absolutely not done. I said, "Shoot it into the sun" and he said, "OK." I thought he'd done it but actually he'd taken the shot without really shooting into the sun. He was pretty close to it but couldn't bring himself to pan that extra five degrees because in thirty years of shooting you avoid the sun no matter what. I wanted the whole screen to highlight at that point. We never did get the shot.

The ending of the film was changed. After Billy's death there is a scene where Pat Garrett's wife says to him, "Come home now." This made almost no sense at all. In the other version we had a little procession start up around the town. What happened was that the camera picked up some of the ladies carrying candles. They start walking from various parts of the town, converging on Billy to look at him. He starts to become a hero of mythic, almost saintly, proportion. That was the last image. But it was the view of Warner Bros. that somehow this would drive everybody out of the theater feeling it was too sad a picture. I don't know how you change sad to happy by having—after the hero is dead—some relatively secondary characters saying, "Come home now." But in the greater wisdom of Warner Bros. they did it anyway.

Mickey One

I'm happiest about the idea of *Mickey One*. It seems to me an exquisite film about the United States in the fifties, about a generation that grew up in the McCarthy era and was profoundly guilty. It was a mute generation, locked up in flight from itself and from its own identity, and exemplified mostly by absolute silence. It seemed that *Mickey One* was a good analogy for this. You've lived high on the hog, you've lived very well, and now—when it comes up against a matter of conscience and morality—you're so into the material things of life that you are obligated to feel guilty because you have experienced all this material well-being. This seems to be a particularly apposite American analogue. It's something I fear in my own life. It's possible to get quite rich in the world of film, whereupon all these material benefits end up incarcerating you. One of the puritanical, rather tight-assed struggles I am engaged in is to keep myself from getting to that stage. I know that sounds almost boy scoutish. Maybe it's because after a lifetime of a lack of such possessions I don't particularly have a hunger for them.

Bonnie and Clyde

I first remember hearing about Bonnie and Clyde when I was a kid, seeing those famous photographs with Clyde on the bumper of the car with the machine gun in his arms and Bonnie with a cigar in her mouth. It was published in all the newspapers and seemed to be a very vivid part of my childhood. Bonnie and Clyde had real drive and historical panache. They wanted to go down in history. I suspect that everybody involved with film has something of that same desire.

Warren chose very strong specifics, a whole body of behavioral things, like the fact that Clyde had chopped off a couple of toes. He had that limp so organically internalized that if I'd had said, "Run, Warren!" he would have run with that limp. He never forgot it. I added a certain kind of quizzicality to the character. I think I was also able to help Faye with a lot of Bonnie's physicality. Again, never calling them psychological gestures, but finding a kind of angry lassitudiness, characteristics for Bonnie that were useful throughout. There was a kind of slackness in her clothes and her view of the world, a kind of sloppiness, at the beginning of the picture. As we went along she grew more and more pristine and cohesive. She was finding her identity, which was to be a moll. There's just no question about it in my mind. That was Bonnie's true destiny.

As I recall it, Benton and Newman—the authors—had an ending for the film. We saw more of the ambush forming. We waited and waited and waited, and then Bonnie and Clyde rode into it, and bang! It happened and that was the end of the film. It struck me that we ought to do something more balletic. By that point I thought we'd had enough of just plain killing, though I didn't know how to do it in a different way to the other killings in the film.

It took three or four hours to get each actor ready. They had all these bullet hits put inside their clothes which would then become visible. All kinds of explosions in the car had to take place. We would get in maybe two takes a day, that was all. We would get them ready for the morning take and go, and then get them ready for the afternoon take and go. Each of the four cameras was cranked at a different speed. The idea was to get a kind of spastic sensation which would verge on dance. That was a clearly formulated idea going in. I felt it in my gut and didn't shoot any alternatives to it. For better or worse this was the way I knew the film had to end. In reality they fired a thousand rounds and I think there were something like eighty-six distinct bullet hits on the two bodies. It was a kind of butchery, but for whatever reason it seems to me that the myth of these people had built up sufficiently in their own time to engender this kind of overkill. You can't just be talking about two people sitting in a car, you have to talk about the myth that precedes them, the possibility that they could escape and outshoot you, because you don't simply break a butterfly on the rack unless the conditions preceding that event have led you to believe it's the only appropriate punishment possible. This seemed to be necessary to document at the end of the film.

I would be the last person to suggest that I wasn't reordering history in order to fit my needs in telling my version of Bonnie and Clyde's story. I couldn't claim historical accuracy for the film for a second any more than I would for *Little Big Man* or *The Left Handed Gun*. You use history and social situations for insight, and also to say, "This is the way I understand the background and foreground of a given situation dramatically." These people worked against this kind of climate socially, economically, historically, and so forth. Bonnie and Clyde were killers, but I think they were killers with an intention. They weren't Robin Hoods by any means, they didn't have those kinds of redeeming features. But they did have the redeeming feature of calling attention to the fact that the repository for the funds of the time were the local banks, and the banks were somehow caught up in that inexorable drive of economic history that caused them to foreclose on the very farms that were keeping the banks alive, and of course many of the banks failed. There was an economic surfeit going on there that was absurd, and I think Bonnie and Clyde attacked the absurdity of their time. I think they were unknowing revolutionaries.

Spontaneity

There is an impulse one has, particularly when confronted with the enormity of a Hollywood movie set, or a movie set anywhere, where you know you're going to run up against ten or fifteen superb technicians all of whom want specific information. It's very easy to feel that you're not doing your job if you don't come in with everything laid out absolutely meticulously. With my television background it would be relatively easy for me to lay it out with actual specific lenses, but I have to fight against that impulse because what I like to do is stay open to what the actors are going to bring and what I'm going to find on the set in the morning by way of a prop or object. It's always a surprise to me. I find that on the occasions when I have been too meticulously prepared a kind of rigidity appears in my work which I don't really like. I'd rather stay open to those happy accidents because they are terrific when they occur.

The big fight scene between Annie and Patty in *The Miracle Worker*, for example, although it had been done in the play for two years, was largely left open for the camera. All we did was say to the camera operator—a very capable and selective guy—"We'll let them go their own way. You go for what interests you." So they really did improvise that fight scene. From that big example to a very small one, like at the beginning of *Bonnie and Clyde* where Warren had a match in his teeth. I never figured on him having a match in his teeth. It didn't mean anything one way or the other until just before she says, "I bet you don't have the guts to rob that store." Then he does that funny thing with the match where it goes up and down. None of that is planned, it just all comes out on the set. It could be anything between the range of something as small as the match or as large as a whole nine- or ten-minute sequence.

In *The Left Handed Gun* the people are ravaging the general store. Almost all of that was really unprepared. We were using two cameras and it turned out that the second camera was the one that got almost all the action. The only thing that had been preplanned was the wife coming in and screaming. The number one camera was on her, and actually the other camera was filming all the wild cavorting and these kids charging. I told the kids to do that but I didn't tell the wife it was coming. It's an example of both the improvisation thing and the other thing of preparing one portion of the scene but not the other, so the actors will be in an alert state to what is liable to happen, rather than in a rehearsed state where only the familiar is acceptable.

I've schooled myself not to be meticulously prepared when I go onto the set. I was envious of that ability of my father as a watchmaker and engraver, and I'm envious in a certain sense of my brother's ability to be that meticulous in his photography. On the other hand I have to recognize that whatever gifts I have lie in the other direction, in the improvisational, working on my feet. Somehow that's my nature.

Alice's Restaurant

I wasn't even sure if I wanted to make *Alice's Restaurant.* We played the record one night and a friend heard something which he found interesting. It was the last refrain Arlo sings, "You can get anything you want at Alice's Restaurant except Alice." It seemed to be a very provocative thing to say.

At the time I was making *Alice's Restaurant* I recognized many of my own experiences. In the film Arlo's father is in the hospital. I thought about my father in the hospital, me at an age of pre-maturity, post-adolescence, those strung out few years of eighteen, nineteen, twenty, the period of my father's death. I thought, "I've done that." I suspect we work on these five or six major crisis periods of our lives again and again in one form or another.

Arlo isn't accepted for the draft and feels the need somehow to discuss and talk about his own moral dilemma in relation to this. We had a very verbose version of the scene between Arlo and his father. Arlo was the first one to spot it and say, "This is kind of the father and son scene out of the Andy Hardy series." I explained that was the way it was being written now, but that we should see what the scene might become after we had gotten to know each other in a few months' time. What happened was that scene became less verbal and more related to these two presences in the room. It's about five sentences but I think they're rather meaningful sentences. "Could I have done that? Yeah, I think I could have. All the good things in my life seem to come out of not doing what I don't want to do." That's about the scene. I think the meaning of the scene is that there's a certain time in one's life when we don't necessarily have any answers, but the right questions occur, questions which lead to the next stage of one's life.

It's very difficult to go into all this without getting extremely personal, and it would be extremely lengthy. My parents were divorced when I was very young. One of the things I sought for conspicuously through my childhood was an association with my father. He was a rather elusive figure and the years I did finally get to spend time with him—from the age of fourteen to nineteen—were the years of his death. He was in a terminal illness for all of that period. It was as if one had finally achieved the goal of one's life only to have it dematerialized, which in his case was what was taking place in terms of the human spirit. So it's a very raw and open subject for me, the quest for the father. That part of my life is very raw and emotional, and naturally shows up in the films. Clearly in the case of this homeless boy brought up by his mother—which is historically the case of Billy the Kid—I couldn't keep this material from washing into the film. And once it did it let loose all kinds of implications in me which at the time I didn't understand. More recently I've come a good distance to understanding it, but it was only through the work that I came to understand it at all.

I don't understand the nature of these themes when I employ them. It's really hard to get that point across because for me it seems so naked after the fact. One looks at my films and says, "But it's so conspicuous and obvious." Well, all I can say is that all of us have to examine our own nature to know how much of it we keep unavailable to ourselves because to open all these wounds lies madness. In a way we withhold so many things from our own consciousness. They become visible when you look at two or three films in order, but at the time I wasn't conscious that they were going into the films. I was conscious of something else: that their dramatic impact seemed right.

Violence and Sex

Eliminating violence from films would be like eliminating one of the primary colors from a palate, particularly in this era when nuclear weapons are poised and ready. When we talk about one missile system knocking out another missile system, we're escalating—in common parlance—to the level of insanity. To say that film is too savage seems to me to be self-delusion at a very deep level. I don't do it for sensational reasons, and I don't think I'm particularly guilty of the accusation of gratuitous violence.

There is a certain character of killing and of violence in *Bonnie and Clyde*, but also a kind of sexuality that I think is meaningful. We were trying to touch on the idea that sexual relations between two people on screen aren't always blissful and sometimes don't even really exist. Clyde is so hurt when she talks about their lack of love-making. It seems to me that this is one of the ways his personality is confirmed to him. It's the private knowledge Bonnie has of him that bonds him to her. They become inextricably connected not because they are adventurers so much as because their identities are so closely interwoven that they can't separate. By this time they have become a single identity.

I think of the sexual life as being very symbolic of the internal life. The sexual experience of the characters in my films is an extension of other experiences of their life. If there is anxiety and hostility and wild aggression in other aspects of their life, then it's going to appear in their sexual life too, in their capacity either to consummate it or—in the case of Clyde—inability to consummate it. It just seems to me something which one includes, as much as you include the way someone dresses or walks or talks. The way someone behaves sexually is a part of the lexicon of that character.

Interview with Arthur Penn

JAN AGHED AND
BERNARD COHN / 1971

Q: *The title* Alice's Restaurant *comes from the name of a song by Arlo Guthrie. What originally drew you to this material?*

A: Recently the United States has experienced a number of far-reaching and important events that we've never had to deal with before. There has always been strong resistance to war in our country, but it had never reached the level it's at today with all these young people refusing to go to Vietnam. Arlo Guthrie's song has had a palpable impact, it expresses the opinions of everyone who doesn't want to fight. But what I really wanted to do was go beyond the meaning of the song. After all, for those who opposed the war in Vietnam, the choices were quite limited. Even though they were courageous, nothing has really changed for them. What I'm trying to say is that their lives have basically stayed the same, that the stand they took has made things even more difficult for them today. That's really what I wanted this film to express.

Q: *The film is not about a single character, rather a city, a country, and the people who live in it. What problems did you have telling the story from this point of view?*

A: First of all I should say that what's going on in the United States at the moment is really very interesting. The new generation has totally rejected the values of the previous one, a rejection that is completely defensible and understandable.

From *Positif* (April 1971). Reprinted by permission of *Positif.* Translated by Paul Cronin and Remi Guillochon.

The question we have to ask is: how do we want to live our lives and what values do we want to hold ourselves to? It's a very important—and difficult—question. I know that the people in the church couldn't answer this question. In fact they didn't even try to answer it. They took everything in their stride and lived day by day. Life, for them, offered many possibilities. Yet what happened was that all these middle-class values, the kind of life they had rejected, reappeared under a different form. They left their parents and their past behind and created new parents for themselves, an environment very similar to the one they had abandoned. It was all pretty much the same stuff. Life unfolded as before. Everyone had left home intent on creating a new, liberated society. It had been quite enjoyable for a few years, but as people get older, life takes new turns and events take on new meanings. The young people in the church started by leading a relatively free life, and pretty soon it all started to get much more complicated. They began to ask questions, like who does this and that girl belong to? Whose mother am I? They were quite bewildered. Who belonged to who?

I wouldn't want to make any harsh judgments but there was something else about these young people. Ray, who as you know managed the church, builds houses. What's intriguing about him is that he can never finish them. He starts building one and then stops. Everyone from the church had very interesting projects, but most of them never came to fruition, and the church soon became a graveyard of unrealized projects. The church should have been completed but never is. They were going to build motorbikes, but this doesn't happen. They start building a house for a local girl, but she never moves in because of a leaky roof. What's important is that everyone was engaged in a new quest, looking for a new way of life. Their search was outside of politics, and I really think these kinds of things aren't possible if you don't have some kind of political framework. I'm not saying you always have to consider the political background to everything, but you need a political motive from day one, and you have to be able to sustain it in order to kindle a new outlook on life. It also provides you with a greater purpose than sheer survival. This is essentially what they lacked, and it's what we discovered while writing the script. The more we tried to define the events as clearly as possible, the less successful we were.

Q: *How did Arlo Guthrie respond in front of the camera to past events in his life?*
A: He reacted the same way he does in the movie. Arlo's a very interesting young man. He isn't an actor and doesn't want to be one. During the shooting he kept on saying, "I can only do what I do." I realized pretty early on that I couldn't ask any more than that from him, so this is basically how we

did things. He was quite content to be on the set working with those lines he liked, pointing out the ones he didn't, and deciding how to say them, including the scenes with his father. We got an actor to play the father because by then Arlo's own father was dead. When we shot the scene Arlo didn't express any emotion, which I think is understandable. His relationship with his father had always been unusual. He was only four years old when his father became ill and had to spend the next fifteen years of his life in the hospital. Arlo really never knew his father, and his feelings for him turned out to be very different from what they might have been under different circumstances. Arlo was always indifferent to whatever anyone said about his father, so when we were working on these sequences he wasn't in the least bit moved. He was living his life as if his father had never existed.

He knew Woody was a celebrity, a legendary artist, but I think he'd drawn a line between Woody the legend and Woody his father. He'd had very little contact with his father, although it was Woody who taught him music. At his bar mitzvah, for example, when he was thirteen, his father couldn't be there but lots of great folk singers were: Pete Seeger, the Weavers. It was a bar mitzvah with folk music. It must have been quite extraordinary, and I would have done anything to include it in the film. It was so extraordinary that people still talk about it today. For them, not for Arlo, it was the best ceremony they'd ever been to. So this is how, in a small way, other people have taken over his father's role, and it's why when Arlo was playing the scenes with an actor as his father, it really had no impact on his behavior in front of the camera.

Q: *In Robert Hughes's film you mention your relationship with your own father. How did you feel about these scenes with Arlo and Woody?*
A: It was quite intense. When I was eighteen, my father went into hospital, and when I went to visit, I hardly spoke to him. It was really strange because the hospital scenes affected me more than they did Arlo. I found it all much more moving than he did and at times was quite close to tears. Arlo remained quite cool. His favorite words are "cool" and "groovy."

Q: *Do you think there is a contradiction in that on one hand an actor is playing the part of Woody Guthrie and on the other there is a strong sense that Woody is actually there? Don't you think it would have been better not to include Woody because his mythic stature is difficult to contain within a fictional story?*
A: Yes, we could have avoided including Woody, something we seriously considered when writing the script. The script was originally quite funny. It was mainly about the military draft and had nothing to do with Woody, Pete Seeger, or any other singers. There were a lot of army jokes, anything we

could think of. It was one big farce. But little by little, as the script developed, I made up my mind and decided that for personal reasons we needed to see Woody.

Q: *Many of the film's characters are residents of Stockbridge. What was it like working with them?*
A: Well, the policeman, for example, was utterly hopeless at improvising. He was too aware of what he was doing, and we'd get only two or three good takes out of him. He kept saying, "I have to go direct traffic." He was very good, very charming, but the more retakes we did, the more uncomfortable he became. He wasn't sure he even wanted to be in the film. He started off quite reluctant, and towards the end of the film, when we would call him, he would say, "I have things to do." We really had to goad him to work, always telling him how good he was on screen, but he was still quite unwilling. He would say, "I've only got an hour, that's all." Then of course he'd stay for two hours. He had his own way of resisting, of not taking part in the film. He had a very theatrical side to him, and I'm sure that deep down he dreamt of being a film star. When I caught sight of this huge policeman in the middle of the road, I instantly felt he was the perfect symbol of the police force. He was the perfect policeman, the embodiment of a police officer, with his large belt and over- the-top acting, something he was well aware of.

Q: *Violence plays an important role in your films, but at the same time you focus on the inner side of your characters. There is a kind of spirituality, even religiosity, in* The Miracle Worker *and* Mickey One, *while the church in* Alice's Restaurant *is very important. What does all this mean to you? Is this film a break from your previous works?*
A: As far as *Alice's Restaurant* is concerned I've tried to show that the symbol of the church represented an entire moral and religious system, an ideological entity that has been rejected and challenged by the young people of today. I also think it's symbolic that they move into an abandoned church. For them it's now just an ordinary building where they can settle, even if before it had been a sacred place of worship. You could say they got rid of its soul and replaced it with their own. It was a good cinematographic device as well as being an effective symbol of human existence.

To come back to the other two films you mentioned, I'm not sure there's any spirituality in them, and I don't think *Alice's Restaurant* is a departure from these films in the way you suggest. I think spirituality means something else in *The Miracle Worker*, and certainly in *Mickey One*, which is the most spiritual of all my films. This is pretty much what I say in Robert Hughes's film. From a political and social point of view *Mickey One* comes right before

Alice's Restaurant. What I tried to deal with in both films is the United States' silence and how we can best respond to that silence. In both cases I wanted to show that the United States is a country paralyzed by fear, that people were afraid of losing all they hold dear to them. It's the new generation that's trying to save everything. These young people have said, and keep on saying, "To hell with this materialistic world. What we want is to act morally and leave behind the despicable side of life. What we want is for our moral position to be at one with our opposition to the war." I believe this is a sign of a great change, of a new phenomenon. This is what's happening with young people of the same age as the characters in *Alice's Restaurant.* The problem comes from only being able to say, "We renounce this world, we reject all its values. We have our own spiritual life, our own morals, our own values." This has to become a reality, part of the political agenda, something I think is only just beginning. At the moment we're witnessing a strong political movement taking shape in the United States.

Q: *The characters in your films have a hard time communicating, something that often manifests itself violently.* Alice's Restaurant *is a film where violence is not so important. Why is this?*

A: I don't think that violence is static and only happens at a certain time and in a certain direction. Violence often stems from frustration. If you prevent a child from fulfilling his wishes, you can be sure there'll be an explosion of violence, something we see in *The Left Handed Gun.* Billy the Kid is violent because he's searching for knowledge that is denied him. The tragedy here lies in the fact that he doesn't actually know what he's searching for. In *Bonnie and Clyde* the characters don't really know what they want, and the means they draw on can only be violent. *Alice's Restaurant* is a film of political transition because the characters know, in some way, what they are looking for. They want to sever ties with a society they utterly despise, a society at war, a war they are opposed to. It's important to remember that the characters in *Alice's Restaurant* are middle-class whites. They aren't poor or hungry or working class, they're not in the same boat as African Americans. But they're not militants either. In this respect the church dwellers aren't particularly threatening. They find it easy to live there, even if most people can't afford such a luxury. From that point of view this film depicts a very specific social class. It's a bourgeois film.

I was thinking about this the other day, that in a sense *Alice's Restaurant* is a lot like Fellini's *I Vitelloni.* Both films are about a group of young people but the characters' opposition to war in *Alice's Restaurant* justifies their behavior. Morally and politically they have a stronger case than the characters in Fellini's films. Arlo was fully prepared to go to prison to avoid Vietnam. *I Vitelloni* is full of people who reject a certain culture but don't put anything in its place. The young people in *Alice's Restaurant* are trying to change things. To go back to your question, the only act of violence in the film is an act of nonviolence, that of draft-dodging. And I should emphasize that it's a film of transition because it takes place at a time of political transition. The young people take a nonaggressive stance. If I wanted to I could make a film tomorrow about what's going on now in the United States that would be so violent you'd jump right out of your seat. There's enough material in newspapers every day to make two hundred films about violence. But even if I did make a film like this it would still show only a fraction of what's going on in the country.

Q: *The protagonists of* The Left Handed Gun, The Miracle Worker, Bonnie and Clyde, *and* Alice's Restaurant *are all based on real people. Your last film was* Little Big Man, *which tackled one of the most loaded issues in American history and also included historical figures. What draws you to these kinds of characters and historical events?*

A: Well, the main character in *Little Big Man* never really existed. Custer did, but he has only a small part in the film. The main characters are the Indians. Custer's role in the film is small because we know that history has the unfortunate habit of repeating itself. Custer was engaged in the battle of the Washita River in Oklahoma where he gave the order to massacre the inhabitants of a village, just as we've been doing in Vietnam. His victims belonged to one of the Indian nations who then retaliated against him at the battle of Little Big Horn which, as you know, was Custer's last battle. These events are included in the story but the rest is fictional. Strictly speaking it isn't a film about American history.

There's something else I want to say about this film. More and more films in America are being made outside the studios. It's hard for me to admit it because *Little Big Man* was an expensive beast of a film to produce. It's absurd. The reason is that we started on the film four years ago, before *Bonnie and Clyde*. The script was ready and studios were fighting for the rights. In the end MGM bought it but they ran into problems and we fought hard to get the script back. It took nearly four years before we could do anything, so in a way *Little Big Man* is outdated, at least more outdated than anything I would do today.

Q: *Do you feel uncomfortable when people draw attention to the violence in your films?*

A: No, I'm not embarrassed. Actually I don't think "violence" is the right word. That's really not what I want to depict in my films.

Q: Violence in America, *a recent book published by the State Department, suggests that one cause of violence in America is due to the wars against the Indians. But Thomas Berger's book* Little Big Man *tries to show that the Wild West was also a pretty funny place. How did you reconcile these two different aspects?*
A: *Little Big Man* is a film about genocide. As for Berger's humor, I'd say it's a confirmation of his talent. You get the feeling that his novel was written with a scalpel. In order to tell the story of genocide he had to use razor sharp wit, something we emphasized in the film.

Q: *Have you made many changes from the book?*
A: We made a few small changes though I hope we haven't altered the spirit of the book in doing so. We also slightly modified some of the characters. The book has lots of characters but we used only some of them. It's quite a long film, more than three hours, but even though the script covers a thirty-year period we didn't exhaust the novel.

Q: *In his book* The Return of the Vanishing American, *Leslie Fiedler writes that the profound guilt of the American people stems from the knowledge that their nation was founded on the massacre of the people who inhabited the land before them.*
A: I haven't read the book but I think this guilt complex is certainly a component of the American personality. You have to be careful because Americans aren't the only ones who've done that kind of thing. After all, nearly all countries have exploited and colonized others. Look at France, think of all the wars that took place in Africa, look back at English history. I'm not familiar with Swedish history but I'm sure—because it's the nature of territorial imperialism—that Sweden had to subjugate others for its land. But in addition to genocide Americans did something more than just kill. What's even sadder is that they also signed treaties. They pretended to be honest and claimed they could be trusted, and made deals along the lines of "As long as grass shall grow, that the wind shall blow and the sky be blue, this land shall be yours."

But they certainly always intended to grab the land away from the Indians a few years later, something that seems to me more American than genocide. Genocide is international. Germany is a good example. Yes, it's true genocide is horrible but it's nothing new. For me what's characteristic of the American mentality is the extent of its guilt and its hypocrisy. Americans say, "I am a morally pure man. I will never commit genocide. I simply will sign a treaty that will rob the Indians of all that was theirs." We can see how the American Indians have lost their identity. I wouldn't say that it's worse, because nothing is worse than genocide, but living without an identity is a horrible way to live.

Q: *This is exactly what we find in Thomas Berger's novel where a man is caught between two cultures. In* Billy the Kid, *and even* The Chase, *the characters are searching for themselves.*
A: Absolutely. The character in *Little Big Man* moves constantly from one culture to another and does so at some very crucial stages in his life: at adolescence, when he gets married, when a child is about to be born and so on.

Q: *Does* Little Big Man *stylistically resemble your other films?*
A: In this sense I'm moving backwards. After *Bonnie and Clyde*, an extremely violent film, I was faced with the problem of depicting the Wild West on screen. There were two ways to do *Little Big Man*. I could either make it very physically painful for the audience or do it without showing a single drop of blood. I chose the latter. In the film nearly all the wars and killings are immaculately clean.

Q: *One of the themes of* The Train, *which you started work on, is that of the place of art amidst destructive violence. How would you have handled this problem?*
A: I'd thought of dealing with the problem in a different way, by looking at trade in a time of war. How do people run their businesses in the middle of a war? I wanted to introduce another character that would have been played by Claude Dauphin, a successful art dealer, though as you can see he isn't in the Frankenheimer film. The character played by Lancaster couldn't care less if it was about art or not. All he cared about was saving these paintings because they belonged to France. As for the German officer, it was also about possession. Between the two there was this merchant who would arrive on a bicycle and who was actually the most important character in the film, but Lancaster cut him from the story.

Q: *You might think this question irrelevant, but to the extent that it is an extremely violent film, what do you think of Peckinpah's* The Wild Bunch?
A: Well, to be honest with you, it's hard to say, but I was disappointed with the film. Peckinpah is a good director—I like *Ride the High Country* and *Major Dundee*—but I feel he didn't know how to deal with the problem that *The Wild Bunch* posed, the problem I'm especially interested in. I think I resolved these issues beforehand more effectively with *Bonnie and Clyde*. All Peckinpah did was follow the technique I used in that film and push it to the extreme, and in this way his intention was to depict violence so fierce that

people would be sickened. That's how he explains it, but I'm not convinced it's what he really wanted to achieve. On the other hand it's an extremely clever film made by a real master of cinema. Peckinpah is a true film director, no question about that. But I'm sure he can do better. Just look at *Ride the High Country*.

Q: *You seem to have great empathy with what we might call "outlaws." But Bonnie and Clyde, Billy the Kid, and the characters from* Alice's Restaurant *also show a kind of immaturity. How do you explain this?*
A: I don't think they're exactly outlaws. Someone who lives outside society isn't necessarily an outlaw, though you can be sure that when circumstances become difficult enough those people who live on society's margins will break the law, something *Alice's Restaurant* makes clear. If circumstances deteriorate enough a whole generation will become outlaws. In fact this is what's happening at the political level today. While we were shooting the film there were several violent demonstrations taking place around us, for example the unrest at Columbia University in which SDS [Students for a Democratic Society], as well as other young people, played a big role. Of course this kind of violence might stem from immaturity, but there are also political causes at work. Political changes are being demanded. Sometimes these changes happen passively and smoothly, and sometimes the opposite happens. Perhaps we need to have a certain number of people climbing on barricades to bring about political change. I'm not sure this kind of thing will necessarily lead to improvement, but I do think it forms part of a wider system that will change things for the better. It's quite sad and I wish people would sit and discuss the issues and decide to lead better lives. But this kind of thing doesn't happen very often, and when it does, the outcome has been a kind of powerlessness, nationally and internationally. Then someone comes along and commits an act of violence that changes the face of history. Violence is innate to human beings. It's an emotional experience that we can't entirely free ourselves from. On the other hand it is completely worthwhile. When there's repression, there's an inability to express one's desires, and this inevitably leads to violence.

Q: *What is interesting about Robert Hughes's film is that it shows how you work with your actors, some of whom come from the Actors Studio. How important is the Actors Studio to you?*
A: It goes without saying that the Actors Studio is a wonderful place, one of the most underrated organizations in the world. It began as an excellent idea, a group of professional actors being able to rehearse together in workshops without having to appear publicly. It's a very sensible idea, especially

for actors who hold the same convictions and can give each other honest responses to the work. The man who runs the place knows his job well. Unfortunately I suspect that the Studio has fallen victim to a journalistic phenomenon. Journalists completely underestimated an actor like Brando when he first appeared. His earlier stage career wasn't particularly successful, and he was even fired from two productions. Even though he was clearly the best actor of his generation no one wanted to have anything to do with him. He was completely misunderstood. People said he mumbled and never came to rehearsals. Brando was trying to develop his inner self.

When you talk about a good film you might think it's a personal film entirely put together by the director, but it's important to recognize the actors' contributions. You might think that when an actor plays a character on film there's nothing of his own personality on screen. If I direct a film about Billy the Kid it won't have that much to do with my own life, but at the same time I couldn't make a good film if I didn't connect to the story in some way. The same goes for an actor and the role he plays. Paul Newman read several books about Billy the Kid before he played the role, but if all he'd done was read a few books and base his characterization on what he had discovered about Billy's behavior and mannerisms, then he wouldn't have been very good in the part.

I feel the director of a film follows the same rules as someone at the Actors Studio. The actor has to play the part and at the same time remain true to himself. He has to convey his own emotions and express his own experiences through his character. This ability is what every actor at the studio has in common. Someone like Dustin Hoffman comes from the same tradition as Newman and Brando, and it's hard to distinguish stylistically between one and the other. We speak the same language, use the same words, and as a result get the same meanings. It'll be like this for at least another decade. The same goes for actresses like Anne Bancroft, Kim Stanley, and Geraldine Page. In my opinion, today we have a generation of great theater actresses and great cinema actors. By the way, I don't know why we have more men in the cinema and women in the theater. At least it's like this in America. I don't know if the same is true in other countries.

Q: The Miracle Worker *played for two years in the theater. Did this create any problems when you directed the film?*
A: The play was on television before it was put on the stage. Back then I didn't know much about filmmaking. I knew I was involved in the production of a most extraordinary play, the work of a great dramatist who had many dilemmas to solve. Helen's parents, for instance, have to communi-

cate with her, but they are able to talk and she's not. Helen's father is a pessimistic person who believes that nothing can be done for her. Gibson was able to create a series of lively verbal clashes between Helen's father and the teacher that allow the play to be carried along by the tension of these two antagonists, but in the film these clashes were superfluous. I was able to put them aside and focus more on the camera work. If we'd spent more time following Helen and pointing the camera at those faces looking at her we would have made a more eloquent film and the tension would have been more convincing. I find the father's pessimism less convincing in the film than in the play because it's not as well integrated into the story. If at the time I'd had a better idea of how cinema functioned, I would have cut half the dialogue and concentrated more on the camera. It would have been a much better film.

Q: *But the film is quite visual.*
A: Yes, but it could have been more so. The visuals of the film should have set off more emotions in the audience but this happened only occasionally, like the close-up of Helen with water running down her face. I think that's good filmmaking but I'd like to point at twenty such examples in the film. I really should remake it. In my opinion the credit sequence when she's running in the middle of all the wet washing is the best in the film. It's better, anyway, than all the shots of Catherine Keller.

Q: *Why have we not seen Patty Duke in other films?*
A: For years she was in a daily American television series. It's terrible that people working in television have to sign lengthy contracts. Fortunately she's just made another film called *Me, Nathalie* so we'll see more of her. I have to say that she's not as good as she was a few years ago. The years she spent working in television have had a bad influence on her. But she was definitely the most gifted actress I'd ever met. Maybe her success was her undoing, even more damaging than being out of work. There was a time when you couldn't turn on the TV without seeing her on every channel.

Q: *You have worked not only with people from the Actors Studio but also with actors from the Hollywood tradition, people like Franchot Tone?*
A: Franchot Tone is an absolutely fascinating actor. Before he went to Hollywood, Tone was the leader of young actors in the Group Theater with Strasberg, much earlier than John Garfield. He was remarkably well trained. I didn't know him before I made *Mickey One*, and he was very ill during filming. I directed him the same way I would have done with Newman, Brando, or Jimmy Dean. It was quite remarkable that the language I used with actors

from the old generation was also suitable for the next one. I was very impressed by the skill he showed even while suffering from cancer. Every time we finished shooting, he would collapse into a chair, out of breath as if he just won a race. For me watching this man at work was unforgettable.

Q: *Would you tell us about the problems you had during the production of* The Chase?
A: The past is past and should be left at that. I don't think it would be interesting to talk about it. Everything in that film was a letdown, and I'm sure every director has gone through the same experience at least once. It's a shame because it could have been a great film. It was during this time that I began to work with my wife at SNCC [Student Nonviolent Coordinating Committee] and for the Civil Rights movement. We were in Los Angeles filming *The Chase* during the riots, when Watts burned for five days and nights. We don't live in that town but it's where we shot *The Chase*. At that time in 1966 Stokely Carmichael was the General Secretary of SNCC. The organization had to find its own identity and not depend on white liberals, so he distanced himself from us, though we still have many friends from SNCC.

Q: *You wrote the script of* The Left Handed Gun *with Leslie Stevens.*
A: It would be fairer to say I helped him a bit as he's the one who really wrote it. I would make suggestions, but I wasn't very confident about it. I've worked with Leslie in the theater but could never have written the script myself. I'd simply suggest a certain behavior or approach, and Leslie would elaborate on this. For all intents and purposes it's his script.

Q: *It seems that with* The Left Handed Gun *you tried to break away from the classic Western. Did you have the same concern with* Little Big Man?
A: No, not exactly. *Little Big Man* is not, strictly speaking, a Western. More to the point, it's a film about Indian culture. I was trying to show that at the time there were two cultures that could have coexisted for the good of mankind. If the whites destroyed Indian culture it wasn't for a geographical or economic imperative. It was for the sheer pleasure of conquest.

Q: *In Robert Hughes's film you explain about filming another ending for* The Left Handed Gun.
A: It was very beautiful. Billy is dead and after we hear the shot there is complete silence. It's dark and Maltree is there in a corner with a handkerchief over his mouth. Standing at a window are the blacksmith and his wife, alongside the sheriff. Then, in one corner of the frame, we see a candlelight, and a woman all dressed in black coming out onto the porch. Another

woman follows her, and another, and another, at least forty of them. They all come forward holding their lit candles. We shot it from several angles and as they were advancing we would widen the shot until it included as many of them as possible. The End.

I always felt this ending showed the connections between Billy and the people of Mexico but Warner Bros. didn't like it and got rid of it, so I had to shoot another ending, the one you see in the film, which was much less convincing. Of course I had to be there, but it was really the director of photography who did all the work. All I did was watch. The actors hated doing it, but it was either that or nothing. We had to do what the studio wanted.

Q: *Are you independent? Can you now do what you want?*
A: Yes. Nowadays directors are freer and what's good is that Hollywood is falling apart because of its ineffectiveness and narrow-mindedness. Anyone will be able to make a film, though it doesn't mean they'll immediately have that kind of freedom. Unfortunately money still counts for something. If you want someone to give you money and suggest they have no other involvement, you'll get nothing. Bergman might get something, but directors like him are few and far between. However, it is getting easier and easier, and eventually you won't need a studio to make a film, just people with intelligence. Films can be made with small budgets. The corporations are just banks, and they should stick to that. Their sole purpose in life is to hand out money, and it's as ridiculous to think I could build a car as it is for them to think they know how to make films, though you can be sure that my car would be better than their film.

Q: *The social background in* Bonnie and Clyde *was well defined. Did you do much research?*
A: I lived through the Depression and was familiar with the era, so my research was based on my own memories. In fact I remember seeing Bonnie and Clyde's pictures in the papers and being very interested in their story. Actually I did some research, but not much. There isn't as much written on the period as one would think, even though it was such an important epoch in American history. There were more and more cars around, and people were starting to listen to the radio and use the telephone. You could easily move from state to state but the police couldn't cross state lines. It was the moment when a federal police force was created, when the police were beginning to play an important role at the national level, when the FBI became known to the public thanks to people like Bonnie and Clyde, Dillinger, and Pretty Boy Floyd. At the same time it was because of the FBI that these gangsters themselves became more famous than they deserved.

Q: *Did you choose Bonnie and Clyde because in some ways they were also victims? Would you ever make a film about Dillinger or Al Capone?*
A: I couldn't make a film about Capone because he doesn't represent the kind of violence I'm interested in. Capone was just a gangster but Bonnie and Clyde were quite different because they represented a social movement. I ought to mention that we used one element from Dillinger's life in the film. When they ask the farmer, "Is this your money or the bank's?" and he answers, "It's mine," Clyde tells him, "Then keep it." These are Dillinger's words. I felt I could use them.

Q: *You seem quite concerned by what is going on around you. How do you see the future of the United States? What sort of films are you going to make from now on?*
A: I haven't given it much thought but I don't think I could avoid making a film about the violent political confrontations emerging in our country today. More and more students and militants are producing their own films and whether we like it or not their films will reflect the current revolution. Coming back to your question about violence, violence allows two interpretations. There is the type of violence we are subjected to when everything around us changes, when we grow up and move from childhood to adulthood. This kind of violence helps us make the transition from family structure to our own discovery of the world. It's a healthy and very positive kind of violence. The other type of violence is repressive. We're imprisoned, we cannot live or act freely. And there's a third kind of violence, one that's necessary, that grows like a cancer and in the end explodes.

The problems stemming from violence are moral ones. It's absurd to say that every form of violence is bad. It is like saying that every law is good, whereas many of the laws imposed upon us in the United States are immoral. The result of this can only lead to violence, the kind of violence Nixon says the students are perpetrating, when in fact he's the one provoking it. The result? We know well enough: the National Guard shooting students.[1] The causes are unclear but little by little the word "violence" has taken on a particular connotation without real meaning. These past few years everyone has said that by definition violence is bad. But violence doesn't necessarily act

---

1. Penn is referring to incidents on the campuses of two American universities. In May 1970, city and state police confronted student protesters at Jackson State University, Mississippi, killing two and injuring twelve. The gathering was to protest the killing of four students and wounding by the National Guard of nine at Kent State University, Ohio, ten days previously.

against man. It can also be part of human nature. It can be healthy. Perhaps we should, if we have the time, find other words to describe this violence. I don't believe that right now the word evokes simply good or bad, just or unjust. It has lost its moral dimension.

Q: *What do you think of movements like the Black Panthers?*

A: It's an inevitability. I personally believe that it's a worthwhile organization, although it has lost most of its young intellectuals and militant members. Within one year they lost twenty-eight of their people, and today it's been reduced to a small movement. No political group can absorb such losses. When the police used firearms in the black neighborhoods, the residents said, "We are obviously not equal before the law so we will take up arms and have as much power as the police." Unfortunately the press and the government have continually claimed that the Black Power movement is made up of irresponsible and vicious people who want to take back from whites what they feel is rightfully theirs. This created a backlash against the Black Panthers which gave the police the opportunity to commit real acts of violence. As Robert Moses of SNCC has said, "When the law becomes an outlaw and the law is a criminal, who then decides what constitutes legality?"

The First Cheyenne Film Director

MICHEL DELAIN / 1971

D: Little Big Man *suggests you are searching for your roots.*

P: Correct. I'm a child of divorce who was torn between two separate families when I was growing up. This dichotomy is still a part of my life. In the film the cowboys and Indians represent versions of my father and mother. That said, I've always been on the side of the underdog, which makes me more Cheyenne than white.

D: *Are you attributing blame because you feel guilty?*

P: Most definitely. More than anything I want to speak out against how the history of the Native Indians has been constructed. There's no point in denying it: we systematically exterminated them. Ninety percent of the Indian tribes perished during the forced marches that took them from East to West. I've been researching what went on and have uncovered facts that my own country would rather not know about. For example, there used to be Indians in Massachusetts, right where we filmed *Alice's Restaurant. Little Big Man* recreates Custer's massacre of Washita where 350 women and children were killed in the space of a few hours. I'm taking my lead from John Ford's *Cheyenne Autumn* that also depicts the Indians' bloody march and the miserable life they went on to lead.

D: *You wanted to demolish all the myths about the Native Indians that most Westerns have perpetuated over the years?*

P: Yes, and that goes for all the myths about whites in general. The cowboys, the hired killers, and the well-meaning priests we see in most Westerns

From *L'Express* (5 April 1971). Reprinted by permission of *L'Express*. Translated by Paul Cronin and Remi Guillochon.

never really existed. For Indians back then substitute the Vietnamese today. The younger generation is tired of us not addressing these issues. *Little Big Man* speaks to those people who want to know why America is always lying to them.

D: *How did the American public react to the film?*
P: The conservatives didn't know if I was being serious or not. For some, the portrayal of General Custer was an absolute betrayal. Others found it inversely racist, saying I'm the first Cheyenne film director. But all I'm asking is that we acknowledge the terrible crimes we committed. American cinema has continually parodied and ridiculed Native Indians, depicting them as savage beasts, in order to justify the fact that we wiped them out. This might ease some people's conscience but I'm having none of it. I'm totally against this form of hypocrisy.

D: *How important is humor in your films?*
P: I see life as both tragic and comic. Making my films funny stops them from becoming too pedantic, which is why I like Samuel Beckett so much. He manages to balance seriousness and comedy perfectly.

Candide in the Wild West

GÉRARD LANGLOIS / 1971

Little Big Man

The title is paradoxical because the main character is actually quite small. There was a famous Indian chief also called Little Big Man but he wasn't the inspiration for the film. This was mainly because we don't know much about him except that toward the end of his life he was a collaborator with the whites and fought against Crazy Horse. There's only a single surviving photo of him. The film does allude to various historical events, like the massacre at the Indian encampment at the beginning and Custer's defeat at Little Big Horn, but it's certainly not trying to be a historical drama. It's just trying to be faithful to Thomas Berger's little-known novel which is packed with humor and fun and which I took an immediate liking to. I wasn't as interested in the historical details as I was in drawing conclusions from them by looking beneath the artifice for something more than raw facts.

A survivor

Jack Crabb is a good example of a survivor. He's white but was adopted by the Indians at a very young age and raised by them. He survived all the massacres that took the lives of so many men, women, and children. He's caught between two different worlds. He wants to die but can't. The image we see at the end of the film, a 121-year-old man's wrinkled face telling us his story, is that of someone condemned to live, a situation the old Indian chief also finds himself in.

From *Les lettres françaises* (7 April 1971). Reprinted by permission of Gérard Langlois. Translated by Paul Cronin and Remi Guillochon.

Faced with the encroachment of the white settlers, his people—the Cheyenne—who he nicknamed the "human beings," are dying out. The old Indian chief would like to die with them. He's blind but can't help seeing all his memories flash before his eyes. When he lies down under the sky and summons up the spirits to carry him away to the heavens, he calls it off because of the rain. But this isn't meant to be symbolic and has nothing to do with resurrection. He simply has to face the fact that our instinct to survive is stronger than anything else. He's condemned to live.

In search of an identity

Jack Crabb doesn't wholly identify with either of the two cultures. He's neither here nor there. At the start of the film he explains that his family has been killed and that he and his sister are the only survivors. He doesn't know who he is, just like people today don't really have a sense of their own identity. It wasn't so long ago that we could define ourselves in relation to our job, nation, and language. But the world has become both so complex and homogenized that this isn't possible any longer. Placing a character astride two cultures is a way to make the narrative more effective, but we may as well be talking about five different cultures since in any case Jack Crabb has no idea where he's going. In the film we meet only strangers and immigrants.

L: *The film is constructed around these encounters. The meetings between Jack Crabb and General Custer are as ambiguous as those with the Indian chief.*
P: We meet the same characters twice but in the meantime their roles have changed. Even though Jack Crabb grows closer to the chief than to Custer he still isn't fully assimilated into the Indian world. He realizes this only when he chooses not to kill Custer and avenge the death of his second wife, who was an Indian.

L: *But doesn't the Indian chief represent old-fashioned values?*
P: Actually, I think we could benefit from such values today. The Indians accepted themselves as who they were. They believed that the world provided for them and that they paid back the world in kind. It worked both ways, a notion that was very important to them. The old man talks about the cycle of earth and water, and at the end he says to the spirits, "Thank you for turning me into a warrior. Thank you for my victory and also for defeat. Thank you for giving me sight and thank you for making me blind." He accepts the paradox. He might appear too passive in our eyes but we could really benefit from some of that passivity right now. It would mean some tranquillity and

time for reflection rather than us continuing to pollute the world with our rampant consumption.

A new form

L: *There seem to be three phases to your career. The first is from* The Left Handed Gun *to* Mickey One, *a metaphysical and Freudian period. The second is* The Chase *to* Bonnie and Clyde, *where we see America in all its horror and violence. The third starts at* Alice's Restaurant *with a search for new values and young people wanting to know how to live their lives. In this sense* Alice's Restaurant *and* Little Big Man *complement each other.*

P: Yes, in a sense. In *Alice's Restaurant* you see the search for a new family set-up and the absence of a father. In *Little Big Man* Jack Crabb is looking for his father—his real father—not the other surrogate fathers, like Reverend Pendrake who takes him in, or the old Indian chief, Bill Hickok, and Custer. As I've already said the fundamental problem in America is this search for identity. In both films we have a small community that's trying to fight against the repressive forces of power.

It's true that *Alice's Restaurant* wasn't the most obvious project for me. After *Bonnie and Clyde* I wanted to make *Little Big Man* but in the meantime had heard Arlo Guthrie's songs which inspired me. I decided to make *Alice's Restaurant* as quick as possible, and we finished it right before filming *Little Big Man*. It was a very relaxed shoot. We talked, drank coffee, smoked, and when we felt inspired, we shot the film. It was difficult to ask people living such a relaxed lifestyle to work very hard.

Beyond the legend

The tale of white settlers is the stuff of legend turned to their own advantage. While the story of the Native Indians isn't part of national legend, the whites have always portrayed them as savages and thieves. In fact this was done to hide the atrocities they had committed against the Indians. The film starts out as a traditional genre piece with whites taken in by Indians. Then the white characters appear as prototypes of traditional figures from the West, though they are depicted in a somewhat contradictory way. You start asking yourself questions about the myths of the West and the way history has been falsified. But you don't have to go back that far. Just look at how the events of May '68 in France have been turned into legend, or the way the peace movement in America, which was so strong, just vanished only a year ago. All the mythic characters of the American West are in the film, but look at how

Buffalo Bill takes the place of Wild Bill Hickok. The more things changed, the more they stayed the same. The sanctioned slaughter of the bison took the place of the slaughter of the Native Indians. In both cases, of course, the Indians lost out. In short, it was the end of the era of the gunfighter and the start of rampant commercialism. Where the world of the Indians was round, the world of the whites was flat. Every character in the film represents an important element of our representation of the West. The priest, for example, is the voice of encroaching Christianity. As I've said, if the characters change it's because they don't really know who they are. Materialism is a substitute for this absence of identity. "I know who I am because this belongs to me." But clearly this isn't right. You can own the entire world and still not know who you are.

L: *But isn't oppressive behavior of the whites against minorities just a way of taking revenge for their own setbacks?*
P: "Revenge" isn't quite the right word. The whites aren't trying to tell minorities to live like them because their identity is artificial. They're living the myth of Sisyphus without realizing there's no top to the mountain. The problem of identity is also relevant to minorities. An Indian on a reservation has lost all reason to live. A black man is treated like a second-class citizen. It's only amidst the white world that the issue is more complex because we have the impression of being free.

L: *Are you interested in contemporary Indian issues?*
P: Absolutely. The suicide rate in the Indian communities is high. I'd like to make a film about a young Indian militant who tries to change things within his own fragile community.

L: *What do you think of "Red Power"?*
P: I think that so long as the problems of the reservations remain unresolved, the problem of "Red Power" will never have a solid foundation.

Humor

Of course the film is funny, but anyone who can start a story with "One hundred and ten years ago, when I was ten . . ." is, to my mind, someone graced with a great sense of humor. Jack Crabb is constantly making fun of himself. And the Indians also have a sense of humor. Take the old chief who says that he dreams of Jack going from one woman to another. How is this possible since there's only one woman? The old chief replies, "That's exactly what I don't understand."

Interview with Arthur Penn

GUY BRAUCOURT/1971

B: *You were working on another story about Indians when you came across Thomas Berger's* Little Big Man?

P: Yes, it was similar to *Little Big Man* in many ways, but at the same time very different. It was about the Americans' commercial exploitation of Indians with a story told from a white man's point of view. The narrative of *Little Big Man* is seen from the Indians' point of view since the hero is brought up by them and lives with them most of the time. It also depicts a war of colonization as waged by Colonel Custer. It's actually a film about the advancing frontier of a nation whose desire for trade and expansion is the real cause of the war between the whites and the Indians. The West was completely changed by trade—especially the trade in bison hides—which is briefly depicted in the film through the character of Buffalo Bill, who was a skilled bison hunter. But in this sequence, and most of the others, Jack Crabb—the story's narrator and hero—is more of a spectator than participant. Rather than being a man of the West he's more like a tourist caught between the two cultures, quite happy to go where events lead him.

B: *You must have had to cut lots of secondary characters and subplots from the screenplay.*

P: Yes, including Calamity Jane, Wyatt Earp, an African American raised by the Cheyenne, and an Italian trumpeter called Martini who was with Custer at Little Big Horn and wasn't able to understand his orders. Berger packed so

---

From *Cinéma* (May 1971). Reprinted by permission of Guy Braucourt. Translated by Paul Cronin and Remi Guillochon.

many characters into his book that you could make half a dozen completely different films from the novel. There's even enough material about Custer and his two officers, Reno and Benteen, who left him in the lurch at Little Big Horn, for a really good drama.

Little Big Man sets out to debunk a key chapter of the history of the West and also of American history, namely the dealings between the so-called civilized white man and the supposedly savage Indian. I want audiences to look critically at the different stages of the story and the characters, from the priests to the traveling medicine vendors, from the gunslingers to the women of the West, like Caroline, Jack's sister. It's clear that through Custer the very myth of America—that of manifest destiny, the conquest of the West and the moral duty of the white man—is brought to light. If Custer's remark after one of his bloody onslaughts—"History will confirm the grandeur and the moral beauty of our actions"—has proven true, it just goes to show that history is written by those who have benefitted from such actions. In fact we owe a large part of the Custer myth to the one person who was without a doubt the greatest publicist in our nation's history. It was Mrs. Custer who concocted the heroic image of her husband when she went to Little Big Horn the day after the battle and declared the area a national monument.

B: *You shot Little Big Horn in a low-key way and without any grandeur, very differently from most other on-screen battles. Almost immediately we move into the turmoil and confusion.*

P: When you see the actual battleground where we made the film, you realize that those small hills and valleys were the worst possible terrain for the soldiers. It took only a few minutes for the Indians to shoot them all down. It's been estimated that the battle of Little Big Horn lasted no more than eight minutes. No director could turn a battle like that into a great spectacle.

B: *The tone of the story is quite picaresque, even parodying, rather than tragic and heroic.*

P: This is because Jack Crabb is something of a picaresque hero who always managed to escape all these events, whether by being a traitor or by switching sides. I don't want to judge him but I'd say quite simply that he's a survivor. The last scene of the film, with this old man sitting alone in a nursing home, is deliberately enigmatic, just as the book's last paragraph allows the reader to make his own choice: "Jack Crabb was either the most neglected hero in the history of this country or a liar of insane proportions."

B: *In the novel the story ends with the death of the old Indian chief, but he doesn't die in the film.*

P: We talked long and hard about this and in the first draft of the script he does die, but this death would have introduced an element of sadness into the film and we didn't want this. The film would have become dramatic, even melodramatic, instead of being picaresque. I also wanted to show that not only were the Indians going to be destroyed, but they were also condemned to live. On the whole, audiences like their entertainment dramatically compact and homogenous, but I want the opposite. A film should remain free and open, not with everything defined and resolved.

B: *Your film includes elements of documentary on the lives of the Indians.*
P: That's because we lived alongside the tribes in their reserves on the site of the Battle of Little Big Horn and talked with the old men about their traditions. Their stories were often contradictory. Whenever we asked them about specifics, they held an elders' council, and the chief would give his consent by giving a set formula whose very simplicity was loaded with meaning beyond the words themselves: "Yes, that's the way it used to be."

B: *Whether Americans or Indians, you have always been very interested in rebels and drifters, and those people on the fringe of society who sometimes break away altogether, like Billy the Kid and Bonnie and Clyde.*
P: That's because even though I'm not like them, I can empathize with all these characters. It's as if I were a Jewish Native American or Black Jew.

B: *Like Arlo Guthrie in* Alice's Restaurant, *Jack Crabb represents an idealized return to an America on the outskirts of society, a nation of the noble savage and open plains.*
P: Yes, the films do have a lot in common, as both main characters are weak people in a harsh world. They also both depict small communities that want to reestablish warmth and love against the backdrop of a cruel world.

B: *But surely the idea of Eden spoiled by civilization and progress is a myth?*
P: Perhaps, but in the history of our country the Native American population has been either decimated or herded onto reservations. And the community in *Alice's Restaurant* doesn't disappear, it just evolves and adapts itself. The history of this country is the story of a nation destroying communities on the one hand and on the other re-creating them and letting new ones evolve. This is why we can't lose all hope for the future.

Conflicts of Conscience

MARIO FOGLIETTI/1971

F: *Adhering to the politics of the New American Cinema, you have made a Western. Why did you decide to shoot* Little Big Man?
P: Maybe I lack modesty but I think that the history of Native Americans has never been told the right way on film.

F: *You have been quoted as saying, "Working in Hollywood with so many technicians is horrible. Each of them needs to know precisely how my ideas need to be realized, and what emerges from this group work is not my idea but rather the archetype of the Hollywood-idea, the commonplace, the triumph of the obvious." If this is the case, why do you keep making films in Hollywood?*
P: I'm not going to make any more films in Hollywood. Actually every time I have made a film within the studio system, I've always tried—and I think succeeded—in avoiding the kind of conditioning that regulates production, all the interference from screenwriters and producers, the eccentricity of "stars," the pressures from friends who don't want to work with this or that actress or actor. Hollywood itself is changing; it's not like it used to be. Today you go to Hollywood only to get your money. The films themselves are made a long way from the producers' offices. This allows for a certain amount of freedom. Working without the fear of some kind of bulldog standing there from morning till night, putting his nose in everything you do, expecting explanation upon explanation.

F: *In 1963 Burt Lancaster had you fired as director of* The Train, *preferring to work instead with John Frankenheimer, a director who was perhaps more likely to go with a more heroic and adventurous interpretation of the story. It was quite a*

From *Rivista del Cinematografo* (December 1971). Translated by Haider Rashid and Paul Cronin.

*scandal at the time and everyone wondered how it was that in America an actor—
even an important one like Lancaster—could decide the fate of a talented director.*

P: Lancaster's "protest" was an act of untrustworthiness. It was a stupid thing to do. The truth is that Lancaster is stuck on his own ideas and doesn't like to work with directors who challenge him. He's a "star," one of those actors who are, thankfully, on their way out. They're becoming extinct. He doesn't like playing real people, preferring heroic supermen instead. It's hardly a surprise that my views on Lancaster are negative.

F: *How do you respond to criticisms that your films glorify violence and encourage rebellion against certain institutions, without suggesting a coherent ideological alternative?*

P: Regarding the accusation about glorifying violence, I admit it's true. I love violence, but only violence directed against brutality. My films themselves are never brutal. It's true that some of them are violent, but then life is violent. The education of children, human civilization, all these things are acts of violence because they all run up against human nature. As for the second accusation, that I'm attacking certain institutions without proposing alternative models, allow me to use *Bonnie and Clyde* as an example. The film has been criticized because I advanced certain ideas against various social and economic institutions, but I hardly think it's my duty to suggest what changes might be made to these institutions because everything in American society was so radically altered by the crisis of 1929.

F: *How do you explain the success of* Bonnie and Clyde*?*

P: Young people feel close to it, and not only in America. It's a social film in the sense that it's about the Depression when young people felt excluded from a society that seemed to be destroying itself economically. They underwent something like an identity crisis and wanted to change things, which isn't so different from what's happening in the United States today. The country is engaged in an action that's absurd, both politically and socially, but rather than reacting violently to demonstrate their existence, young people today act passively and sometimes self-destructively.

F: *Perhaps this explains why the characters in your films—with the exception of* The Miracle Worker*—seem to be constantly involved, sometimes because they are so weak, in situations they cannot control and therefore resolve. Does this have anything to do with your own personal view of the world?*

P: I don't agree that the destiny of the characters in my films are determined by weakness. Everybody—including Annie and Helen in *The Miracle Worker*—struggles tenaciously against his or her destiny, something that's intrinsically related to the human condition. We all struggle to improve our lives. We don't always succeed in our attempts, but we nonetheless continue struggling. This is the basic idea behind my films.

F: *Some critics have written that you belong to the romantic tradition, that your work is all about impulse and instinct. Do you agree?*
P: Partly, yes. The spontaneous impulse of human nature that tries to overcome limits and destiny is something I've always felt and appreciated. Bonnie and Clyde, for example, stand for anything we can think of, and even though we consider them outlaws, it stands out that at the root of their behavior is the feeling of there being something unjust about the world that needs to be changed.

F: Mickey One *could be described as a parable of modern man's metaphysical fear. Is there a link between this idea and the tensions of the era in which it was produced?*
P: Yes, the film was made during a precise historical and political moment which was marked by highly repressive political activity. It was the end of the McCarthy era, a period when a generation that was afraid to talk was growing up in a country that has always respected individual freedom and allowed people freedom of thought and expression. What were they afraid of? My opinion is that they didn't want to lose sight of those things that, in fact, they had never earned. That's why the film was a kind of parable but also a description of what I hope has been the last generation of unhappy people in American history.

F: *It seems as if today's American cinema is moving toward real critical reflection and in this respect is looking to the great tradition of social realism of the 1950s. Do you agree?*
P: Yes, in the fifties the optimism born out of winning the war and euphoria during the age of prosperity came to an end. Since then cinema has exalted a kind of heroic optimistic American, heir of the tradition of Frank Capra's characters, for whom everything was possible. Then the American people started to look around and understood that everything that was said and done in those films didn't correspond to the truth. They understood there was another America, the ruggedness of the rich and opulent America, the unraveling of happy America, that there are disinherited, poor, and disenfranchised people. That's how social realism was born, based on the example of Italian neorealism, which was a way to hold tight to reality. Today, as our nation is going through a period of great crisis, there is a tendency to look inward. With the war in Vietnam, racial intolerance, and social disparity,

America in the seventies is tormented by conflicts of conscience. It seems that nothing has changed in all these years. Cinema, at least a certain kind of responsible cinema, is facing this reality again, a reality that holds a mirror up to humanity. This, I think, is the best way—and perhaps the only way—to make films.

Rising out of the Ashes

JESSICA VAN HELLER / 1976

Q: *Most of your films share similar themes. Your characters share similar emo-tional conflicts and problems. Do you see your films as essays on alienation and emotional isolation?*
A: No. I don't see them as essays at all. As a matter of fact, if we're talking about the process of creativity, I can't even detect similarities between the films until they're well behind me. Each time I think I'm doing an absolutely brand-new film, and it's only with hindsight of fifteen years or so that I can detect there are very clear lines of similarity between them. I think of them as simple stories, yarns.

Q: *How did you come to make* The Left Handed Gun?
A: It had been done originally as a television show, and they couldn't get anyone else to direct it. Fred Coe was going to produce it for Warner Bros., and he tried a couple of other guys, but they wouldn't do it. I agreed to do it if I could get a friend of mine, Leslie Stevens, to help write it. We just thought it would be interesting to take the story of a Western juvenile delinquent— which is the way Billy was always regarded—and see if we couldn't find a basis for authenticating that existence. Why did he remain so legendary and so much a part of the national consciousness and the legend of the West? Taking that as our departure point we decided we would highly personalize it by giving him a distinct family. Then we thought that if we gave him a fam-ily we would have to go back to his infancy, which is relatively unknown, though it's believed he came from New York. We thought it would be bet-ter if we chose a surrogate parent, as we all do in adolescence. We tend to choose a substitute parent, somebody who becomes a rather idealized friend.

Previously unpublished interview conducted on 30 August 1976. Printed by permission of Philip Porcella.

So that's what we did, and chose Mr. Tunstall from whom Billy solicited affection. I thought we would learn a lot from that relationship. Then when Mr. Tunstall is killed, Billy takes on a cause as if it's been his lifelong cause. In fact Mr. Tunstall hardly knew Billy. But we always tend to pick up the cudgels of certain injustices we feel committed to, and I think that's what Billy does.

Q: *Do you think there was a psychological necessity for Billy to seek revenge?*
A: Sure. There was a psychological necessity that preceded his relationship with Mr. Tunstall. I'm sure it was a psychological prerequisite that was formed in his early childhood.

Q: *I always felt that James Dean would have been the perfect actor for that part.*
A: Before we made the film, before Paul Newman was a movie star, he'd done *The Silver Chalice*, and then Warner Bros. had dropped his contract. We had worked together in live television, and a new series was being produced, a show called *The Battler* to star James Dean as a forty-five year old punch-drunk prize fighter and Paul Newman as Nick Adams from the Hemingway stories. Ten days before we were to leave for California and do it, Dean was killed so we asked Newman to play the fighter and got Dewey Martin to take the Newman part. Paul played it extremely well. Robert Wise saw the show and asked him to do *Somebody Up There Likes Me*, which essentially was the beginning of Paul's movie career. So perhaps James Dean was the obvious choice for the role, but he was dead and Paul inherited that part.

Q: *What was James Dean like?*
A: In *Giant*, when he's playing a shy, vulnerable coiled spring who's going to explode, that was exactly what Jimmy was like. He wore glasses and was shy and hung around, not talking very much, but inside was a bomb ticking. He was wonderful.

Q: *Why didn't you edit* The Left Handed Gun?
A: Look around. I don't think there are five directors in the United States who have that right. It's part of a problem, one that has economic and political overtones. The American film industry—which is a word I loathe—is the only unsubsidized film enterprise in the world. Every other country subsidizes its film industry and filmmakers to some degree. We don't, so to that extent as filmmakers we're subject to the banks as our primary source of financing. If you go to a bank for a sizeable loan—two or three million dollars—they want to know if you're going to survive. If you say the loan is to construct a building, they might say, "Wait a minute, he might never finish the building. We want a third party who can guarantee us that he'll finish it."

That's what the studios do, and they say to you, "We can't give you final cut otherwise we can't get the money from the banks." Of course this is nonsense but it's the kind of psychology that operates in the film industry. I think there's an uneasy accommodation between trying to be a good artist and a commercial artist that pervades all my films.

Q: *How do the studios know how to edit the footage?*
A: They don't. The shots have a mathematical continuity that is detailed in the script but following that to the letter doesn't produce a finished film, as you know. There could be two shots listed in the script, but you might have actually filmed eight or nine. It's only once you get to the set that you really start seeing things. The shot that's on the page is only an indication of what's to come. So we're really at the mercy of the editors. They call themselves editors, but they're really just studio employees. They spend their lives editing in a little toilet out back of Warner Bros. with a pair of scissors. They're a hopeless lot and should be distinguished from the people I deal with who are not just editors but collaborators, people like Dede Allen.

Q: *Are your editors with you during filming?*
A: Not usually. Maybe Dede will come out for a couple of weeks to get the feel of the film and the atmosphere of the set.

Q: *What do you think about the idea of there being a homosexual subtext to* The Left Handed Gun*?*
A: There was never an explicit intention of homosexuality but in the case of Billy the Kid the absence of a father figure allows for that kind of an emotional investment in what we call a peer group or a group of contemporaries. There's a desire to emulate people in Billy's own age-group. Only in the most abstract sense is that homosexual. A far more appropriate way to describe it would be a state of arrested development, in that Billy has never fully completed that traditional Oedipal experience with his father. The failure to do so has left him overly investing in his friends with these kind of familial as well as friendly values, so that with their deaths a piece of him also dies.

Q: *What about the scene of Moultrie's betrayal of Billy?*
A: What a scene that was! He goes to Pat Garrett's bar after Billy has knocked him down into the dust and kicks him. Moultrie is an alcoholic and hysteric, but he's also in an acute state of anxiety. He's a disheveled and dusty figure who's been profoundly rejected by this figure who he'd had a large hand in elevating to an almost God-like status. So he comes into the bar, Pat Garrett is behind the bar, and says in that faintly Southern way, "Something has to be done." Garrett says, "Yes" and puts a bottle of whisky onto the bar. It was

a crucial scene. He's drinking his booze, weeping like a baby, betraying Billy, and getting his own sense of pride in order. An insane episode, a prototypical Judas experience. It was meant to be something that touched a real cultural nerve.

Q: *What has Billy learned by the end of the film?*
A: I think he has the sense that he's doomed to endless pain. He has slept with Saval's wife, thereby committing a primal sin that really destroys his parents. He's overwhelmed by guilt. He has the feeling that somehow he's a leper and that whatever he touches causes other people misery.

Q: *Many of your characters seem to be alienated loners. The themes keep on repeating themselves in your films.*
A: I guess what I'm resisting is the word "alienated." I don't think of it as quite the appropriate word. If anything the characters in my films—particularly in the early films—exist in a society that's alienated. But I don't mean to make too much of it because I think of them as outsiders, as deviants and people on the edge of society and culture.

Q: *So society is to blame?*
A: I don't think it's a one-way street. I don't think these people are the only ones at fault. They're the mavericks of society, having been created by that society. They can't blame society, and at the same time society can't be entirely exonerated because it exerts so many contradictory influences on a person growing up. In the case of *The Miracle Worker* the social attitude toward the deaf and blind to this very day is "Put them away, we don't want to see them, we don't want to deal with them, we don't want to have to confront that horror." In fact, at the Perkins Institute for the Blind they constantly have people out in the field following up rumors of children who have been locked away and are living like animals in filthy conditions because the parents are so ashamed and unable to deal with it. Of course this isn't the fault of the child, and I don't think it's society's fault either. What we have is just an unenlightened herd instinct. All of us would rather have an attractive child who does nice clear-minded things. If you have an aberrant anomaly who comes out of you that can't hear or see—or worse, both—then you feel somehow so intimidated that most of these children are locked away. The conditions in which they live are unimaginable.

Q: *How did* Mickey One *come about?*
A: The film started out about Joe McCarthy. Everyone was walking around so afraid of McCarthy, but what the hell did we have to be afraid of? Before

anyone accused us of it, society was saying, "I'm not a Communist! Not me!" The whole damned society was incapacitated. We were all acting like a bunch of fools. Those who had radical pasts were trying to destroy their earlier identities. But if youth is not radical who's going to be radical? Why repudiate that? How that drunken fool was able to bring the country to its psychological knees was one of the most irritating things I've ever encountered.

So I decided to make a film about a guy who starts out running, hiding, burning his identity, getting rid of himself, trying to pick up another identity, trying to get rid of some ancient guilt. He doesn't know what he's done or why he's done it, but he feels guilty and wrong, just as the whole country did under McCarthy. And by the end of the film he says, "Fuck it, I've had it. I'm going to stand up and take it. I'm going to deal with it." Of course, the minute anyone did that—when Lillian Hellman went in front of the [House of Un-American Activities] Committee and said, "I cannot and will not cut my conscience to fit this year's fashions"—within a matter of days that hit through the cultural community like a shot in the arm. People said, "Where's the sense in running?" There was no sense in running.

I think the essence of the film is about the courage to be. The sum of our actions determines how we see ourselves. It's almost an act of will to have the courage to exist. My private sense is that the film is about having the courage to speak out. If you find something so deeply offensive, then you must have the courage to respond to it. To some extent I suppose I was really challenging myself to see if I would have the courage to speak out if I were, for example, living under Hitler. Today, with hindsight of the war, we keep saying, "If you get an inhuman order, you shouldn't carry it out." I certainly agree with this, but it's a lazy judgment for people to make with hindsight. I think a lot of people in our government—and a lot of us in our own lives— get orders that we find difficult to refuse. We don't say, "I don't think I can do that, Mr. Nixon" or "I don't think I'll go to Vietnam." The thing that really startled me about the generation of *Alice's Restaurant* is the balls, the guts, they have to say these things. My generation had been backed into the corner, and with *Mickey One* I just thought it was time to turn around and say, "Wait a minute. What I think belongs to me. What I do belongs to me." I was inspired by people like Hellman, Arthur Miller, and Zero Mostel who had the guts to stand up in front of the Committee and tell them to go fuck themselves.

Being in control of your destiny means trying to live your life the way you want to live it. The thing about Mickey is that he has no control over anything. There's a scene in the film when he sees a little Japanese man who has taken pieces of junk—the detritus and debris of a civilization—and is beginning to put them back together again. Even if it falls apart or blows up, the fact is that he is going to survive. His impulse is to put it back together again and again, that even the bombs that fell on Hiroshima and Nagasaki are not as terrible as the paralysis that results when everybody who is appalled by these events doesn't know what to do about them and just stands around slack-jawed and gaping. If one man rises out of those ashes and says, "I can make something beautiful here if I put this on top of that and that on top of this. It might last only until tonight when someone'll come and knock it down, but for thirty seconds it'll be just stunning." If Mickey takes anything from this it's just to put something together. You might be a lousy piano player and a weak comic, but if that's the best you've got, put it up there. Don't run away from it.

Q: *I read that you and Warren Beatty did not get on while making the film.*
A: Not exactly. If an actor and director are arguing, the journalists who come around the set interpret it as not getting along. But that's not what it is at all. We're fighting because we're two volatile people with strong, passionate feelings. The last thing I want an actor to do is mute or suppress his own attitude. Nor would I want them to ask me to suppress mine. So we kind of go at it. Warren and I have such an open relationship that goes back to the days of *Mickey One* where we simply fight everything out. But when I'm making the film the ultimate decision rests with me. If he were directing the film the final choices would rest with him.

Q: *Where did you find Alexandra Stewart who plays Jenny?*
A: Truffaut recommended her to me. I had someone else in that part, but ten days before we started shooting, the studio said we couldn't use her. I had seen her in Louis Malle's *Le Feu follet* and thought she was nice looking. I knew she was Canadian so I called Truffaut from Chicago and said, "I'm in trouble. Is Alexandra Stewart any good?" He said, "She's terrific." Little did I know that she and François were having a fling.

Q: *Do you like* Mickey One?
A. I hadn't seen the film for years and then saw it recently and thought it was very good. I don't know why people thought it was so obscure. In Robin Wood's book about my work it's the only film of mine he doesn't like even though he likes *The Chase*, which is far less my film than *Mickey One*. People said they didn't understand *Mickey One*, but it really doesn't seem that hard to understand. It's a very simple film. It happens all the time that comedians get bought up by the mob. They don't know how to get out or what they

owe or why they owe it. I could give you names of some very conspicuous comedians who are owned by the mob.

The Left Handed Gun was such a flop in the United States that I thought I'd never make another film again. The New York Times review was just scathing so I went into the theater and was going great with Two for the Seesaw and The Miracle Worker and another couple of plays. Then I made the film of The Miracle Worker and began to get the reviews from Europe of The Left Handed Gun, from André Bazin, from Cahiers du Cinéma, and they were terrific. They really understood the film. "Jesus Christ!" I thought, "There's a world out there!" I got carried away and went to Columbia Pictures and said, "I'll make you two movies for practically no salary. They'll cost less than a million dollars each. The only thing is that you can't read the script, I'm just going to make them." They didn't like that but agreed to it because of the two films I'd already made. Annie and Patty had both won Academy Awards, and I had all these Broadway hits at the time. I was being treated like a hot young director. They figured, "For a million bucks we can't go wrong." So I made Mickey One. I was suffering from an excess of freedom. I didn't give a shit whether they understood it, I just wanted to do my number. And I did. And I never made the second picture for Columbia. They reneged on the deal. That was the end of that and Mickey One disappeared quicker than any film you've ever seen. I do remember it was at the New York Film Festival where Judith Crist really liked it, for which I've been eternally grateful to her. Anyway, for me it's almost a really terrific picture, even if it does suffer from what we might call youthful excesses.

Q: In The Miracle Worker there are many contrasting images of light and dark. Was this a very conscious decision?
A: I was trying to isolate the acuity of seeing something. Every moment when we could take advantage of that idea, we did. In the dream and fantasy sequences Annie could see only a portion of light. It was done with a very complicated process where we altered the image to the point where the emulsion broke down so you could just barely discern a figure. We had it blown up, I think, thirty-two times its size. In order to shoot a close-up we used a very wide lens from all the way across the studio. We had a little dot in the viewfinder knowing that the dot would eventually fill the screen because we would blow it up to the size we needed. We did a lot of tests to determine what the optimum degree was.

Q: I always wondered about the character of Helen's brother and if you ever spoke with William Gibson about the brother. Why was he such an outcast?

A: The character of Jimmy is entirely Bill's creation, constructed from Annie's notes and letters at the Perkins Institute. It's chilling to read them, such
beautiful letters. Bill spent a lot of time reading them.

Q: *You have spoken of the film being "too theatrical." What do you mean by
this?*
A: Let's go back to the play. Bill had this terrific problem which is that everything has to be articulated verbally. Problems and counter-opinions need to be
expressed, you have the protagonist-antagonist configuration. In the theater it
was necessary to have Captain Keller be a kind of irascible shortsighted, short-
tempered man who kept putting qualifications and limitations on every event
that occurred. A line right out of the play is "Two weeks Miss Keller, and then
the child comes back to us." Well, I'd done the play, I'd watched it for two
years, and when I came to shoot the movie, it never occurred to me that we
didn't need all that stuff. We didn't need a protagonist to verbalize everything,
all we needed to do was show it. We needed to show Helen's condition. We
just needed to photograph a child in that condition, which would be more
eloquent than Captain Keller saying what he did. His character could have
and should have been very different in the film, far less father-knows-best. He
should have been a man in shock, kind of stupefied. I should have filmed it in
some other way, reducing what Captain Keller had to articulate by showing it
with the camera and then him watching it. It would have been ten times more
eloquent than him saying anything.

Q: *You seem to have a fascination with mirrors and glass. Every film seems to
contain images of glass, window panes, mirrors, glass store fronts. Do these objects
symbolize something or do you use them merely as visuals?*
A: I use them because they're visual, but I suspect that I have a very strong
voyeuristic streak. I don't see how anyone who makes movies isn't some kind
of voyeur to some extent. One of the things about theater and film is that we
take the occasion to study other people's behavior. It's kind of a primal desire.
The basic essence is that we'd like to see our parents screwing if we could. I
think that's the heart of it.

Q: *That might explain why someone might make films, but it does not explain
why there are so many mirrors in your work.*
A: No, it doesn't. As you see in *The Left Handed Gun* I use the language of
"Through a Glass Darkly" very consciously and conspicuously. I think it's
an apt phrase, and when Bergman used it for the title of one of his films
several years later, I was thrilled that we had both come up with this Biblical
reference.

Glass seems to be a wonderful way—without getting tricky—of doing things like doubling an image, obfuscating an image, producing an image in fragments, in a kind of distortion, all without getting fancy with the lens. I don't think we should mess with the basic medium of the lens itself. I think we should see it as we actually perceive it. Then perhaps we can interpolate some other medium into that vision, some other ingredient that helps say, "Wait a minute. There's the objectivity of the eye and the subjectivity of the mind operating at the same time." And that's what I think glass provides as an opportunity in film. In *The Miracle Worker* there's a shot of Annie Sullivan looking through the glass window and we see her reflection in it. Since we didn't know what the light conditions would be on any given day I think we had six or seven panes of glass with different degrees of reflective filter. It's still transparent but we designed it to get just the degree of intensity I wanted.

Q: *Mickey is trying to escape himself in* Mickey One. *There are so many instances of glass that I wonder if the point is that when you look into a mirror you absolutely cannot escape yourself.*
A: Let me tell you an anecdote. Warren Beatty is a very handsome guy. Someone pointed out to me that every time he got on an elevator and there was a mirror, Warren would look at himself. Before we started shooting, I said to him, "Why do you do that?" He said, "I don't know. I think to make sure I'm still there." I thought it was a very astute thing to say and a terrific characteristic that Mickey would have. So we borrowed it.

Q: *Your films are clearly strong personal statements and reveal a strikingly consistent personality. You don't write your scripts but do you personally select them all? How much of the characterizations come from you and how much are in the scripts?*
A: I select them all. This is one of those *bêtes noires* that bothers me. There's a very artificial line of distinction between who writes what. I have written a large part of my films but happen to feel it's not moral for a director to take credit for this unless he is the original author. So I don't tend to share screen credit. Increasingly in this country—and more so in Europe—we're now seeing three or four writers and the director being credited as if there were a distinct writing function that he or she was performing. For years, in theater, television, and films I was actively writing scripts, but with the exception of *Alice's Restaurant* I thought a director's credit was sufficient. With that film I literally had the original idea and started the entire project and wrote some of the script with Venable Herndon.

Q: *But are the ideas about your characters being outsiders, or searching for parents and looking for an identity, all your own?*
A: They are my ideas communicated to the author. It's also part of the reason why I selected the script in the first place because it appealed to that aspect of my personality. I don't think you can isolate any of these things. It tends to be part of the entire process.

Q: *How do you work with your actors?*
A: As little as possible. If you select actors, the best thing a fledgling director can do is stay out of their way. If you're working with good actors and you're not a fledgling actor, the best thing you can do is help them discover it for themselves. If they don't discover it for themselves, if it's imposed from the outside, what you have is an actor performing a task assigned them by the director.

Q: *What would you do if an actor had a completely different interpretation to your own?*
A: I would give him a very good hearing because certainly you can learn something from a completely different interpretation. But if you find the interpretation is really going to be so at variance to the kind of movie you want to make, I think you have to separate. But I don't really think there's any reason for that to occur. If you discuss it at the outset and really don't see eye to eye, I don't see any reason to continue because you're going to end up with half what you want to do, half what he wants to do.

Q: *Someone once wrote that your films show an emotional isolation that has become physical. Do these mannerisms come from the actors or is it part of the collaboration?*
A: I think those are actors' choices. How they use their bodies is an extension of their knowledge and feelings about the part. I wouldn't tell an actor how to walk or make a gesture. Very rarely I might do it and say, "This is how I would do it, now you find your own equivalent for it." I might make a fool out of myself by doing this, but this is something I would recommend every young director do. The idea of acting in front of a camera, day in and day out, is such an isolating, terrifying, and lonely experience. Actors have to stand up there and do it, whether it's weeping or being funny or attractive or seductive. It's such a burden, it's really the loneliness of the long distance runner in front of the camera. It's pathetic to say this about movie stars, but there's nothing lonelier than being out there in front of the camera. Let's say you're about to make love and you look up and there are seventy-five men standing around who have watched a lot of people make love before and

they're wondering, "Let's see how you do it." That's what a movie set is like. My heart goes out to movie stars. I think it's extremely valuable and probably the director's principal function in relation to the actor is to help break that isolation.

Of course someone like Brando refuses to submit to the role of being interrogated by the camera. He has the guts to fail. He insists on saying, "What I feel and believe at this moment is what I'm going to play, and that's all." In his so-called failures I always find a high degree of success. It never disturbs me when Brando doesn't match our expectations of him. There's always something magical going on.

Q: *After a success do you feel under pressure to match your past achievements?*
A: Sure, but it's much easier for the director than for the actor. I get pressure from the critics, but it's relatively easy to deal with. Cole Porter said the critics always wrote that nothing was as good as his last show. That's how he went through life, writing a series of great songs and always getting panned for his show not being as good as his last one. I've made some good films and some not so good films. You never have hundred percent hitters in baseball. They hit once out of every three or four times at bat. That's the way the game is played. But movie stars are always expected to bat at a very high level.

Q: *You once said, "I owe a certain debt to the psychoanalytic world." What did you mean by that?*
A: There's no question that I employ a lot of what I would say are Freudian insights in my work, insights of what I know of the psychoanalytic process, which is considerable, and what I have experienced myself. It's one of the more remarkable systems to give us an adequate explanation or accurate description of human behavior.

Q: *I know that* The Chase *was taken away from you before the film was edited. I just wonder what your original intentions were for the film?*
A: *The Chase* resembles what I had in mind and thematically isn't very different from my original intentions. In the film everybody's going along with the establishment. That's the way it is: you rub my back, I'll rub yours. Calder, Marlon Brando's character, was meant to be someone who said, "Wait a minute. I go along with this up to certain point and then suddenly find myself owned by someone else? To hell with that!" He wasn't owned by anyone but discovers that E. G. Marshall is giving his wife a dress, that there was a certain expectation of being owned. You don't know how you get bought up and owned by someone in this culture. You don't know who's going to call

in the debts that they think you owe them. If I call you tomorrow and say, "You're in Boston, could you do me a small favor . . ." then you're caught, right? That's the way these kind of relationships start out. "I'm a rich man, you're not a rich man, Calder. I would like you to come to my place tomorrow night. It's a fancy do and I know your wife doesn't have a dress so what the hell, let me pop for the dress." The assumption now on the part of the guy who bought the dress is that if he gets a parking ticket he can get Calder to tear it up. These kinds of things go further and further and further. This is what the film was meant to be about. Marshall's character is a man who in other relationships—most particularly with his son—absolutely possesses somebody else's soul and identity.

The only thing wrong with *The Chase* is that they used all the wrong takes of all the right scenes. That's my only objection to it. It's not that I would have made a diametrically opposed film. I would have made something very like that but different takes and better acting. Certain scenes I would have cut down, other scenes I would have built up. It's a deformed creature.

Q: *Which of your films is your favorite?*
A: I think *Bonnie and Clyde* because it's the best one, but it's hard to say because there are aspects of all of them that are favorites. I don't really know. What I do know is that I'm more passionate about the thing I'm doing now and the thing I'm going to do next. By now *The Left Handed Gun* has slipped twenty years into the background. I can't talk passionately about it. It's like someone talking passionately about his child's diapers. My kids are grown. I'll talk about them now but I'm not going to sit here and say they were cute when they sucked their thumbs.

Q: *What are some of your favorite films by other directors?*
A: Almost everything Bergman has done in the past ten years. *Citizen Kane.* Jean Renoir. Fellini. Some of Truffaut's films, some of Godard's. Ford, Hawks, aspects of Kazan. I couldn't say how they've influenced me. As far as working with actors I think Kazan has probably influenced me more than anyone. We work similarly, I think he's a superb director of actors. Perhaps the best. I hope I've been influenced by Welles, but I don't know yet if I can point to one of my films that is particularly like his work.

Q: *What is your favorite period of art?*
A: I would have to say the Italian Renaissance, but that's only because I studied it. For me it's probably immediately juxtaposed to modern art: Picasso, Matisse, Cézanne, Léger.

Q: *How has your television and theater work affected your film work?*
A: I tend to prefer relatively simple camerawork, not long elaborate dolly shots or zooms. I tend to think the camera should be as anonymous as possible. I'm not saying that what we see on screen shouldn't be highly selective, but at the same time I don't think a director should endlessly zoom or dolly or track in and out. I don't find that interesting.

Q: *All of your films have moments with dialogue and certain shots that are very powerful and emotionally affecting.*
A: They come at crucial moments. When the image is appropriate to the emotion and there's a genuine sympathy—and I mean this about painting and photography and certainly about cinema—and they come together, there's such a consonance, a kind of sublime state. It's what we mean, I think, by aesthetics, when the good and true and beautiful all come together in a transcendent way. I'm not talking only about isolated incidents in my films, I'm talking about all films with those moments that remain in your mind forever.

Interview with Arthur Penn

CLAIRE CLOUZOT/1976

C: *In his review of* Night Moves, *Max Tessier talked about what he called your "hiatus." What exactly were you doing between 1970 and 1973?*

P: I went through a really difficult period after *Little Big Man.* For three years I didn't shoot any features except for an episode of *Visions of Eight,* the collective film about the 1972 Olympic Games in Munich. I didn't shoot anything for television or direct a stage play. Absolutely nothing for three years. Nothing. That's a long time. Actually . . . I lost my identity. I just gave up on things. I lost myself. For three years I stopped doing what really made me happy and what I really wanted to do.

C: *Were you overwhelmed about the successes of* Bonnie and Clyde *and* Little Big Man? *Did you feel you had failed in some way?*

P: *Little Big Man* really wasn't such a success in America. Everywhere else, yes, but not in America. As always the film worked better abroad, especially in France, than it did here. After its success overseas *Little Big Man* got a better reception in the United States. The reasons I got depressed are very personal, it's pretty complicated. I hope to be able to make a film about it one day but don't really want to say any more about it right now.

C: *What was it about* Night Moves *that got you going again? Presumably you must have been sent many scripts during those three years.*

P: Most probably a whim. Yes, I'd been sent several scripts, but I turned them all down. When I decided I wanted to direct again, I just chose the first

---

From *Ecran* (15 December 1976). Reprinted by permission of Claire Clouzot. Translated by Paul Cronin and Remi Guillochon.

script to hand. Impulsively and without really thinking about it I just told myself I was going to direct Alan Sharp's screenplay.

C: *Is that really true?*
P: Yes, I swear. That's exactly what happened.

C: *Is this why it flopped in the United States? Or was it just because it wasn't a very good script?*
P: No, I really liked Alan's script and think it's an interesting film. The problem was it was put into production too quickly. We just weren't ready. And there were other problems I had with the production, like a writers' strike just after I'd agreed to direct.

C: *A writers' strike! Impossible to imagine Jean-Loup Dabadie, Jean-Claude Carrière, and Francis Veber on strike in France!*
P: Just before the script of *Night Moves* had been really worked through, the Writers Guild went on strike for three months. We only had time to develop the film's central idea, in other words the "enigma without a solution" element of the plot. The strike lasted until we started shooting, and when it ended, we had to work really quickly. I really would have liked to have spent more time preparing the film.

C: *How confident were you about making a thriller?*
P: *Night Moves* is really an anti-genre film. In what I call cinema's "innocent" period the thriller was focused on an anonymous character, the "private" detective like Philip Marlowe. He was omniscient, cunning, impersonal, and by the end of the film, we didn't know him any better than at the start.

I found it philosophically interesting that Harry Moseby, Gene Hackman's character in *Night Moves*, influences the investigation and the way it's carried out. The point is that solving the case depends on the qualities and flaws of the detective. I asked Alan Sharp to make certain changes to the character. In my version, Harry Moseby became an angry and jealous person. The mythical character is transformed into a real human being who isn't always entirely likeable.

The public wasn't ready for a film that challenged the sacred laws of genre at a time when most films were slavishly following conventions. We were a few years too late. In 1973, in the midst of the Watergate scandal, people wanted to see traditional heroes. Anti-thrillers weren't in fashion.

C: *Are you used to your work being better received in Europe—and especially France—than in the United States?*

P: I find American critics very strange. Vincent Canby in the *New York Times* said *Night Moves* was confusing and bad. And then, at the end of December, he classified it as one of the twenty best films of the year. It's the second time he's changed his mind about one of my films. When *Little Big Man* came out he wrote a bad review and then at the end of that year put it on his list of the top ten films. It's really all very odd, especially in a country where critics have a zero margin of error. The only good review of *Night Moves* was in the *New Yorker* by Penelope Gilliatt, who actually understood the film, along with some European critics.

When it came to Europe I thought my chances were best at the Cannes Film Festival. I showed the film to [Administrator General] Maurice Bessy, but he turned it down. I've never actually had a film screened at Cannes, and this was the first time I'd asked to be included in the festival. Of course, I wasn't expecting to win the Palme d'Or and was actually prepared for a strong reaction against the film. Still, I was quite disappointed when he rejected it outright. As much as I appreciate the French critics, I don't appreciate the idea of a single individual deciding what gets screened at such an important festival. Who is Maurice Bessy after all? He's nobody. It's ridiculous.

C: *You didn't screen* The Missouri Breaks *at Cannes even though it was ready in time. Why is that?*
P: The film was ready in time and Bessy wanted to show it, but I turned him down as an act of revenge. I have very different feelings about film festivals than he does. As I say, I'm against the idea that a single person can decide the fate of a film.

C: *Was The* Missouri Breaks *a film you really wanted to make?*
P: Absolutely not. Like *Night Moves* it all happened completely by chance. It's something that could only happen in Hollywood. Elliot Kastner, a producer in the true sense of the word, sent me Thomas McGuane's script which I really liked, but at the time I wasn't really in the mood to make another film. He sent the script to Brando, then to Nicholson, and all three of us had the same reaction: interesting, but not filmable. Kastner, who can be quite unrelenting, came to see each one of us and asked me if I'd do the film if Brando did it. When I said yes, he went to see Nicholson and asked him if he'd do the film if Brando and Penn did it. And so on. A deal was struck that said each of us would do the film only if the other two were on board, and everyone agreed. We weren't actually interested in the film so much as working with each other. This probably isn't the best reason to embark on such a massive project. To tell you the truth, I don't really know why I made *The Missouri Breaks*.

C: *But wasn't it an exciting challenge to work with Brando, whom you knew, and Nicholson, with whom you had never worked before?*

P: From the start it was business, pure and simple, though after a while the idea of working with the two of them was exciting, yes. But I couldn't honestly sit here and tell you that at any point we were conscious of working on a project to which we were really committed.

C: *Did you have any problems with Thomas McGuane? American critics were very harsh on his script. Some said it was just an old-fashioned remake of his film* Rancho Deluxe *which also takes place in Montana.*

P: I really liked working with Tom McGuane. I like him and his novels, but I think that maybe his scripts aren't quite all there. Like *Night Moves*, we didn't do sufficient pre-production on *The Missouri Breaks*. At the point when I wanted to start working with McGuane on the script, he was in London editing his second film *92 in the Shade*, so we didn't have much time to work together. I think contracts were signed at the end of April and we planned to start shooting at the end of June or beginning of July. We just didn't spend enough time on pre-production. Another case of a contract being pushed through too quickly. We had five weeks to build the sets and do the screen tests and really didn't have enough time to work on the script. The powers that be at United Artists, and the two financiers, Richard S. Bright and Lester Persky, expected everything to be sorted out on set and that we'd be able to compensate there and then for the problems of the screenplay. It's the kind of studio mentality that's totally anachronistic today.

C: *You have the reputation of making only films you really care about. Were you passionate about* The Missouri Breaks?

P: I was never passionate about the film. I basically did it for three reasons: I wanted to work with Brando and Nicholson, I needed the money, and I wanted to shoot something in the summer of 1975. I also wanted to film in Montana where I'd made *Little Big Man* because I really like it there, but I couldn't tell you what significance the film has for me. Sure, there are some things about it that may someday become clear to me, but I don't find the general theme of the story terribly interesting. I don't really know what I was doing making the film. It was like passionless sex.

C: *But are you at least happy with the final result?*

P: No. Oh God, when United Artists read this they're going to kill me. Luckily this interview isn't for a big selling American magazine. Look, to be completely honest with you and a little guarded at the same time, in the original script Brando and Nicholson's characters met only once during a short scene. That's all. But when we faced up to the fact that we had two huge stars in this film, we realized one scene wasn't enough and feverishly set about rewriting the script so they met four times. Dramatically speaking, there was no reason for them to meet again and again. Once would have been enough. What was needed was a rising line of tension in terms of the character relationships, but there just wasn't one. Brando, Nicholson, and I did all we could to make up for this. The way they met had to be more dramatic, and if we'd had more time, I'm sure we could have sorted it all out. We thought we could put the whole thing back on course when we were on the set. No easy task. We worked like dogs and did our best to sort out these script problems, namely the lack of passion, but our solutions were based on knowledge and technical expertise, and none of this makes up for passion.

C: *Did Brando and Nicholson help you rewrite their parts?*
P: Not exactly, but they did give lots of suggestions along the lines of "What if the character said that?" or "What if he did that?" Brando in particular was full of ideas. He was completely devoted to the film, which is why I'm so bothered about all this talk of his bad behavior on the set. We actually worked very hard, more than we would have on a film which we believed in and knew intimately. And it was more difficult because we were working intellectually rather than emotionally.

C: *Can you give examples of the contributions Brando and Nicholson made?*
P: Brando works from a visual point of view. I saw his character Lee Clayton as a hermit crab, a man lacking his own real physical identity and who's always disguising himself as other people. Clayton has no style or outfit that makes him recognizable. Brando immediately seized on this idea and decided he'd change his costume each time he appeared on screen. The idea of dressing up as an old woman was his idea.

Brando was right in thinking of Clayton as a man without a center of gravity, something that's quite obvious due to the fact that he keeps on changing his persona. He spends his time looking for extravagant outfits that give him an unusual outward appearance. We finally end up recognizing him through these borrowed identities, not any one in particular.

Jack's contribution to the film was different. His thing was to establish a close relationship with the members of his gang. During filming they always hung out together, spending their evenings drinking and having fun at Jack's place. They spent every waking moment together and textured the film with their own lingo, inside jokes, and banter. The best way to explain Jack's gang is that it's like a bunch of kids playing in the street who suddenly see one of their friends convicted of a crime and sent to the gas chamber. They're not cowboys, they're just guys who have stolen a few horses without really thinking about it. And they certainly aren't that good at it. Jack's character isn't a natural leader, he becomes one only because everyone else is so useless. Jack brought a lot to the role and came up with a lot of dialogue himself which really contributed to the general atmosphere of the gang. He's a very inventive actor. All in all what I liked most about *The Missouri Breaks* was being able to work with the two of them.

C: *How different are they to work with?*

P: Nicholson was methodical, rational, and very logical in the way he approached his role, which doesn't mean he necessarily acted in a methodical and logical way. He needs an intellectual starting point from which he can let his instincts take over. But he never strays from his conception of the character. Brando is different. He doesn't like to plan out his role or set anything in stone beforehand. He uses images as a starting point. The idea of the hermit crab that moves from one shell to another is just the kind of image Brando would use. He's really a great actor.

In fact if the two of them hadn't respected each other the whole thing would have been virtually impossible. Instead of clashing they listened to each other and took one another's opinions into consideration. I was very happy to work with Brando again. As for Nicholson, I found a friend in him. He's someone I have deep respect for.

C: *The American critics were cruel about Brando's physical appearance. They also said that the scene in the bath, where you show his flab, was your way of getting even with him.*

P: My God! What the hell are you talking about? Who says these things? Brando is anything but difficult. I really can't stand things like that. I didn't have any problems with him when we were working together on the film. We were very much on the same wavelength the whole time. Get even with him? No way!

All this gossip about Brando is downright unfair. The American press is always running him down, but he's a great actor and a true professional. Journalists have targeted him ever since he decided he didn't want to be their friend, and he's certainly suffered because of this. He deals with the press either by clamming up or playing the clown. The press doesn't have enough of a sense of humor to understand him, certainly not those who covered the filming of *The Missouri Breaks*. You should have seen them. Some really acted like idiots.

C: *How do you choose the actresses you want to work with? You tend to cast women who are unknown in France alongside seasoned professionals like Hackman in* Night Moves *and Brando and Nicholson in* The Missouri Breaks.

P: I chose Kathleen Lloyd for *The Missouri Breaks* over some well-known actresses whose names I'd rather not mention. She's worked in television in California where someone brought her to my attention. She has a strong personality and wasn't intimidated by the fact that this was her first film or by the presence of the two stars she was working with. She was very natural with the two of them, even if she was a little scared. I like her a lot for her direct and honest approach. As for Jennifer Warren, I chose her for *Night Moves* after having seen her in a play in New York. She's a marvelous actress, and I really can't understand why she hasn't done anything since. In America you're tainted if you make a bad film. It's as if the actor carries some mark of failure with them. It's a shame and I really find it incomprehensible. The critics think of her as a decent actress but since *Night Moves* no one has given her a job.

C: *Do you think you upset the American public with* The Missouri Breaks? *If not, why did the press attack you, and why did the film play in theaters for only a month?*

P: First of all the American public isn't ready for a film that doesn't have a big shoot-out at the end. And second I think the film is more easily understood in Europe because Americans don't have a recent, immediate experience with colonization. They're terribly naïve and think that expanding America's sphere of influence is a good thing. Personally I don't agree. To me *The Missouri Breaks* holds a mirror up to the American people. The thing is they just don't want to look. Critics thought this image was just too unpleasant for them to deal with. Europeans, on the other hand, know what colonization means.

C: *Is that the real meaning of the film for you?*

P: During the process of colonization there is always a moment where the colonists and the wealthy set about establishing a system of rules and laws to protect their property. *The Missouri Breaks* is the story of the West where, all of a sudden, new laws appear without warning which automatically lead to splits and opposing camps. It certainly isn't your average Western. It's like *Night Moves* in that it runs against the genre. It's an anti-Western, an idea I toyed with in *The Left Handed Gun*. Apparently the Western is one of those sacred and untouchable genres. You should read what the critics wrote about that film back in 1957. They were absolutely vitriolic and humiliating. When he reviewed *The Missouri Breaks* in the *Village Voice*, Andrew Sarris wrote I shouldn't have made a Western because I don't understand them. It seems as if there are only two people in the entire world who understand Westerns: John Ford and Andrew Sarris.

C: *Is it true you went way over-budget on* The Missouri Breaks?
P: Absolutely not. Well, maybe sixty or seventy thousand dollars, which is nothing for a film that cost eight million. And that was only because United Artists wanted to release the film early. They thought it would be advantageous to get it out at a certain moment when there wasn't much competition from other films, so I had to finish working on it three months earlier than planned. We had three editors each working day and night on a third of the film in three different editing suites: Jerry Greenberg, Stephen Rotter, and Dede Allen, who is my regular editor and who wasn't available until late because she was working on the new Mike Nichols film, which ended up being delayed. So we went over budget because of the editing, not because of the shooting, and certainly not because of Brando and Nicholson, whose behavior was exemplary and who were both very disciplined.

C: *You're directing a play at the moment. Is theater something you are particularly keen on?*
P: It's been eight years since I worked in the theater. There was that period when I didn't do much at all, then the time when I was working on *Night Moves* and *The Missouri Breaks*. I just finished rehearsals for *Sly Fox*, Larry Gelbart's adaptation of *Volpone*. It's very funny. Gelbart wrote *A Funny Thing Happened on the Way to the Forum* and the TV series *M*A*S*H*. Volpone is in California during the Gold Rush. George C. Scott, Trish Van de Vere, Jack Gilford, Bob Dishy, and Hector Elizondo all appear in it.

I'm still working at the Actors Studio in New York where I moderate classes with Lee Strasberg and Elia Kazan. There are two sessions a week with between twenty and forty actors. There are nearly four hundred actors at the Actors Studio. Once you're in, it's for life. No one can ever throw you out. Graduates often come back, like Estelle Parsons, Rip Torn, and Shelley Winters, who you might see working through a script with a young unknown actor with a promising future like Steven Railsback. It's a place where hostility, cruelty, and politics have made their way in, but that's normal. For me the whole point of the Actors Studio is to present scenes publicly and in a democratic way, and that's why I'm still part of it.

C: *Have you cast any actresses from the Actors Studio? People complain there aren't enough parts for actresses. Where are the women in your films?*

P: Listen, for the small role in *The Missouri Breaks* I saw at least ten actresses who could have become big stars overnight because of their talent and presence. They were all beautiful and talented, but unfortunately they all work in television, where they basically become indistinguishable. As for the Actors Studio, all the students there who want to be in films are at the Los Angeles branch. People come to the one in New York to improve their theater skills.

C: *You could write a substantial female part and discover a new talent. Since* The Miracle Worker, *which featured two great female roles, your heroes have been men, who all went on to become famous.*

P: Throughout my life I've always been much more interested in women than men, probably because I was raised by my mother and not my father. When it comes to my theater work, I've concentrated on plays with female characters: *Two for the Seesaw*, *The Miracle Worker*, *All the Way Home* with Kim Stanley, Patricia Neal, and Eva Marie Saint. Women are what I know best. I know my mother very well but not my father. I think I've got a better understanding of women.

C: *So what about a role for a woman?*

P: Well, I'm currently working on two screenplays. One is about a woman in the Appalachians who suffers at the hands of the men around her. She doesn't know where she stands, caught between a father and husband who are rivals. Loss of identity is the theme. The other one, which I'm probably going to make next year, is about the Attica prison revolt. It's based on Tom Wicker's book *A Time to Die*. I'm writing the script for Warner Bros. with Don Peterson. We've already completed the first draft, and we're looking for money to do the second. There have been other similar projects announced, but I think mine will be the first to get made. I saw Cindy Firestone's *Attica,* which is very interesting, but it's a documentary. Mine will be fiction.

C: *So no more thrillers or Westerns?*

P: Let's just say that *Night Moves* and *The Missouri Breaks* are not what I really feel close to. I feel removed from New York and too close to Hollywood. I don't like the feel of the studios over there. My last two films haven't been very good because I've made too many compromises with Hollywood, something I really need to stop doing. I'm going to devote myself to changing the direction of my life and in turn my films. Not so I can get back to the way I was before my "crisis," but so I can be true to my interests and to myself. I'll never again work on something I'm not truly passionate about.

Arthur Penn

JEAN-PIERRE COURSODON/1977

C: *Apart from* Visions of Eight, *the documentary film about the Olympic Games in Munich, between* Little Big Man *and* Night Moves *you weren't around on the filmmaking scene for five years. Yet* Little Big Man *had been a commercial and critical success, as was* Bonnie and Clyde *three years earlier. Why this silence?*
P: I stopped working for rather serious personal reasons. It was a period when it seemed more important to spend more time with my wife and children. It was more important to me to devote myself to my family than to filmmaking, so it was a deliberate choice on my part even though—as you point out—I was riding high at the time.

C: *Were you working in theater during this period?*
P: No, the Stockbridge experience had ended around 1970–71. I basically did nothing for several years.

C: *Reading interviews you did between 1968 and 1970, there is a sense of great enthusiasm, an enormous confidence in the new generation. You spoke of consciousness raising and political organization. You even suggested that the country was moving toward a revolution. Things developed very differently, and I was wondering if your retreat from public life might be explained in part by the disenchantment that, for many, followed such euphoria.*
P: Perhaps indirectly, but again my reasons were mainly personal. As for the revolutionary ideal of the sixties, very little about it was actually revolutionary. There was certainly a concern about putting right obvious social and racial injustices, but it was still motivated by bourgeois ideals. The protesters were middle-class students and intellectuals whose movement never extended

From *Cinéma* (May 1977). Reprinted by permission of Jean-Pierre Coursodon. Translated by Paul Cronin and Remi Guillochon.

to the underprivileged, and their ideology didn't have a solid economic basis. Today it's a drained, exhausted revolution, and you have people like the Weather Underground who resurface and try to rejoin society, leaving their once revolutionary positions behind. In this atmosphere it becomes difficult to make truly committed films. For example I'm trying to make a film about the Attica prison riots based on Tom Wicker's book *A Time to Die*. Paramount has already invested quite a bit of money in the project, but I don't know if they'll have the courage to follow through. It'll be quite disturbing, many people won't like it. For the time being everyone thinks audiences want only escapist entertainment.

C: *Your last two films were very pessimistic.* Night Moves *could be described as a parable on the impossibility of knowing oneself and other people. Elsewhere it has been referred to as "a commentary on the post-Watergate era." The same could be said of* The Missouri Breaks.

P: It's true about *Night Moves*. It's the reason why the theme of the Kennedys is so central in the film. John wasn't the kind of hero we turned him into, even if he did personify the hopes of all those who had ideals back then, to the extent that we projected those hopes onto him. With his death, and then Bobby's, a part of our existence and aspirations came to an end. It's in this way that *Night Moves* is pessimistic, although I don't normally look at my work from an optimistic or pessimistic point of view. My intention with *Night Moves* was to make a seventies detective movie as opposed to traditional detective films that always present a problem followed, at the end, by the solution. *Night Moves* presents a problem whose solution doesn't exist to the extent that the character searching for the answers carries within him the impossibility of finding them. Harry Moseby's inability to understand his own problems, to discover his own identity, leads to his inability to recognize that the problem—the case he has been hired to solve—shouldn't actually concern him. Or, to put it another way, that he shouldn't approach it in a way that is likely to allow him to solve it or even to understand its nature. Being a rather conventional person, he insists on approaching it conventionally.

C: *You said in an interview with* Sight and Sound *that you considered Harry to be a "normal" character as opposed to the majority of your heroes who are rebels, misfits, outsiders. But do you see a connection between him and the others?*

P: What interested me about Harry was being able to show a man who, without being a true outsider, is nevertheless alienated from the society in which he lives. He's unable to establish meaningful connections with the world and other people. The alienation of a rebel like Billy the Kid is different. Harry's alienation is somewhere between that of an outlaw and that of a "regular" guy.

C: *In the same interview it seems as if you despise Harry, although the film doesn't give this impression at all. Besides, doesn't Harry do what all your characters do, to the extent that he wants to break out of the darkness?*
P: I don't despise him but rather his job, the very concept of a detective. With a few notable exceptions, detective films bore me and detectives are rather despicable people. They grant themselves the right to violate other people's secrets, which is very different from a quest for truth and knowledge, a theme evident in most of my films. In that interview I think I was just expressing a kind of revulsion for men like the Watergate conspirators, people who spend their time spying on each other. Harry seems to want to find out the truth about himself, but in reality tries to separate this self-awareness from the criminal case he is investigating. By doing this he demonstrates what I was trying to say about this kind of man who imagines he can compartmentalize his existence, to build a wall between his private and professional lives, which of course is impossible. Detectives are a particular breed of person. Real detectives have personality, something that most detective movies before *Night Moves* denied.

C: *Did the original screenplay include Harry's search for his missing father?*
P: No, I suggested that.

C: *Even though the screenplay has an extremely complex structure, everything is expressed visually and most of your recognizable preoccupations are there. Yet you say you made few changes to Alan Sharp's script?*
P: I must have been misquoted. What I meant was that the general spirit of the script remained the same but that I made a great number of modifications and additions in collaboration with Sharp. The film is very different from his original script.

C: *The film's entire structure seems to rest on binaries, whether oppositions—East-West, air-water, day-night—or duplications. There are his two trips to Florida, two deep-sea dives, two plane accidents, two visits to his wife's lover.*
P: I tried to express Harry's polarity, his contradictions, the fact that he lives two compartmentalized lives—interior and exterior—through various thematic motifs, visual or dramatic. The film is full of these oppositions and repetitions. The same goes for the triangular relationships between the characters. In my mind the film needed a certain cubist quality with superimposed and overlapping planes.

C: *For example the scene in the beginning where Harry is in his car, listening to his client's tape as he drives past a movie theater playing Eric Rohmer's* Ma Nuit chez Maud. *Here are three superimposed three-way relationships: Moseby's client's adulterous affair, mentioned on the tape, Harry's wife's affair as she is in the theater with her lover, and the triangular relationships in* Ma Nuit chez Maud.

P: Exactly. This is actually the reason why I chose Rohmer's film. Sharp suggested a Chabrol film in his script, I forget which one, but it made no difference as far as the psychological point was concerned as Harry is no "intellectual." But the Rohmer reference does add something thematically.

C: *The relationships between the characters are unclear and opaque. We never really know how they feel toward one another and why they do what they do.*

P: Same as in real life. In detective movies the characters are always transparent. They have no tangible reality, they exist only in relation to clues, to the investigation. We tried to make a detective movie that's situated in ordinary life, with characters reacting to each other in a complex manner. It was going against all the rules of the genre, which perhaps explains the critical and commercial failure of the film. People thought I'd tried to make a traditional detective film but done it very badly. Actually the film represents my exact intentions. I'm just sorry it didn't find its audience, but what can you do?

C: *Speaking of "anti-genre," the final sequence is extraordinary, the opposite of all those detective films with a drawn-out explanatory scene at the end.*

P: I tried to tackle this problem right from the start by deciding that there wouldn't be a traditional all-is-revealed scene at the end. In this film nothing can really be explained, and it seemed to me that we had to find a way of suggesting an explanation that would be purely visual. Harry's and the spectator's discovery of the pilot's identity is a revelatory moment in the strongest sense of the word. It reveals the connection between Harry's blindness in relation to himself and his blindness in relation to the identity of the guilty party, or parties, in this story about which he understands absolutely nothing.

C: *At the moment when Harry makes out the pilot's face through the boat's glass bottom, one thinks of the Biblical quotation from* The Left Handed Gun: *"Through a glass darkly." This time it is a play on words: "Through a glass-bottom darkly."*

P: That was certainly intentional.

C: *Editing is very important in all your films, especially so in* Night Moves, *where shots are extremely fragmented and dislocated.*

P: Very early on I felt that the film needed abrupt, disjointed, almost con-vulsive editing, something that might suggest a nervous tic. I don't know exactly why but I wanted to make a movie based on this kind of rhythm. I discussed it with Dede Allen and we agreed on this idea.

C: *Perhaps because of the discontinuous structure of the plot and the characters, the film is made up of pieces that come together only at the very end.*
P: Exactly. The film is a kind of mosaic.

C: *Some critics feel that choppy editing like this is detrimental to the continuity of the actors' performances.*
P: The editing may have been a bit too excessive, but I don't think it hurt the performances, which turned out to be exactly the way I wanted them and are quite extraordinary. Jennifer Warren is wonderful, and Hackman is a superb actor for whom I have immense admiration.

C: *There is a particularly moving scene where Harry and his wife are lying on their bed talking about the day when he was reunited with his father. Hackman does something truly incredible, I have seen nothing like it in any other film. Susan Clark asks him a question that embarrasses him and for a moment he puts his hands over his face to avoid his wife's gaze. When he removes his hands his face expresses something indescribable, a look that suggests shame, embarrassment, and guilt. But there seems to be no real "acting" going on, and Hackman conveys this all in a single gaze. You even get the impression that he is blushing. Did you give him specific directions for this scene, or was it a moment of inspiration on his part?*
P: I remember the scene very well. It was a difficult one, and we needed several takes because Susan had trouble with it. With an actor like Gene I don't need to give precise directions. He is able to produce the kind of re-action I'm after quite spontaneously, something he can do differently take after take. It just comes naturally to him.

C: *And the fight in the kitchen?*
P: There was nothing particularly difficult about the scene except it was a moment of intense violence. It's the moment when tension between the two characters is so high that they're capable of the absolute worst. Hackman has an extraordinary power that can be excessive, and I had to restrain him. There's sometimes something murderous about him.

C: *Whose idea was the crushed glass in the garbage disposal?*
P: Alan Sharp came up with that.

C: *The screenplay was originally called* The Dark Tower. *Was it you who came up with the title* Night Moves?
P: Yes. It was suggested in the dialogue itself, with the reference to chess, which was in Sharp's script.

C: *It was originally a Sydney Pollack project.*
P: Actually I only found out about this quite recently. Apparently Pollack was associated with Mark Rydell, but they had some disagreement. The company folded, and the script became the property of producer Bob Sherman, who sent it to me and produced the film.

C: *Did the film lose money?*
P: I don't know. That's what "they" tell me. It's quite possible though, since no one saw it.

C: *Did you work a lot on the screenplay of* The Missouri Breaks *and did collaboration with a writer who had a strong personality and who had just directed a film himself create any particular difficulties?*
P: Not really. We didn't get a chance to work together the way I would have liked. I'd hoped that Thomas McGuane would be around for the entire filming, but he was away for quite a long while. When he was there, he was with [his wife] Margot Kidder, who was expecting a baby. I think he came on the set only once during filming.
     The main problem with the film was the lack of time and preparation. The project was put together too fast due to the fact that Brando, Nicholson, and I found ourselves available at a given time, and we only had six weeks of pre-production. Then McGuane had to go to England for the editing of *92 in the Shade.* We thought we could handle it, but we were being too ambitious. In reality the project needed more time for preparation and reflection. Throughout the shooting I had a feeling of not being truly ready, of not knowing what I was supposed to do. It's not a bad film, but it is only a sketch of what it could have been.

C: *Did you generally agree with McGuane on what you wanted to do?*
P: I thought we agreed, but I know he doesn't like the film.

C: *There are several differences between the film and the screenplay published by* Random House.
P: I haven't seen the book. (*I show him a copy, which he skims through rapidly*). It seems to me that the book is a compromise between the original script and the film itself. The final scene is different but there was another ending

that was never filmed. It was an ironic, even comical, scene where Logan and Jane are sitting in deckchairs in front of the house, talking about opportunities of escape from the West. As for Brando's scenes that aren't in the script, they were improvised, usually on Marlon's suggestions, which I found to be excellent. In fact the script had to be modified to fit the scale of the two stars we managed to get. Originally there was only one important scene between Clayton and Logan, but with actors like Brando and Nicholson we needed further confrontation between the two characters.

We wanted to establish a situation built on historical fact involving the kind of men typical of the period of the West's conquest, those men of considerable power, first economic, then political. This is clearly apparent in the books on the history of Montana that McGuane gave me to read. There was at first a small "territory" that a small number of men who had become powerful wanted to turn into a State of the Union by creating laws to serve themselves. This passage from a lawless society into one in which the powerful gather to say "We're going to create laws that will protect the lawmakers" is an interesting moment in history. At one point, McGuane and I thought about ending the film with Braxton elected governor of Montana.[1]

C: *With* The Chase *and* Little Big Man *you expressed your frustration in working with a large Hollywood crew on a big production. The technicians might be highly qualified but they screened your decisions based on their own interpretations. It seemed that you always had to fight to get what you wanted. Did you have a similar experience on* The Missouri Breaks?

P: *The Missouri Breaks* wasn't really a big production. The budget was high only because of Brando and Nicholson, and with less prestigious stars it would have been a rather modest film. Actually as far as the crew was concerned, it was perhaps the most enjoyable experience I ever had. All the technicians were young, talented and enthusiastic. I had a particularly fruitful and friendly relationship with Michael Butler, the cinematographer, whose photography for *Harry and Tonto* I had liked and who had also filmed Tom McGuane's *92 in the Shade*. Tom introduced him to me, and we got along well from the start.

C: *Chronologically* The Left Handed Gun *is your first film but one wonders whether* The Miracle Worker *might be a more important work to the extent that you worked on it as a television drama before* The Left Handed Gun. *It is striking*

---

1. Montana obtained the status of "territory" in 1884 and became a state in 1889. *The Missouri Breaks* is set in the early 1880s.

that Helen Keller is literally what your other protagonists are metaphorically: blind, stumbling, inarticulate, almost animal-like, in search of her own identity without knowing it. And Annie Sullivan represents an extreme, even insurmountable, development of the pedagogical function, that of master and guide, also seen in such characters as Tunstall in The Left Handed Gun. *It is also the one film of yours that contains the most extreme physical violence, even if it isn't as bloody or murderous as your other films.*

P: It's true. All those elements come through in *The Miracle Worker*. Still, I consider *The Left Handed Gun* to be my first film, and not only chronologically. When I directed the film version of *The Miracle Worker*, I felt more confident with myself than when I directed *The Left Handed Gun*, in part because of my lengthy experience with the stage version. The TV drama was done before *The Left Handed Gun*, but it was only a sketch, something quite simple and schematic. The film is much closer to the stage play than to the TV version. I really see it foremost as a filmed stage play. The dining room scene when Annie forces Helen to use a spoon had the same violence on stage and was just as lengthy. I believe it lasted nine or ten minutes.

C: *In the film the scene is astonishingly fluid, filmed in long takes, often with a hand-held camera. Yet you have said that the film was not cinematic enough and that you would like to redo it. How would you go about doing this?*

P: I would change the part of the father. I think he talks too much and represents a contrived threat, a gratuitous element of antagonism. Once I understood that the camera—and here I mean a film camera, not a television camera—could shoot a face, in this case Patty Duke's, and make concrete all the characters' difficulties, I should have realized that this physical presence was enough to express the huge task facing Annie. We could do without the theatrical character with his wordy speeches that try to verbalize his ideas. I regret not having more judgment and self-confidence at the time.

C: *We are struck by the contrast between the staginess of the dialogue scenes between the parents or Annie and the parents, and the extraordinary physical power of the clashes between Patty Duke and Anne Bancroft. One gets the sense that dialogue should have been entirely dropped, making an almost silent film, concentrating on the Helen-Annie relationship.*

P: Absolutely, and I regret not having had the courage to do it. As it is, the film is a hybrid compromise.

C: *Was it done live on television?*

P: Yes, like all TV dramas prior to the introduction of the Kinescope. Actually, when you ask which came first, *The Left Handed Gun* or *The Miracle*

Worker, I would be tempted to answer that what came first were some hundred and fifty live TV dramas. It was an extraordinary period in the history of American television during which I learned a lot about performing, directing actors and technique, and the possibilities of the camera as well as its limitations on TV. When I started making movies, I was fascinated by the expressive resources of the camera which were incomparably broader than on TV, where you always had to take into account the limitations of the equipment, like filming while being careful to avoid the other cameras in the frame and so on.

C: *Some names recur regularly in your filmography, particularly in the early years: Fred Coe, Leslie Stevens, William Gibson.*
P: Fred is an old friend, we served together during the war. After the war I came back to the United States, studied for a while, then went to Italy where I studied literature at the University of Florence. Upon my return to the States I worked in television, at NBC as set manager on comedy shows, for example *Martin and Lewis*. One day Fred called and asked me if I would direct dramas for a series he was producing. This is how our friendship was renewed.

C: Portrait of a Murderer *is one of your most well-known episodes.*
P: By Leslie Stevens, yes. Leslie was a playwright I knew who had written a play called *The Lovers*. This was long before *Portrait of a Murderer*. During the out of town tryouts of the play he had a fight with his director, who was I believe Michael Gordon, and he asked me to take over. The play failed, but Leslie and I became good friends. A few years later when I went to California to work for TV, I was asked to recommend possible screenwriters, and I suggested Stevens.

C: *Was the narration of* Portrait of a Murderer *done by the killer on whose case the script was based?*
P: The man who brought us the subject for the show had been a cellmate of the actual murderer and had taped his confessions. He made the tapes available to us, but I don't remember exactly if we used them directly or if we had the transcript read by an actor. But it's true that the murderer's words were used for the commentary.

C: *How did you come to direct* The Left Handed Gun?
P: Originally it was a television drama directed by Robert Mulligan and produced by Fred Coe. Warner Bros. asked Fred to produce a movie version, and he approached Delbert Mann to direct but Mann wasn't available so he asked me. I accepted provided we hired Leslie Stevens as a writer, and this

was how the three of us found ourselves on the credits. Leslie and I worked for four or five months on the script before shooting.

C: *You had a modest budget and the shooting schedule was tight, yet the direction is very elaborate, particularly with the actors.*
P: All the actors including Newman took pride in the film. They regarded it as an invaluable experience and insisted on rehearsing for a long time without pay before we began filming. The rehearsals took place at my home or theirs. We had to hide since it was against union rules.

C: *It's difficult for me to ask you specific questions about the film because I haven't seen it in a while, but I'd like you to talk a bit about the famous shot of the foggy windowpane where Newman makes a cross with his fist, and then the switch from the street to another scene inside, in the same shot.*
P: I remember this shot very well because it was my first experience of a purely cinematic and creative act, the pleasure of achieving a visual and temporal stylistic effect through the camera. I had a very conceptual idea of the effect—to suggest the passing of time spatially, through a movement—and when I explained it to the technical crew, at first they didn't understand me, saying it couldn't be done. Then I realized I had to describe my idea in very concrete terms, and everything became simple.

C: *After The* Miracle Worker *there was the unfortunate experience of* The Train. *What was it that first attracted you to the project, particularly considering that you have often said you couldn't make a film in a foreign country where you weren't familiar with the language and customs.*
P: I would make an exception for France, at least occupied France, because I spent some time there toward the end of the war while in the army and stayed there for a while after the end of the war before returning to the United States. I didn't view *The Train* as an action film, nor even a film with a message. To my mind it was a study of the economic status of a work of art in a troubled period and more generally of war profiteers. The negotiations surrounding the paintings should have been developed much further, and I was planning a lot of work on the screenplay, but as you know Burt Lancaster had me replaced by John Frankenheimer after a few days of shooting.

C: *Did he explain his reasons? Did you discuss the matter?*
P: No, he didn't talk to me about it at all. He called United Artists, and they let me know I was off the film. I think Lancaster felt too uncomfortable about the whole situation to discuss it with me. Clearly we didn't have the same film in mind. Actors who were my friends and who had accepted parts in the film in order to work with me—Jeanne Moreau and Paul Scofield—

found themselves engaged in a project that was quite different from the one I initially spoke to them about.

C: *What do you think of Frankenheimer's film?*
P: I don't like it much. It's not bad, it's a decent adventure movie, but not much remains of what had originally attracted me to the project.

C: *You then directed, one after another, two very different films.* Mickey One *is a low budget film made with complete freedom, while* The Chase *had a big budget which didn't allow you too much freedom. How did the first of the two come about?*
P: After the success of *The Miracle Worker*, which got two acting Oscars, Columbia offered me the chance to direct two films with a budget of one million dollars each. I agreed to receive a very modest salary in exchange for complete freedom in the choice of the subjects, screenplay, casting, production, and editing. I wasn't even required to submit a screenplay. The first of the two films was *Mickey One* and the second one never happened since Columbia neither understood nor liked the first one. The critical failure of *Mickey One* affected me a lot. For the first time I'd tried to break traditional narrative structures while telling a story I thought was worthwhile. I'm far from satisfied with the end product, but I don't think it's a bad film. Some critics thought I was trying to make a European-style film in America, but actually I consider it to be a profoundly American film.

C: *Robin Wood wrote that the film's fundamental mistake was to start from an abstract idea and to try to conform reality around it, whereas the natural movement of your films is to go to the contrary from the concrete to the conceptual.*
P: That's correct. I think I'd come up with a much better film if I could remake it today. I was still quite inexperienced at the time of *Mickey One*. I'd really only directed one film, *The Left Handed Gun*, as I don't really consider *The Miracle Worker* a real cinematic experience. So *Mickey One* was my second film, so to speak, and it's often with their second film that directors stumble. I thought I could work with abstraction, not realizing that my forte was the concrete, the real.

C: *Where did the screenplay come from?*
P: From an unproduced play by Alan Surgal called *Comic*. The manuscript seemed to have more possibilities on screen than on stage, so I asked Surgal to turn it into a screenplay. We did make a lot of changes to the play which took place entirely, or almost entirely, in the main character's room. We used exteriors in Chicago not only because we wanted to open the play out. It helped make the whole thing more cinematic. I felt that the character's problems,

his paranoia and fears, would look more real once he confronts the outside world.

C: *You have made contradictory statements about* The Chase *in the past. At times you have completely disowned it. How do you feel about it today?*
P: I can't disown it entirely. After all, I did shoot everything you see in the film. But I wanted to give it a very different look, rhythm, and style. The actors had improvised many of the scenes, and the way the film was edited rarely corresponded with what I had in mind. Certain things were put in that I would have thrown out and certain things were thrown out that I would have kept. I should have supervised the editing as I'd done with all my other films, something Spiegel actually promised me I could do. But I naively took his word for it and didn't insist he put this in writing. When shooting was over, Spiegel took the film to London to edit it. I had to stay in New York where I was committed to direct the play *Wait until Dark.*

C: *What attracted you to the project?*
P: A number of things. First, the opportunity to work with Lillian Hellman, for whom I have great admiration. We'd had an excellent relationship when I had directed her play *Toys in the Attic.* Equally, the opportunity to work with Brando and some of the best American movie actors around. It truly was an extraordinary cast. At the beginning I had a lot of respect for Spiegel because of his reputation, but I had a rude awakening. It was my first clash with traditional Hollywood methods, and the only time I've worked with an old-fashioned producer who considered himself the author of the film. He treated me like a drudge. Maybe it was naïve and stupid of me, but lots of things happened during production that I never expected. For example, I wasn't aware that Spiegel had hired another writer, Ivan Moffat, to work on the script. When I found out about it, I immediately told Lillian. She resented me because she imagined I was in cahoots with Spiegel. Shooting hadn't yet started, and I should have dropped out at that point. My big mistake was to accept the compromise.

C: *Lillian Hellman has said that you and Spiegel rewrote some scenes without consulting her.*
P: I didn't write a single word of the script. I only suggested a few locations. I know Hellman has always believed in a conspiracy between Spiegel and me against her, but I swear I didn't even know Moffat before Spiegel introduced us. By then he'd already been working on the script for weeks. I don't think Hellman ever really finished the first draft anyway, it was incomplete. During filming I started getting scenes from all these different writers:

Hellman, Moffat, Horton Foote—the author of the play and novel the movie is based on—and even Spiegel himself. You could say that I took part in the writing of the script to the extent that I had to connect all these sometimes contradictory scenes. It was a new and very disturbing kind of experience to come to the set every morning and be handed scenes I wasn't familiar with. Brando told me some time ago, "This is the image I have of you during the shooting of *The Chase.*" (*Penn mimics Brando, mimicking Penn, arms dangling, shrugging his shoulders with a distressed look of helpless disbelief*).

C: *Yet Robin Wood regards the film as your first "unquestionable masterpiece."*
P: I'd say it's a "questionable" masterpiece.

C: The Chase *is your first color film. At the time did you have specific ideas about the use of color?*
P: Again, things didn't happen the way I would have liked. I had hired Bob Surtees as the cinematographer because I admired his work. Ten days before shooting started he came to me and said, "I can't explain to you why but I can't do the film." I never found out his reasons. I heard he didn't want to work with Brando again, but he knew Brando was cast when he first accepted to work on the film a few weeks earlier. And speaking of Brando, I want to say, in parenthesis, that having worked with him on two films I can say that he's an actor who demonstrates exceptional professionalism, punctuality, and team spirit. So anyway, we had to find another cameraman very quickly. They sent me Joseph LaShelle who turned out to be hopelessly slow. We had a lot of night scenes to shoot. We'd arrive at sunset, and it would be one in the morning before he'd lit the first shot. Obviously by the time we finally started shooting, everyone was exhausted. I should have been more authoritative with him, but I was quite intimidated. I felt like a beginner, and I remember thinking, "These people know what they're doing." It taught me a lesson. I realized it's the director who has to know what he's doing and what he wants. Later, with *Bonnie and Clyde*, I was determined to impose my views on the cinematographer. I had long preliminary discussions with Burnett Guffey. We didn't agree on everything and fought several times.

C: *You have said that you had a very precise idea of* Bonnie and Clyde*'s visual style before shooting began. Was it the result of those conversations with Guffey or a sort of intuition?*
P: It was more the result of conversations with Newman and Benton, but I also remembered Bonnie and Clyde themselves in the newspapers when I was a kid. I think from the beginning I had a mental picture of the texture the film needed.

C: *It is evident today that the film was a turning point in the evolution of American cinema. Among other things it challenged the notion of genres.*

P: Mixing the genres was an essential aspect of the screenplay. It surprised and confused a lot of people. They didn't know how to deal with the abrupt breaks in mood. Of course today it all seems almost banal. More generally the film played a lot on reversals of values. Stylistically I feel it harked back to a very old-fashioned way of filmmaking, that of the silent era.

C: *The photography and the color palette have this sort of polished, almost overly pretty edge to them. It tends to keep the characters, their environment, and the entire time period at something of a distance from the audience. Some critics felt it was an attempt to idealize the era.*

P: This was all precisely because we weren't out to make a historical reconstitution of the thirties. We wanted to make a film that would conjure up the spirit and atmosphere of those times through the modern sensibility of the sixties. Ingmar Bergman said the film should have been done in black and white, but we wanted color because we didn't want it to look like a documentary. The distancing effect was very deliberate.

C: *Even the violence in the film is embellished through slow motion, for example. The result is a certain ambiguity, which is perhaps inherent in any representation of violence: it is at the same time an object of moral condemnation and aesthetic pleasure.*

P: Yet the film was criticized when it first came out because its violence was too "realistic." But violence is treated in two different ways in the film. I wanted to move from a very brutal and I think quite accurate approach in the beginning—for example the bank clerk Clyde shoots point blank in the face—to a lyrical and poetic violence in the final scene which indicates the birth of the myth.

C: *I was also thinking about something that goes beyond the frame of violence proper that is often found in your films, the pleasure of disorder, destruction, and messiness, a pleasure found by the characters or yourself and which you want to communicate to the audience. There are so many examples: ripped up bags of flour in* The Left Handed Gun, *the food that Helen spits in Annie's face in* The Miracle Worker, *horrible bloody wounds with Hackman in* Bonnie and Clyde *and Brando in* The Missouri Breaks. *Also the self-destructing sculpture, the cars being compressed in* Mickey One *and the chaos at the draft board in* Alice's Restaurant, *the burnt-out houses.*

P: I've always disliked the pristine look of traditional cinema, the cleanliness of violent deaths or the tidiness of the sets characters live in. When I started making films, I wanted to react against this and bring some disorder into real life. In *The Miracle Worker* the child's monstrous, animal nature is an extreme case, since we're dealing here with a pathological situation. But it's an aspect of human nature that exists in all of us, and I feel it's legitimate to represent it aesthetically. That's why a certain form of childishness is an essential trait of most of my characters.

C: *This is particularly obvious in the muddle-headed, adolescent behavior of the gangs in* The Left Handed Gun, Bonnie and Clyde, *and* The Missouri Breaks.
P: That's the influence of my New York childhood. I grew up in neighborhoods where there always were gangs of youths, steered by their repressed or rechanneled sexuality that expressed itself both in unconscious quasi-homosexual relationships and in outbursts of playful violence. Every time I have a gang in one of my films they tend to show up like this.

C: *The gangs re-create rituals, a kind of family unit. There is a nostalgia for family in all of your films. But parents, when you show them, are always disappointing, useless, or even harmful to the protagonists.*
P: That's exactly what my own experience of life taught me.

C: *Which brings us quite naturally to* Alice's Restaurant, *in which the gang becomes a kind of parallel society. It is an ambiguous film to the extent that you stress both the positive values and the limits of that—if I can use an old-fashioned word— "hippie" infrastructure. There is a feeling of perpetual disenchantment, where all the characters' efforts to build a new lifestyle through play, ritual, celebration fail rather miserably.*
P: There was something noble and admirable in the attitude of those kids who rejected war, the army, and society. But at the same time their revolt was bound to fail because in their semi-communal life they were trying to re-create the family they had rejected in the first place. They were looking for mentors, parents, and their choice of Alice and Ray for the part could only lead to dissatisfaction, since Alice and Ray were themselves too immature to satisfy it. The film deals with those contradictions and the disappointments they create.

C: *The characters in Arlo Guthrie's song were inspired by actual people living in Stockbridge, where you spent your summers.*
P: Yes, people I saw every day. I knew Alice and the police chief well. I'd never met Arlo but did know several of his friends. One of them came over to our place once and played Arlo's album for us. A few days later I heard the record again at another friend's place and suddenly got the idea that it could be turned into a film. I started discussing it with my wife, and later I asked

Venable Herndon—a playwright who had never written for the movies but whom I knew—to come spend some time in Stockbridge to help me develop my idea for a screenplay. We wrote the film together.

C: *Even more than* Bonnie and Clyde, Alice's Restaurant *breaks away from the notion of genre and traditional structures. It's a very deconstructed film.*
P: Yes. I feel this was in the spirit of the time. The best films between 1965 and 1970 were in that spirit. Maybe that's why the film didn't really find its niche or audience and wasn't a box-office success. It did fairly well in the United States but had no audience in Europe. It's never even been sold to television here.

C: Little Big Man *is perhaps the closest film equivalent to a picaresque novel, something often attempted but rarely successful in cinema. Do you think you succeeded?*
P: I believe I did. It was certainly a dangerous endeavor because the lack of dramatic unity makes the picaresque form terribly difficult. I think that *Little Big Man* comes closer to a genuinely picaresque movie than any film I know. It would have been much easier to boil down the material to a simple story about Indians, but Thomas Berger's novel was too valuable to be treated that way, and anyway, it was an interesting challenge.

C: *In a* New York Times *interview during the production of* Little Big Man *you stated that film narrative should deal with "the repetitive characteristics of patterns of living, of the cyclical problems of a changing nature that people are confronted with." Could you clarify this statement in relation to the film?*
P: I was thinking about the film's form itself, about this reaction against the sacrosanct "beginning-middle-end" linear construction which every idiot in Hollywood repeatedly says we can't live without. Actions and behaviors tend to repeat themselves although in different forms. We keep doing the same things to the extent that in real life there is never a feeling of a beginning, a middle, and an end, something that belongs to the conventions of a certain type of narrative. It seems to me that the picaresque novel feeds on a non-linear, cyclical motion that plays with mutations that are related thematically rather than dramatically. The result is that seemingly unrelated events take on meaning. That's why the film is organized in a deliberately disorganized way with constant shuttling back and forth, multiple levels, movements from comedy to tragedy, from satire to drama. It's a film that should and could have been made six years earlier. The rights had been bought as early as 1964, but there were disagreements within MGM where some people wanted to do the film and others were against it. It took us nearly six years to get back the rights and set up a relatively independent production.

C: *It's hard to imagine the film as we know it being produced around 1964–1965. In its form and spirit it is much more characteristic of the mood of the late sixties.*

P: But we had the screenplay ready by 1967. *Little Big Man* had the misfortune of being released towards the end of 1970, a few months after films like *Soldier Blue* and *A Man Called Horse*, and even some of the best critics around—I'm thinking of Pauline Kael, for example—complained that it was just another film about Indians and massacres. But how can you make a film on the relationship between the two cultures without dealing with the massacres? They are, unfortunately, the essence of the relationship. I actually went out of my way to make the massacres look as bloodless as possible and keep things seemingly picaresque. The intention wasn't to shock the audience with a display of brutality, which we could have done quite easily. If you really wanted to make a documentary-style movie about the Indian massacres the result would be horrifying, probably unbearable. In doing research for the film I discovered incredible things. For example, according to one author, scalping the victims was not, as is always assumed, a traditional practice among Indian tribes. It may have originated as a form of retaliation against "civilized" soldiers who made belts for themselves with the dried-up vaginas of Indian women they had massacred or tortured. This kind of thing, assuming you could even show it, would obviously be out of place in a film like *Little Big Man*. The film is a kind of *Candide* where you had to preserve the lightness, the ironic distance of the picaresque style even when showing atrocities.

C: *We have discussed all your films except* Vision of Eight, *which I haven't seen. I think your sequence was about pole vaulting?*

P: Yes. It was one of the events that hadn't started when I arrived in Munich. But my initial project was more interesting. The idea was to follow a black boxer during the weeks before his being selected for the Olympic Games, showing his daily life, his family and circle of friends. It would have been a strictly sociological document with the Games themselves coming in only toward the very end. There would have been one closing shot showing either his winning or losing. Unfortunately at the last minute he lost a fight and wasn't selected, so I left for Munich without a subject. But all the material for the sequence was filmed. We went to Charleston, South Carolina, his hometown, where he was doing time in jail. We shot on location inside the jail and filmed his grandparents who had raised him. The very day we came back to New York I got a phone call telling me his grandfather had just died, and we immediately flew back to Charleston to film the funeral. It was a traditional black service with singing and an extraordinary atmosphere. Altogether we had about two hours of footage.

C: *Did you keep the material?*
P: It belongs to David Wolper, the producer, who'll probably never do anything with it. It's too bad because that shoot was a unique experience for me. We had the makings of a wonderful film.

C: *In your films the camera moves are much less numerous than in most contemporary American films. You seem to prefer short, static takes, with the emphasis on editing.*
P: I don't move the camera much, although there is always the temptation of setting up complex crane and dolly shots. But I feel it's important to resist things like this and do them only when something specific is needed. It's precisely because camera mobility is such a precious resource that it can have such extraordinary emotional impact. To take examples from one of my films, the final sequence in *The Miracle Worker* was filmed in a single dolly take. The camera follows Patty Duke all over the place as she runs from one object to another after discovering the relationship between words and the objects or elements they describe. And at the end of *Alice's Restaurant* I combined a long tracking shot moving out with a zoom in to create the impression that we are pulling away from Alice while she occupies the same screen size. In other words it's superimposing a subjective space on an objective space. I prefer to keep camera moves for this kind of effect rather than use them mechanically to follow movements or move from one location to another, which can always be done more economically through editing.

C: *Do you prepare your camera moves ahead of time? Are they indicated in the shooting script?*
P: Very seldomly. Before shooting starts I discuss the general visual style of the film with the cinematographer, but during production we start each day with a rehearsal of the scenes to be shot. I decide on framing and camera moves, if any, in relation to how the scene develops. Generally the same applies to the choice of lenses. I like to work in this semi-improvised fashion. After years of work in television where each frame, each camera move, each cut had to be preplanned, I felt I was freed from jail when I started making movies.

C: *Can you talk about your collaboration with Dede Allen?*
P: We have a very close collaboration. Hers is not the work of a mere editor, just like mine is not limited to shooting. We really make the film together by discussing it at length in pre-production and keep communicating

throughout the shoot. She comes on the set for at least a few days to get an idea of location, characters, and general atmosphere. On *Bonnie and Clyde* she spent two weekends working with the crew and a whole week on *Little Big Man*. Then she goes back to New York and starts putting the footage together. Once the shoot is over we sit together and talk nonstop. The first cut isn't a mere assembly, we try to give it some of the rhythm and style that will be found in the finished product. There's a lot of friendship and affection in our working relationship, even when we disagree. We're as close as two collaborators can be.

C: *Would you feel uncomfortable working with a different editor?*
P: Intensely. In fact I have a hard time imagining it. It would be almost impossible. I worked with other editors on my first three films, but Dede has edited everything since then, starting with *Bonnie and Clyde*. I just can't see myself working with anyone else.

C: *Do you think she has influenced your conception of film structure?*
P: Yes, to a certain extent. Most of all she has had a liberating influence. What's wonderful about Dede is that for her, everything is possible. There are no rules. She's the least dogmatic person I know. If I ask her, "Can we cut from this shot to that one?" she'll look surprised and say, "Of course, why not?" Whatever the technical or stylistic problems she never considers it hopeless. "I don't know how to handle it," she might say, "but let me think about it. Come back in three or four hours." When I come back, she has a solution.

C: *Do you shoot with a preconceived idea of the editing?*
P: Yes, I do this automatically. I couldn't do otherwise even if I wanted to. Again you see habits I developed during my television days. I always know more or less how my shots are going to cut.

C: *Yet people who have watched you filming say you shoot a lot of coverage, that you shoot the same scene from lots of different angles.*
P: It may look that way to an outsider because I do shoot a lot of film, but it's not because I'm undecided. I film with a certain style of editing in mind that demands a lot of material. Most of the takes that are technically usable actually end up in the completed film. Of course it's always good to protect yourself, but I don't systematically make multiple takes saying to myself, "I'll choose one in the editing room." I like to have a lot of material to deal with because with lots of shots it's possible to work on the film's rhythm, to change it, to speed it up.

C: *Do you ever shoot with several cameras?*

P: Rarely, and if I do it's always for a specific reason. For example the cavalry charge in the snow in *Little Big Man* had to be shot in one take, as doing the scene again would have been extremely costly, so I used four cameras in order to get enough varied angles.

C: *How do you decide what the color style will be?*

P: I'm just beginning to! I used to think that we were very limited in our choices of color. I wasn't satisfied with the color in *The Chase*, so I had an incentive to try to control it more in *Bonnie and Clyde*. But I'm not entirely pleased with the color in any of my films. I'd like to use very vivid colors in the future. For a number of years filtered, misty, and muted colors have been in fashion which makes you think it's the only acceptable style. I'd like to try De Kooning-style colors, the kind of bright colors Godard uses. And Agnès Varda uses color very convincingly. Her films are the ones that have most impressed me as far as color is concerned. I'd like to make a color film in the same spirit, using primary, blunt colors and using them organically, giving them a dramatic function.

C: *Could you talk in more detail about the Attica project you mentioned earlier? Who is your writer?*

P: Don Patterson, who wrote the prison play *Does a Tiger Wear a Necktie?* He worked in prisons himself for a while. Don is an excellent playwright, and we're happy with the screenplay so far, but it's only a first draft. There's a lot of work still to be done.

C: *What is your notion of the adaptation? How do you plan to handle the balance between documentary and fiction?*

P: I don't believe in documentary objectivity. I think we always have our own point of view and bring our own prejudices. In this case mine is that the massacre was a brutal, insane, inhuman tragedy that should never have happened, a political and human absurdity. That point of view will be put across so powerfully that a documentary would expose us to lawsuits, while with a fictionalized version it will be easier to convey what we have to say. We won't use the names of actual people, only their function, which is what matters.

C: *But you'll follow closely the course of events, or more exactly, Wicker's vision of them in his book?*

P: I intend to go beyond his vision, to broaden it by using other documents. Wicker's book is very personal, and I'd like to make it a little less subjective. One of the book's most interesting aspects is the way Attica has influenced and changed Wicker himself, but that's obviously not the subject of the film I want to make.

C: *If the film is made do you think that some political pressures, whether direct or indirect, will manifest themselves?*
P: Certainly. I would think, for example, that we'll have a hard time finding a prison to shoot in. There are a few abandoned prisons we might be able to use but getting permission to shoot will undoubtedly be difficult.

C: *You said you are going to collaborate with William Gibson again. Is it a screenplay or a stage project?*
P: It's a play about Golda Meir and Israel. Gibson has just completed it. Actually we had lunch together today to discuss it.

C: *Your relationship with the theater is an on/off one. You've just directed* Sly Fox, *your first Broadway production since* Wait until Dark *in 1966.*
P: From 1966 to 1970 I was busy making movies but I must say the difficulty of finding interesting plays had something to do with it. At the time Broadway was swamped with psychedelia, mixed media, and even pornography. It turned off the serious playwrights, although I didn't lose touch with the theater. I was still working at the Actors Studio and at Stockbridge in the summer.

C: *Can you give some details about the Stockbridge experience and its evolution?*
P: It was an exciting but unfortunately short-lived experience because of the lack of money. We wanted to form a semi-permanent company that would stage both repertory plays and original works by young playwrights. The first year we received $50,000 from United Artists plus grants from the federal government and various private foundations, but those sources quickly vanished or were considerably curtailed, and it was a long-range project that could only survive if it was financially supported over the long haul. Yet it was a labor of love for all the members. Just imagine: the first season we managed to bring together people like Dustin Hoffman, Anne Bancroft, Gene Hackman, and Estelle Parsons, who all worked for two hundred dollars a week.

C: *You made a comeback to Broadway with* Sly Fox, *an adaptation of Volpone.*
P: Yes, by Larry Gelbart who transposed the action to San Francisco at the end of the 1880s, after the Gold Rush. It's simple entertainment, but I love Gelbart's humor. I enjoyed directing a comedy for a change and working with George C. Scott who is a born comic even though he too has made very few comedies throughout his career.

C: *In an interview for the* New York Times *a few weeks ago you said something to the effect that film was the ideal medium for the sixties and theater for the seventies. Isn't this an oversimplification? Weren't you rationalizing and justifying your own evolution?*

P: It's possible, but I wasn't quoted quite accurately. I meant that in the sixties everything happened very physically. People acted, theater was in the streets, and film was the best way to document this activity. I think we've entered a more complex period where action and reflection are combined, and it seems to me this is an area where theater can prove to be resourceful. Actually I think that theater and film should be complementary. That's what we're going to do with Gibson's play. It will have filmed sections using three or four screens simultaneously. It's been tried before of course, but never quite satisfactorily, and I think we'll bring something new and worthwhile to this area.

Arthur Penn

RICHARD COMBS/1981

C: *Before we talk specifically about your background, there is one trivial question I would like to ask about* Mickey One. *I believe you did a number of television shows with Dean Martin and Jerry Lewis, and I have seen it suggested that Jerry Lewis has some connection with Warren Beatty's character in* Mickey One. *Is that true?*

P: It never occurred to me until this minute. It's quite possible that it did. Jerry Lewis made a strong impression on me and a lot of other people, particularly in his earlier days as an irreverent raucous comedian. He was absolutely remarkable.

C: *But there was no drawing on his character for any of this?*

P: No. We came across a little article in some newspaper about having found a body in the trunk of an automobile in Chicago. The man had had some peripheral contact with show business, and I think that's what started us on it.

C: *You've also said that when you worked on television in the early fifties, because there wasn't much money around, you felt free. Just how free were you on things like the* Colgate Comedy Hour *and the* Philco Playhouse *series?*

P: *Colgate* was a great variety show, there were no boundaries. It was a Sunday evening program that went into all these homes but was designed to be simply an amusing variety show. On the *Philco Playhouse*, an hour drama show, we did some drama which was—for its time—quite extraordinary, and a number of those pieces went on to become films, like *Marty*. A number of them also became theater pieces. We had a remarkable group of writers during that period.

Unpublished seminar from the National Film Theatre, British Film Institute (30 August 1981). Printed by permission of Richard Combs.

C: *Were they contracted to do particular series or were they individually hired?*

P: They each were contracted. It was actually a very civilized arrangement. A remarkable man named Fred Coe, who died just recently, was the producer. He spoke to the writers at the beginning of the year and said, "How many would you like to do this year? Would you like to do three, four, five?" One of the nicest things about it was that whenever the authors said, "I'll do six or seven," if indeed they managed to do only four or five there was no recall on the money. It was all contracted and they knew what their life was going to be like.

C: *Fred Coe was instrumental in different points in your life, including taking you into film. You met him in the army?*

P: I was stationed in the South, and he was running a small theater in Columbia, South Carolina. It was the nearest thing to an oasis of civilization that existed in Columbia at that point. I met him there and then went off to the war and came back, and by then Fred was a very conspicuous television producer. We had a great reunion, and he gave me the opportunity to start directing. I didn't direct on the *Colgate Comedy Hour* with Martin and Lewis, I was the assistant director.

C: *Is there anything in your background that prepared you for a theatrical career? I believe at one time you were studying to be a watchmaker, like your father.*

P: It was one of those happy events as far as I'm concerned. I was in high school and was pressed into service by the drama teacher who also happened to be my French teacher. I ended up participating backstage mostly in scenery building, that kind of thing, and eventually discovered that I really rather liked the life. Then it was interrupted when I went into the army in Europe for three and half years, and when the war in Europe ended, they somehow saw from our military service records that some of us had been interested in the theater so we ended up in something called the Soldier Show in Paris. From there I decided it was a pretty good way to make a living. It beat watchmaking, at which I was totally inept.

C: *You brother is Irving Penn, the photographer. Do you see any visual connection between his work and yours?*

P: I suppose there must be, though I've never been able to detect it. The odds were against it that both the children in this family—and we didn't even really grow up together—would end up in visual media. It's quite extraordinary, I think.

C: *You didn't discuss it together?*

P: No, never. Not at any point. There was mutual support but that's all. We're very close.

C: *You also did a lot of work in the theater and still maintain links with the Actors Studio in New York. When you went into film did you find that theater was more of an influence on your work than television?*
P: No, I would think television was more instrumental than my work in theater. I'd always been disposed toward working in the theater but was much less intimidated going into film than I think I might have been had I not had that period in television where the choice of camera angles and how to work with actors on camera had been available to me. If I'd gone directly to film from theater, I think I would have been petrified. Fortunately I went the other way.

C: *There is a style of acting in your early films like* The Left Handed Gun *that seems to come out of the Actors Studio, rather than television.*
P: Yes, it does. It was a very happy time and perhaps resembled London more than it does the United States today in that we had this television program on Sunday nights and were able to use the actors who were performing in the legitimate theater. That's something like what I hear the life is like over here for actors. Now that this no longer exists in New York, there is hardly any television emanating from that city. It all comes out of Hollywood in some form or another. Those very good actors have either moved to Hollywood and have, I'm afraid, perhaps become less good actors, or have stayed in New York and don't appear on television.

C: *What was the impetus to do* The Left Handed Gun *on television rather than as a play?*
P: When Gore Vidal wrote it, originally for Philco, it was designed for the cameras. I didn't do it originally, Bob Mulligan directed it. Fred Coe had the opportunity to make a film and asked me to join him. I thought it would be fun, although it ended up not being much fun because I'd never really had any idea about major film studios. Warner Bros. was still headed by one of the Warners. Jack was still very much in evidence there, and life was quite different. There were a number of notable directors making films on the lot at that time, but we were a tiny film by comparison and enjoyed a degree of freedom that wasn't characteristic of the period. But once I finished shooting the film, I was disinvited from being present at any part of the editing, which astonished me. It was something I hadn't even foreseen, that anyone would even have to contemplate such a thing. But it was very much in the old studio

manner. Directors directed, editors edited, and they did not necessarily communicate with each other. This man showed up on set very near the end of shooting and said, "Good day. My name is Folmar Blangsted, I'm the most artistic editor in Hollywood."

C: *Was that very different from your experiences in television?*
P: With live television we were our own editors. We were choosing the cameras live on the air. It was a simultaneous experience. We were working with the actors, and in the control room where we sat with a variety of images coming up from the camera it was clear that we had to be in a kind of empathic relationship with the actors. We'd know when the moment would come to go for the close-up. It was a deeply symbiotic relationship that we enjoyed with the actors. It's very different from what I suspect an editor who had never been around a group of actors would ever experience.

C: *What was the producer's role in television?*
P: It was merely propriety and hand-holding and trying to prevent us from having heart attacks, which we were prone to do. It was rather like flying test planes. You'd go on the air at eight o'clock and bang! Across the country! The state of the art was not highly refined, and it wasn't uncommon to have laid out this entire show with three or four cameras and suddenly two of them would be out, and you would try to make do with two cameras talking your way through the show. The neighborhood bar enjoyed terrific business at a minute past nine o'clock.

C: *You have frequently returned to the theater, but the plays you have been involved with have not been as controversial as your films. Do you perhaps return to the theater to refresh or reaffirm your autonomy as an artist? The films seem to be more of their time than the plays have been. Is there a difference between the two forms?*
P: Yes, a distinct difference. The opportunity to be more individual and controversial exists in film. It doesn't exist on Broadway very much. Broadway is very much a rather machine-produced center for the well-to-do middle class. That really seems to be the major audience, those people who can afford to pay what is now forty dollars for a ticket. I suppose you have something like that here. It's not quite up to that figure, but it's coming fast. By definition this pre-censors your audience, although there is something very pleasurable for me in working with actors who are there and live and not only an image a year later when we're editing the film.

C: *In terms of subject matter, do you feel yourself to be less experimental with your theater work?*

P: Much, yes. The American theater is very conservative, though Off-Broadway is different.

C: *In* Mickey One, *your third film, you seem to be trying to get away from theater and television, and also from American cinema as it was at the time. Did you consciously adopt a European style?*
P: What happened was that after making *The Left Handed Gun*, having that experience with that editor, I decided film was a silly medium and went to work in the theater. Then *The Left Handed Gun* appeared in Europe, and I began to receive critical reviews that were astonishing in their perspicacity, despite the mangling that I felt had taken place in the editing of the film. European critics, particularly those in France and Belgium, responded so well to the film that I came over and met with them. I wanted to find out how they were able to see film in their particular way. It was so different from the way the New York critics had seen it and had dismissed the film with the back of their hands. So I met these people who at that time happened to be named Truffaut and Godard and André Bazin. What I got was, I'm afraid, a bit of an overdose of rapture with the European film. Then I came back and made *Mickey One* which has an excessive degree of obscurity about it.

C: *You even used European technicians.*
P: Yes, Ghislain Cloquet was the cameraman. When I look at it now after all these years I'm astonished at how derivative it is of European films. The symbolism almost makes me queasy.

C: *Your next film,* The Chase, *was your most Hollywood-ish film. Was that partly a reaction against* Mickey One?
P: No, it was not intended to be a reaction against anything. I thought I was going to have the opportunity to work on something quite wonderful. It was a chance to work on a Lillian Hellman script, and with Marlon Brando. We had the good luck to choose a lot of very good actors who were fairly new in those days. Jane Fonda, Robert Redford, and Robert Duvall are all in that film. We brought quite a few of them out from New York and for some it was only their first or second film. I thought it was going to be a terrific experience, but it turned out to be a nightmare because I had never worked in the Hollywood system. As I said, with *The Left Handed Gun* we were this tiny little film off in the corner here and nobody bothered us. We made *The Miracle Worker* in New York and had already done the play so they assumed we knew what we were doing and they left us very much alone.

When I came to deal with *The Chase*, I ran into something that was new to me: a Hollywood producer. That's really quite something to encounter, in this case a gentleman called Sam Spiegel. It was a rather shattering encounter. Script rewrites were being done in closets and in other places by other writers. Spiegel made off with the film at the end of the shooting and brought it here, to London, to be edited, which was not at all our agreement. So I was back in a situation that resembled the first picture, except that in this case I had invested a high degree of emotional and—I hope—artistic impetus, and to be somehow deprived of it was quite extraordinary.

C: *Had you been involved in the setting up of the film?*
P: No, it was brought to me by Spiegel. The screenplay was by Lillian Hellman whose last really good play, *Toys in the Attic*, I had just done on Broadway. We had a very nice working relationship which became one of the other victims of this terrible experience of *The Chase*. Our friendship stretched quite thin from that moment on.

C: *Ivan Moffat received a co-screenplay credit on the film.*
P: That was one of the other scripts being written in Scandinavia where Ivan Moffat was making a film. I never met him until months later. Such were the ways of Hollywood, enough to send me away from the place. Although I've described the Broadway theater as being less then adventuresome, it nonetheless had a degree of integrity. One knew with whom one was working, at least. You could encounter the playwright and deal with the actors, so I simply left the idea of making films behind until Warren Beatty acquired the rights to *Bonnie and Clyde*. He came East and bludgeoned me into making that film. I hadn't really wanted to make another one.

C: *You actually functioned as a producer on* Mickey One *but you haven't really tried to consolidate yourself as a producer/director since then.*
P: I did on *Four Friends*.

C: *Was there any point between those films where you felt you could have made your footing somewhat firmer in Hollywood?*
P: No. What happened was that *Bonnie and Clyde* was such a success that I was able to have final cut in my contract, which meant nobody could touch the film after I had finished with it. That meant having virtually all the assets of the producer without having to do the business part of it, for which I have no skill at all.

C: *What you seem to have done most often since* Mickey One *is to take on genre subjects and turn them on their heads.*
P: That's a perception I seem to have only after I've made the film. When I'm making a film, I'm not particularly aware that I'm sort of reordering the

genre. I seem to be just doing the film that I see in the material, and then I read these scholarly articles which tell me what I've done, which I recognize after the fact. You'd think after I don't know how many films I've done by now I would be able to predict this before the fact but it completely eludes me. I look at a script and say, "I know how to do that" and know damned well it's going to end up being written about in the same way later on, but I'm not aware of the process while it's taking place.

C: *Do you think there is an unconscious element in you that has made you seek out situations where you will have to struggle against something?*
P: There's probably something in my nature to be something of an outsider and struggle against the establishment, whatever form it takes. I know that for me the characters in my films tend to be heroes. For instance, in *The Left Handed Gun* I took Billy and turned him from an urban hoodlum into something quite different. I was quite aware we were altering the nature of myth there, but I figured that myth is anybody's fair game. You can do whatever you want with myth. I don't have a lot of faith in history. Something I've quoted before—and I think Napoleon is the source for this—is "History is the lie we choose to believe." I tend to feel this way most particularly about mythic and historical characters.

C: *There is no historical or legendary character in* Night Moves, *rather sometime who fits very well in a particular mold, the private eye story. Yet at some stage you begin to turn him around. I read you changed the character in the original script so you could somehow be more critical of the kinds of things that Harry Moseby represented.*
P: Alan Sharp and I did go to work on the script because it wasn't finished. So many detective films end up with the detective as an anonymous figure who somehow, through his perspicacity and wisdom and misanthropy, solves the case, but you never really know anything about that detective except that he talks like Humphrey Bogart. This struck us as one of the things that seem to be not appropriate to a modern detective story, that one of the things we should have in a modern detective story is that the detective's own story becomes intimately involved with the basic plot.

C: *In a way you're saying that this drive to solve the crime, the need to know something, is corrosive. There sometimes need not be solutions to these riddles he goes after. It is actually Harry's drive as a detective that is the most destructive thing in the film.*
P: I guess I'm a creature of my times. When I started making films, we were just coming out of the McCarthy era. It was a very bad period. I'm not sure

we're not going back into it at the moment, at least I hope not. The kind of burning existential questions seemed to be about knowing yourself, knowing what your motives are, trying to work out—as Mickey One asks—"Who owns me? In whose thrall am I? What have I done that has put me in a state of obligation that confines my freedom of choice?" That seems to be the basic theme, one that comes up again with Harry Moseby, who seems to think he knows. What happens is that he goes to pick up his wife who has gone to see *My Night at Maud's*, supposedly with a companion, and as she comes out of the theater he discovers she is with another man and suddenly discovers his marriage and everything else is in a very different state.

C: Mickey One *and* Night Moves *seem to mark out two areas of pessimism in your work. There is a slight charge of optimism with* Alice's Restaurant, *but the heroes of both films are in flight. In* Mickey One *it is outward, with Harry Moseby it is inward. They both refuse to confront their problems.*
P: In *Mickey One* the flight is resolved more positively. At the end he comes to have possession of his life, but Moseby doesn't and ends up flying around in a circle like a wounded bird.

C: *To go back to the European influence on* Mickey One, *does it have anything to do with the fact that Benton and Newman brought* Bonnie and Clyde *to you after having first taken it to Truffaut and Godard. Did they see you as being the most European of American directors?*
P: That's not exactly accurate. It was brought to me first, before Truffaut and Godard, but I couldn't do it. Then it went to Godard who said he would shoot it in two and half weeks. That, I think, chilled Benton and Newman's blood, so they took it to Truffaut. They worked on it for a long time, and then Truffaut decided at some point that he couldn't handle the American aspect of it. To this day he's never quite managed to learn English, even though he now pretty much lives in America. I saw him a couple of months ago at a party, and he speaks about as much English as he spoke back in 1957, which was none. So then Warren acquired the script and that's how it circled around.

C: *You once described* The Left Handed Gun *as Oepidus in the West. Would you say that in a loose and picaresque way* Little Big Man *is the same? Jack Crabb goes through as many father figures and family relationships as Billy the Kid does. More, in fact. The film is structured around a whole series of finding fathers and families and losing them.*
P: It's a perfect example of never recognizing what comes out of one's own life. I became enraptured by Tom Berger's novel but didn't recognize this recurrent theme in it, though it's obviously something out of my own child-

hood. My parents were divorced when I was very young, and I lived with a number of families and a great number of people in a great variety of cultures, and to my amazement that shows up here. But I promise you at the time while I was making it I didn't perceive it at all.

C: *In* Mickey One *there is a destruction of his old identity and search for a new one.*
P: Yes, I'm afraid it's true. It shows up in all the damned films. I wish it would go away.

C: *You have made three Westerns which might seem something odd for a director based in the East and associated so closely with the theater. But there is a way in which the heroes of all your Westerns seem less like true Westerners than like displaced urban juveniles, for example Jack Nicholson's gang in* The Missouri Breaks.
P: Again, one reads out of history what one chooses to read. I read in a number of books that the West was not this great, clearly defined place where there were all white hats and black hats and that's how you knew who was good and who was bad. It was made up of people who had been driven out of the cities. They were immigrants coming from all over the world. That great artistic editor of *The Left Handed Gun* took out what was for me one of the most pleasurable scenes. Billy passes a man who is driving a wagon, a peddler. They say almost nothing to each other, but the peddler is wearing a Western hat and a long coat and looks like a full figure of the West. At the end of that exchange Billy tips his hat, and the peddler tips his hat, and he's wearing a yarmulke. Well, that was unheard of in those days, that we would have any kind of ethnic groups of any kind in the West. Not in the West! The West was made up of people immediately sired by John Ford, you know? Ford and Hawks and Walsh all did spectacular Westerns, but they were all of that Western bent. They were working with their clean, pristine images of good and bad with a very clear line of morality. I brought to it the street urchin mentality that I'd grown up with. As I say, I read in history books that many of these gangs were made up of guys who could barely ride horses, which is what you see in *The Missouri Breaks*. Nicholson gets together a gang of people who were smuggling horses, some of whom couldn't ride them let alone be able to draw a six-gun and shoot from them.

C: *The other fascinating thing about* The Left Handed Gun *is the metaphorical thing about "through a glass darkly" which is the way Billy sees the world. Was that in the original teleplay?*
P: No, it was just one of my favorite passages from the Bible and I wanted to use it. I've found that tends to be true of my kind of visual style. I tend,

to some degree, to impede the image. It's something fundamental to acting, it grows out of what we use at the Actors Studio as our method. We are interested not only in what the character wants but also ask what is the obstacle to achieving that? When I moved over to film, I felt there was a visual correlation to this one, something that shows up in one form or another in almost every film.

C: *Does this relate to what you said earlier, how you yourself like to feel resistance when dealing with a subject?*
P: Yes. Unless I have to fight my way through something, I tend not to be attracted to it.

C: *Religion crops up quite a lot in your films, as a repressive force but also more positively in the sense of community, for example in* Alice's Restaurant *where the commune is set up in a church. I wonder how ambivalent your feelings are about religion.*
P: Well, they're pretty ambivalent. There is a part of religion to which I am very deeply attracted but not the sense of believing in a direct line to the Deity. I do have a strong sense of communal engagement and contact, something that has been a very pleasurable part of my life. I went to a peculiar college—Black Mountain College in North Carolina—where we grew our own food and shared everything. It was a place made up of quite a remarkable community of people, less than a hundred of them, faculty and students. Buckminster Fuller, John Cage, Merce Cunningham, and Willem De Kooning were all there at very much the same time. It was a pretty extraordinary community that the fates tossed up at that moment.

C: *Another parallel between two of your Westerns is when Dustin Hoffman goes to kill Custer in his tent but is put off when he discovers Custer naked. The vulnerability of the man means he cannot go through with it. There is something similar in* The Missouri Breaks *when Nicholson goes gunning for Marlon Brando and finds him in his bath.*
P: One element to this, in both cases, is so we can have some more movie. If Jack Crabb plunges a knife into Custer's back, we'd have the end of the movie after an hour and ten minutes. We had the same trouble with Brando and Nicholson. Brando is there as a man called a "regulator" who wipes people out from a great distance. We had to get them together in the same place. But if we did this, Jack would be able to take Brando out unless he were so disarmed, so we put him in a bubble bath. It's a rather strange sequence.

C: *The defenselessness of each victim puts the other off.*
P: Yes. We had Hoffman meet Custer under other circumstances but never

as nakedly as that, and it seemed to me a good character definition for Jack Crabb. But equally it drove Nicholson crazy when he had to play this scene alongside the bath tub where Brando is blowing soap bubbles and playing around with him.

C: *Is it one of the scenes you worked on during shooting?*

P: Some of it is in Tom McGuane's script, though it wasn't originally set in a bathtub. The idea of Marlon sitting there like a great Buddha attracted all of us to the idea that it would make a good film scene. McGuane's script existed in a fairly rudimentary form. It was sent to each of us individually, and we all said no. Then Elliot Kastner, the entrepreneur, got Nicholson and said, "If I can get Penn and Brando, will you do it?" Then he got me and Nicholson and went to Brando and said, "If Penn and Nicholson do it, will you?" And bang! Pretty soon we had a picture. But the picture was based on a script all three of us had rejected. We got to Montana six weeks after we'd completed the deal. More time was spent writing contracts than was spent writing the script. Marlon said, "Listen fellows, I hate to bring this up, but there is no Robert E. Lee Clayton character in this picture. There just isn't anyone here. He's a regulator who shoots people from a great distance, but we never see him encounter anybody. What is he supposed to be when we meet him?" I didn't have a good answer. Marlon said, "What if he's an Indian?" I said, "I don't think that's so good." So we began to play around with the idea of somebody who was different every time you met him. That's how we started out with Brando playing different characters inside of the role he plays in the film. Finally, with his audacity, once he was triggered to this, when it came to the scene where he kills Harry Dean Stanton he said, "How about I play it as a woman?" He couldn't wait to get into this great calico dress and hat and came down and played it as old granny. It was a delightful night, I must say. Many of us spent hours just rolling with laughter because Marlon was absolutely wild that night.

C: *The film was criticized as being a typical Hollywood package and for Brando being allowed to do his own thing. But in some sense the performances are quite structured.*

P: The film certainly has severe limitations, but I'll be damned if it's just a Hollywood film. It's not that at all. It was made by three people who were really working very seriously, at the top of our form. We were trying, desperately, to take what was really a vestigial script and turn it into a movie under the enormous pressures of having to start and stop at a certain date. Those obligations are ones we took on consciously and professionally. Admittedly any one of us might have said no to the given circumstances, but once we accepted them, I worked as hard as I've ever worked on a film and so did Marlon and Jack. We didn't stint on digging up some of the personal stuff. There was a lot of invention that went on. When Marlon and I made that choice about his character, I had to be able to provide him with stuff to work with. He said, "How about I show up in the first scene with a toothache?" I said, "Fine. Terrific." Now, what are we going to do with a guy with a toothache? It's not terribly interesting. He'd just walk around with his hand up to his mouth. But it happens to be at a point where somebody is laid out in a casket. The foreman of this farm has just been killed off, so I loaded up the casket with ice and put this body in it. When Marlon walked on set, his eyes went right to the ice and I could see where it was going. That was the kind of invention we were feeding each other back and forth but wouldn't tell each other about. It was about trying to keep that thing alive on the set. I leave it to the rest of the world as to whether or not the outcome was any good, but the work was hard, creative, and very nourishing. We had a terrific time making the film, even though we were like three drowning men. How were we going to keep our heads above water and get a movie made?

C: *Is* The Missouri Breaks *in any way a negative version of certain characters in* The Left Handed Gun? *There is a sense in* The Missouri Breaks *of the West being divided up and ruled by corporate interests.*

P: The abiding idea in the original script, one we used throughout the film, was that this was the period when they were carving up Montana with as few owners as possible. They succeeded in doing so. There were enormous ranches owned by people who didn't hesitate to bring in armed gunmen to enforce their law. These were laws unto themselves. This man Clayton is based on a man named Tom Horn who was indeed a regulator. McGuane wrote another script about Horn, and Steve McQueen played him in a film.

C: *Do you allow the actors to improvise on the set?*

P: I'm not wildly taken with the idea of improvisation. I think that what a group of actors can make up on the spur of the moment is not going to measure up to what the author can do with a few months of contemplation. The scene in *The Missouri Breaks* with Marlon with the horse and mule is entirely improvised. We realized he was about to get his throat cut, and we hadn't seen him for five minutes in the movie so Marlon got the animals some carrots and food. He said, "I'll figure something out." He started and we just kept the cameras going. We went all day, just rolling cameras. The horse urinated, and he said, "Ah, that's lovely my darling." He had this love affair with the horse and absolutely rejected the mule. He built this entire scenario himself inside of that one scene. But this is one of the few occasions where I've ever done something like that.

C: *Do you rehearse with the actors?*
P: Ordinarily I like to rehearse, but one of the curses of working with big stars is that you can't rehearse. You can't get them even one week before the start of photography. They'll give you a couple of hours of costume fitting, that's all. I'm not really talking here about the stars as such but about them as the center of an enterprise. They have attorneys and agents and body-guards and people who keep them from you. They are like some kind of creatures in an ant colony that are there only to be unique and treated in that way. It's rare to get a bunch of actors together if the picture includes movie stars. They just aren't available. I do like to rehearse on the day of shooting with the actors. After I see what they do I tend to lay out the camera shots, except in a very clear case like the shooting in *Bonnie and Clyde*. I planned that weeks and weeks before we shot it, but usually I try not to do this. I like to be at least as improvisatory in my work as I want the actors to be, despite the fact that I suggest they basically stick to the text. I like them to get to the text through a process of improvisation, and I think I should have at least some of the same pressures put on me.

Arthur Penn

JACQUES FIESCHI/1982

F: *There are often lengthy gaps between your films. Is this a conscious decision on your part?*

P: No. I spent two years working on a film about the Attica prison riots but the producers got cold feet, and the project fell apart. I also spent a long time preparing *Altered States* with Paddy Chayevsky until the very last minute. I've known Paddy forever, we knew each other during the war in France at Châtou but had some disagreements over the project, and I withdrew *in extremis*. When Ken Russell came on board Paddy also pulled out.

F: *The original title of* Georgia *is* Four Friends, *although the film is actually centered around a single character.*

P: The story was originally as much about the three other characters as it was about Danilo, but then the screenwriter Steve Tesich decided to dig into his own memories. His father left Yugoslavia before he was born, and Steve met him for the first time at the train station in Gary, Indiana. Bit by bit Danilo became the central character, though Georgia also plays an important part. At the start she is the ideal image of these three youngsters, and we made sure she was in every episode, including Danilo's failed wedding.

F: *What idea of America do you think* Four Friends *conveys?*

P: All things considered it's an optimistic one. When Danilo arrives, he truly believes in the American dream but then becomes aware of all the ferocity surrounding him. He becomes a blue-collar worker like his father, climbing the ladder step by step. By the end of the film he's able to make some fundamental choices.

From *Cinématograph* (February 1982). Translated by Paul Cronin and Remi Guillochon.

F: *How did you work with Steve Tesich?*
P: We wrote together for three months, and Tesich was always around during filming. We would discuss things and look at the rushes together and do rewrites in the middle of the night. Sometimes the actors would get confused and recite their original lines.

F: *Have you worked like this on other films?*
P: Not really, no. A little bit on *The Left Handed Gun* and *Bonnie and Clyde*, but only on specific lines. With *The Missouri Breaks* it was different because we didn't have a script, only two big stars.

F: *You have worked with as many nonprofessional actors as you have with stars. Does your directing change with each actor?*
P: The approach is the same, it's about spontaneity and confidence. Naturally stars are more difficult to handle because they have precise ideas about how they want to look. When I directed Paul Newman at the start of his career, I didn't have any problems, and Brando couldn't care less about his image. He'd say, "I'm obese, so make me look obese" and Nicholson would say something like, "My teeth are too white. I look like I'm in a toothpaste commercial. We have to blacken them up." Noon and night we would paint his teeth. Warren Beatty is also very conscious about his appearance. One day I asked him, "Why the hell are you always looking at yourself in the mirror?" I found his reply a little odd: "Because I'm worried I won't see anyone there."

F: *When it comes to stars, how do you deal with conflict? In 1963 you were fired from* The Train *by producer-star Burt Lancaster.*
P: Yes, and I've often asked myself why. Lancaster and I originally didn't have any problems with each other. The first day of shooting, here in Paris, seemed to go just fine. That evening the scriptwriter told me I was fired. Lancaster had never said a word, there was no disagreement between us. And it was me who'd brought the story to Lancaster in the first place! Frankenheimer took over immediately. I've always wondered how he got there so quickly.

I was always on very good terms with Warren Beatty who produced *Bonnie and Clyde*. "We can discuss things at length if you want," I said, "but my decision is final and will always carry the day. I'm the director." Warren always wanted to talk things through and wield ultimate control over the film. Sometimes I just had to shout, "Enough! We're doing it my way!" Having said that, it's important to argue about certain things. Sometimes you lose sight of what you're thinking, and objectivity goes out the window. We're like excited children in a nursery. Sometimes toes get stepped on, but you have to get beyond all that. At the end of the day I adore actors. I find them courageous, even heroic, for facing the camera.

F: *What is your relationship with actors like once filming is over?*
P: During filming I have no time for anything but work. We start at seven in the morning, finish at six in the evening, and watch rushes until nine o'clock. The actors don't work every day which means they have a little time for socializing, but I live like a monk. After filming I run into actors here and there. I've seen Warren, Nicholson, and Dunaway, but I've lost track of Brando at the moment. I think he's in Tahiti.

F: *Do you still feel close to the Actors Studio?*
P: Yes. I started work there in 1953 with Strasberg and Kazan and still go regularly. It's a family affair for me. Kazan has seen *Four Friends* and is very enthusiastic about it. We live close to each other, and I see him a lot in New York. He lives a block away. It's unfortunate that he no longer makes films. I know he wants to write. His books are OK but not as good as his films.

F: *When you direct actors do you give psychological direction?*
P: No. I have a precise plan in mind but keep it a secret; otherwise there wouldn't be any creativity on the part of the actor. I wait until they suggest things, and we test them out together. Brando would show up every day with something new. He would change his accent or just mumble. In *The Missouri Breaks* he got the idea that he would be completely different each time we saw him, with radically different accents in each scene. His character became absolutely crazy. The whole crew doubled over with laughter, and when the cameraman couldn't keep up with what he was doing, he'd just say, "Don't worry, we'll just do it over."

F: *In a film like* Four Friends *how many takes do you need in order to capture the hysteria we see in the actors?*
P: Not many, maybe six or seven. I'm not fond of rehearsals. I don't want to start shooting when an actor is too relaxed, so I'll say, "Action!" before he's ready, which makes the technicians nervous. The hysteria you see in the film emerged mainly during editing.

F: *Did the rushes sometimes surprise you?*
P: Not often, but when the shot isn't quite what you expect, it's time to get rid of the camera operator, and quickly. You have to be careful when it comes to the internal energy of the image. One wrong move can be fatal.

F: *Where are you during filming?*

P: Sometimes next to the cameraman, sometimes underneath the camera. Warren would always tell me, "Stay there. I feel better if I can see you."

F: Four Friends *was cameraman Ghislain Cloquet's last film.*

P: Yes, I'm very sad he's gone. We worked together on *Mickey One* and were good friends. He was such a hard worker, arriving very early on set, working on the lighting, climbing ladders, changing everything. It angered the technicians in America because, as you know, everything is regulated by the unions and you can't violate the boundaries of all these different groups. A technician could get penalized if he drove a car. This is one reason why *Four Friends* was so expensive. The truck and limousine drivers cost us a million dollars alone. It was a tenth of the entire budget.

F: *Do you miss black and white?*

P: Yes I do, and might use it again with the right film. *Raging Bull* worked well in black and white.

F: *Do you ever make structural changes during editing?*

P: I find editing the most interesting part of filmmaking, more so than the actual filming, which to me is like fighting the Second World War. I'm very close to my editor, Dede Allen, and just jump into the scene and explore it to the maximum through a magnifying glass. In *Bonnie and Clyde* Warren made some gesture of dissatisfaction at the end of one of his lines. We decided to keep it because of the strange effect it created.

F: *You often return to theater.*

P: Yes, directing for theater is completely different from working in film but paradoxically the two are quite complementary. On set you shoot two minutes a day, and in the theater you play out the whole story in one evening. Sometimes this overall view is more interesting, working with the actors from the origins of a story through to the very end.

F: *And what about television?*

P: I'm very suspicious of it. American television is so dreary. The three main networks are all exactly the same, but there is some hope because pretty soon there will be sixty channels, some without commercials. If this happens I'd love to get back into live television, like the way it was in the fifties, and direct a play or a Faulkner short story.

F: *What did you make of Hollywood in the fifties?*

P: Jack Warner was head of the studio at the time and the hierarchical system was dominant. When I made *The Left Handed Gun* William Wellman, Fred Zinnemann, and Raoul Walsh were all shooting nearby. We had a tiny crew, and I met with Jack Warner only twice during filming. When we asked to see the rushes, they said, "Not possible. Mr. Warner is looking at them." We'd await his verdict, usually something like "Too many close-ups" or "Too many long shots." With *The Chase* I had a lot of things to consider. It was a huge Sam Spiegel production starring Brando, Redford, and Jane Fonda. The pressure was unbearable as all the studio executives were on the lookout for something. Today the whole studio system is in ruins. The Fox lot has just been sold in a real estate business deal. They're making more money through distribution than production. People are leaving and crews are constantly changing.

F: *Did you like living in Hollywood?*
P: No, and I only lived there while making those two films. There was a time when Lumet and I were the only ones living in New York. Today there are lots of directors living and working there.

F: *What do you think of American cinema today?*
P: We're being besieged by huge budgets. I never thought of George Lucas as being a director. He's interested only in producing and money. I like Coppola and Scorsese, especially *Mean Streets*. Altman can sometimes really impress me, though other times he drives me crazy. He needs to work on the form of his films. His last three films seemed to float in time and space, but when he's working with interesting subject matter, like *Nashville*, he's great. I loved *The Deer Hunter*, especially the first part. I only saw the cut version of *Heaven's Gate*. The characters aren't at all well defined, but there are some wonderful moments in it. I'd like to see more European films in the United States, but these days it's rare they get distribution. From my point of view the last decade was a disaster. America is caught in its own growing isolation.

Interview with Arthur Penn

MICHEL CIMENT/1982

Q: *It's been five years since* The Missouri Breaks. *Why such a gap?*

A: Despite appearances I wasn't sitting around doing nothing. I was working on lots of things. I was supposed to do *Altered States* based on Paddy Chayefsky's novel, which we spent months working on together. Paddy and I have been good friends ever since we were drafted into the army together. I told him I wasn't interested in special effects and wanted to concentrate on the human dimension of the story. We had some disagreements about this, and I pulled out two and a half weeks before shooting was due to start. I told Paddy there were just too many risks. The producers then contacted Ken Russell, after which Chayefsky tried to take his name off the film.

I was also going to make a film about Cambodia and went to the Far East to do research, but we just didn't have enough money. It's about a group of journalists from all over the world gathered in the French Embassy in Phnom Penh and shows how each of them filters the information they send back home through their prejudices and allegiances. It starts with the involvement of the U.S. army in Cambodia and ends with the fall of Phnom Penh, the finale being the journalists escaping to Thailand. The script was by Larry Gelbart who wrote the play *Sly Fox*, which I directed on Broadway.

I was also going to make a film about Attica. The story was fascinating, but no one was prepared to hand over thirteen million dollars to make it. It was an ambitious project. If we could have pared it down, we might have been able find the money, but I just couldn't imagine doing it any other way.

From *Positif* (March 1982). Reprinted by permission of *Positif*. Translated by Paul Cronin and Remi Guillochon.

I'm also still considering a story close to my heart called *Appalachia* which has parallels to the oil crisis in the Middle East today. Coal is found in a very poor region, corporations move in and pay a small fortune for the land, and the people living there in sheer destitution suddenly become very rich. This new-found fortune throws their lives into upheaval. It's meant to be a comedy about capitalism. A young playwright from the South called James Lineberger is writing it for me.

Q: *And you have also been working in the theater?*
A: Yes. You see, I was far from idle! As I mentioned, I directed *Sly Fox* and also *Golda*, a play about Golda Meir with Anne Bancroft, as well as Strindberg's *The Wild Duck* at the Brooklyn Academy.

Q: *How did you manage to get a studio to finance* Four Friends? *It's hardly a mainstream film and is full of unknown actors.*
A: It wasn't easy, especially because it wasn't cheap. The producers liked Steve Tesich's original script, and once the project was accepted we worked on it together. At the start the basic idea was the life of four friends. Then we added the historical dimension and turned what was originally a sentimental and psychological story into something broader.

Q: *What do you like about Tesich's work?*
A: He's a great writer with an open mind. He'll try his hand at something even if he doesn't really feel it's right. In a narrative film like *Four Friends* that covers such a long period of time, the problem is how to allow characters to live out their emotions while making it absolutely clear to the audience exactly what year it is. This is sometimes done in the most banal way with lovers in bed with one telling the other "The Algerian war has ended" or "Bobby Kennedy was killed last night." But that wasn't the kind of film we wanted to make. I thought of having voiceovers to comment on the action without being part of the main thrust of the film, but Tesich was against this. He thought I wanted a proper narrator, though I was really only talking about voices throwing in casual remarks, as if we're almost overhearing what they are saying. Eventually Tesich, not entirely convinced, started to work on it and came back with excellent ideas like the lady next door who speaks about the three boys, then about Danilo going off to college at the beginning of the year. Through these hints we managed to move through history without the main characters telling us directly what year it is. Once Tesich started going in that direction, nothing could stop him and he was delighted with the result. He worked with me nonstop, even during the shooting, except for short periods when he had to go to New York for performances of one of his plays.

Q: *There is always a problem with re-creations in films set in the recent past. The distant past is often easier to represent on screen because it is so different.*

A: As far as the language, Tesich has a wonderful ear and a good recollection of how people talked when he was in high school. For wardrobe I had the assistance of Patricia Morris, who'd done wonders with *The Missouri Breaks*. Elisabeth Swados helped us with the music. It wasn't easy to bring together all these talented people who really understood a period which obviously wasn't my own.

Q: *Is the film based on Tesich's own background?*

A: He came to the United States from Yugoslavia around the time the film is set and lived in a small town in Indiana where he attended the local school. Then he went to Roosevelt High School where he became part of a group of friends. The links between reality and fiction are both concrete and general. Of course the details of the film aren't exactly his own story, for example his parents didn't go back to Yugoslavia. I myself went to the Midwest for three months to soak up the atmosphere before shooting began. I was raising my two children at the time and know that beyond superficial differences, American high school students are very similar.

Q: Four Friends *reminds us of Kazan's* America, America *and especially of* Splendor in the Grass *which is set during the Depression, an era not entirely dissimilar to the sixties.*

A: Tesich and I often referred to *Splendor in the Grass*, and when it came to an historical representation of immigration, we looked at Kazan's *America, America*. But beyond these references I had my own close connection with the sixties. I was living in New York and Stockbridge, and was involved in that era of upheaval and protests against the Vietnam War. It was interesting to tell the story of these people in the Midwest who weren't really affected by what was happening at the time. For them the era was about this delicate transition from adolescence to adulthood, something that's rarely been dealt with on film. The girl never knows what the boy wants and vice versa. The comic and real-life aspect of the story touched me. I've often admired what happened during the sixties, even though for many it was a cause of much anxiety. I never thought any of it would actually lead to a revolution, but it was exhilarating to witness the moral distress of a generation who so vigorously refused to go to war. Unfortunately the country went back to sleep afterwards. Making films in the seventies was difficult because all the action was happening in Washington, where Nixon was directing a better film than any of us possibly could have. I think these kinds of things will happen again in this country and that the young people will play an important part in it all.

Q: *The working class is rarely portrayed in American cinema, which is strange because it makes up a substantial element of American society.*

A: This is mainly because so many films are shot in Hollywood, where the working class doesn't exist and where there are mainly white-collar workers. Tesich and I are both from the working class, and we wanted to explore this. My father was a watchmaker, and my parents divorced when I was a child. I lived with my mother in New York during the Depression, and we were extremely poor. It was only during the war, when I was in the army, that I managed to escape this environment.

Q: *What is Indiana's working class like?*

A: A lot of them work in the steel mills. They work hard, drink hard, and don't have it easy. Nowadays most of them are Latinos. At the time when the film is set they were mainly from the Balkans and Central Europe. There's an actual Serbian festival in Libertyville which we filmed. They've since turned it into a Steve Tesich celebration day. The cemetery where people say their farewells to Vera is where Tesich's father is buried. What we also liked about the story is that generally people think of immigrants as something from the past, even though America is full of people who have just arrived. Tesich is a good example of this. He loves America.

Q: *Doesn't living out the American dream cause problems for immigrants at a time when the American dream is so shattered?*

A: Danilo is out of touch with reality. He thinks he can live out the myth of social mobility and self-improvement through his marriage to this rich and elegant young girl, but it all leads to disaster. On the other hand his father teaches him about hard work and progress which can be attained step by step. This interesting confrontation of two points of view about the United States ultimately leads to a fragile peace between father and son.

Q: *The sequence in New York has a dreamlike quality about it.*

A: This is mainly due to the shock Danilo receives when his inner world is destroyed. We also wanted Georgia to be caught up in the New York counter-culture of the era that eventually descended into madness where people were literally throwing themselves out of windows.

Q: *The film has a structure not unlike* Little Big Man.

A: I'm fond of films that extend over a period of time. I prefer them to sto-ries that are perhaps too condensed. When people ask me what influenced *Four Friends*, I always answer *Gunga Din*. In that film an entire culture is seen by an ordinary person who is also a part of that culture. Basically, *Little Big Man* is *Candide*.

Q: *As someone who comes from the theater this is all quite different from a play with individual acts and dramatic episodes.*
A: Plays need to be compact, although this can become boring after a while. I love theater and like to see a production unfold in rehearsal over a short period before seeing the actual performance. All this work is compressed in time and that's fine. But a film isn't a play with a beginning, middle, and an end. If I could choose the form to work with I'd go for *Little Big Man*, *Alice's Restaurant*, and *Four Friends*.

Q: *But at the same time intense and dramatic moments hold a special place in your films, like the wedding scene for example.*
A: This is perhaps because of my origins in the theater, but these moments really are necessary in film. In the case of *Four Friends* violence best expresses the era, a time when the Kennedy brothers were assassinated. When John Kennedy was killed, the Vietnam War hadn't yet torn the United States apart. You had this romantic figure, this intelligent man with his beautiful wife, this lover of the arts who emphasized the importance of culture. And then suddenly everything stopped. It's as if the country had suffered a heart attack. After that nothing would be the same again. My five-year-old son came home crying and said to me, "I don't want to become president because I don't want to killed." In one sentence he expressed the shattered hopes of many Americans.

Q: *In* Four Friends *you don't seem to judge the parents with as much severity. You show them with more understanding.*
A: I never wanted to depict generational conflicts in black and white, but I suppose I was quite let down by my own parents. Of course today it's different because it's my turn to be a father, which might explain why I'm more sympathetic. My father died a long time ago, and my mother died two years ago. When you lose your parents you begin to think of them with tenderness. I also think that the idealization of youth has gotten out of hand. This is what Georgia means when she says, "I'm tired of being young." The kids of the sixties are in their forties today but are still living in that era. They feel lost. It's like they're frozen in time. On the other hand—and this is also a problem—the youngsters from *Alice's Restaurant* who grew up in the climate of the counterculture, these people who turned their back on their bourgeois upbringing and chose to live in an idealized community, this abandoned church, have become landowners. Some have even made fortunes in the real estate business. They've become the older generation. It's just part of life.

Q: *The soundtrack to* Four Friends *is particularly interesting.*

A: I worked with a new mixer, a truly remarkable man, and I worked with Elizabeth Swados on the music, a wonderful composer who has worked in theater. She's constantly coming up with new ideas. I really miss not having Dede Allen, who has edited all my films since *Bonnie and Clyde*, but she was working on [Warren Beatty's] *Reds* at the time. Barry Malkin, who I got to replace her, has had the same training and comes from the same background. He was perfect for the job.

Q: *Since* Alice's Restaurant *your films have become more relaxed and serene. Are you aware of this change?*
A: You know, I'm a theater man. I'm always inclined to make each scene in my films as intense as possible. In a way I've never stopped learning and today have a lot more faith in cinema as a medium in its own right. This has come to me quite slowly, especially as I entered filmmaking relatively late. There's a certain ease about the earlier films of young film directors who were brought up around cinema that you don't find in the movies of Bergman, Kazan, or mine. We all have stage backgrounds.

Q: *You wanted all your actors to be unknowns in this film.*
A: We chose our actors from an audition where three hundred people showed up. The parts of Georgia and Louis were the most difficult ones to fill. Jodi Thelen had just arrived in Los Angeles from the Midwest. She worked in a theater where she also lived because she had no money. She was seventeen and a half. I made her audition along with five other actresses which shows how uncertain I was. I don't usually do castings. I spoke to the actors and talked about their roles but didn't ask them to act in front of me. I look for the atypical and quickly get an idea of whether a person is suitable for a role. I don't think that well-known actors would have been as convincing in this film. The only one who had some film experience was Craig Wasson. Michael Huddleston had a line in a Mel Brooks film. He is [actor] David Huddleston's son. Jim Metzler and Reed Birney are newcomers. They were available so we had two weeks of rehearsals before the shoot, something I'm not usually able to do because well-known actors cost a lot of money, and they're usually booked up. We didn't rehearse according to the script, otherwise it would have been too contrived. We improvised around the script and imagined what was going on in the story before or after the actual scene to be filmed.

Q: *Writer James Leo Herlihy plays the role of Mr. Carnahan. Did he already have some acting experience?*

A: We were students together after the war at Black Mountain College in North Carolina where the painter Willem de Kooning taught us. Leo Herlihy was taking drama classes that I was meant to be supervising, but we actually just read books. He went on to perform in Edward Albee's *The Zoo Story* in Paris after having written *All Fall Down* and *Midnight Cowboy*. He came to mind when I was looking for someone to play Carnahan.

Q: *The story moves along very quickly, for example suddenly seeing Tom married to a Vietnamese woman.*
A: Everyone expected him to die in Vietnam or at least come back wounded or paralyzed, but I thought it would be more interesting if he returned home married to a Vietnamese woman with children who are apparently not his own. This is the kind of story that could go on for three hours, but I like being able to make leaps in time. The action covers nearly two decades.

Q: *It was the last film that Ghislain Cloquet photographed before he died.*
A: We stayed friends after working together on *Mickey One* and were waiting for another opportunity to work together again, only this time in color. I sent the main special effects person and the head electrician to Paris to see what type of equipment Ghislain wanted. They weren't very keen on going as they didn't think they would learn anything from him, but they came back full of enthusiasm. When setting things up on set, Ghislain has a very fast and economical way of working. I think American cinema could do well with being a little impoverished, something the rest of the world has to deal with all the time. We're too lavish. Our film crews are too big and we spend too much money.
    Ghislain and I wanted the color to change as the story unfolded. The first part would be like those movies from the fifties with slightly diluted color. For the New York episode we decided to bring it up to the same intensity as the soundtrack, which was quite loud. Six weeks ago Ghislain came back to look at the film in the laboratory and checked the color. I'm happy he had this last opportunity to add the finishing touches to his work.

Q: *Your films always have a realistic approach, but at the same time each scene takes on a symbolical dimension.*
A: I believe there are times when you have to leave realism behind and let symbolism take over in order to express the spirit of a scene and the different levels of meaning that might otherwise be hidden. Realism is horizontal, symbolism is vertical. Take, for example, the murder during the wedding. There are many different levels, echoes, and changes in image, sound and

attitude. This is the kind of cinema I'm fanatical about. A film opens up completely when it explodes like this. This is what film is really about and what distinguishes it from theater.

Q: *Is it still the case that you shoot a lot of film?*
A: Nowadays much less, but these days some young directors shoot so much footage. Take Warren Beatty, for example. He shot millions of feet for *Reds*. Compared to these people I look positively thrifty!

Q: Bonnie and Clyde *and* The Miracle Worker *are full of static shots, but starting with* Alice's Restaurant *your camera seems to be more on the move.*
A: As I was telling you, I never stop learning. I'm more familiar with theater and live television than film. With televised plays you couldn't move your camera around because space was limited and the other cameras would be seen. We didn't have the means to do another take so the shots were rather static and you had to cut directly from one camera to the other. It was only toward the end of *The Miracle Worker* that I thought about shooting with a moving camera, even though I still wasn't terribly sure of myself. People discouraged me from doing it, but I was pleased with the end result. It's only after *Bonnie and Clyde* that I became more confident with the camera. We mustn't forget the money aspect too. Preparing shots with the dolly is time consuming in the United States, although with Ghislain Cloquet it was incredible. The speed at which he sets up shots! What got me down with the shooting of *The Chase* was the slowness of the crew. If I changed my mind and wanted to change the angle of the set-up by only a few centimeters it would take them at least two hours to sort things out. It becomes a question of money and energy. The actors simply can't be expected to keep up with this long process, and there's a kind of breakdown. Michael Butler, the young cameraman of *The Missouri Breaks*, had a small team of five or six people and with his help I could shoot any way I wanted.

Q: *You belong to the generation of filmmakers from the fifties who demanded greater artistic control over their work. But you differ from the younger directors who claim total responsibility in that you believe more in filmmaking as a collaborative venture.*
A: A completely independent author? I don't know any. Let me know if you do. Maybe Coppola comes closest, but I think he'd be the first to admit that filmmaking requires teamwork. I have quite an open mind when I work with set designers, cameramen, and sound engineers. Technology is progressing at such a pace that I can't keep up with it unless I devote every second to it. But my life is also about writing, working on the script, and discussing things

with the actors. As a matter of fact I'm always in contact with my scriptwriters. Tesich was even there during editing and we would compare ideas. On the whole I don't produce my own films, with the exceptions of *Mickey One* and this one. I wonder how objective you can be if you produce and direct a film. But in this instance no one knew the problems as well as Tesich and me. In all honesty, nobody could make the proper budget choices, and this is why I decided to produce the film alongside Gene Lasko. Otherwise I think the movie would have gone far over its budget of $10,700,000. Everything was shot on location in eighty days. It was relatively cheap compared to what other American films cost.

Q: *Do you prefer location to studio filming?*
A: Definitely, if by studio you mean Hollywood. I won't go back to Hollywood. Making *The Chase* there was a hellish experience! For *Four Friends* we built two or three sets, not at the studio but in a garage. We had to construct the dormitory where Georgia comes to see Louis because we couldn't rent the university for such a long period. In the original script Danilo's house is close to the steelworks and constantly lit by the blast furnaces, so we went to East Chicago in Indiana where we found out that steelworks no longer had houses close to them and that most of them had closed down due to the recession. After we had built the house, U.S. Steel closed its steelworks, and we had to light up the sky ourselves. We tried very hard to re-create reality but it was tough. We had to settle for a half realistic–half theatrical solution.

Q: *Do you see* Four Friends *as something of a follow-up to* Little Big Man, *after the interlude of* Night Moves *and* The Missouri Breaks?
A: Yes, I think *Four Friends* is in the same tradition as *Alice's Restaurant* and *Little Big Man*. The two movies I made after those are quite different from anything I did before and have done since. The seventies really shook me up. It began in 1972 when I was shooting a sequence about the Olympic games, and I witnessed the massacre of the Israeli athletes. I lost my bearing that decade, just as several interesting new directors were coming to the fore. I seemed to lose my grasp on reality. I could see people like Altman and Coppola doing so well, and it made me feel disoriented. I couldn't for the life of me remember what it was that attracted me to filmmaking in the first place, and that's why I made *Night Moves* and *The Missouri Breaks* so I could find my bearings by working on these more traditional stories. I trusted their classical structure which was familiar to me. I didn't really know how to go about tackling a new kind of structure. I consider *Four Friends* to be a new departure for me, the first since *Little Big Man*. It's a film about the continuity and discontinuity of time.

Q: *Was this uncertainty the reason for your inactivity at the beginning of the seventies?*
A: I had some projects I was working on, other than the one on the Olympic Games, but nothing came of them. I also made another decision: my son was a teenager, my daughter was growing up, and I wanted to spend more time with them. I decided to stay at home after having been on the move for so long. Besides, I didn't find an interesting enough film project to make me change my mind.

Q: *You have always kept one foot in the theater. What does working for the stage give you?*
A: First of all I enjoy working with actors. The theater is a place where interesting ideas can be developed, and each play I stage teaches me something. At the moment I'm directing *Monday after the Miracle* by William Gibson. It's about what happens to Annie Sullivan and Helen Keller, the original characters of Gibson's *The Miracle Worker*. A man enters their lives and in the end marries Annie Sullivan. It is a true story with Ellen Burstyn, John Hurt, and Karen Allen. Living actors, a new play, a new form, a short endeavor that will take up no more than two years of my life—this kind of project is always very rewarding. We'll prepare the play at the Actors Studio without a set or costumes, then rehearse on Broadway in January 1982 for the premiere in March.

Q: *Are you still involved with the Actors Studio?*
A: Yes, although Strasberg is in charge and runs it. But if he is away Kazan, Lee Grant, or I come in and teach. For me there is no real difference between acting for the stage or the screen. The same principles need to be considered, the same emotions. A good actor is a good actor whether he works on stage or screen. It's only a bit more challenging on stage because the acting requires more endurance and of course there's no second take. I'm impressed by people like Ellen Burstyn who can act with such intensity for two whole hours. Of course the focus is different as well. Thanks to the camera and close-ups there's no need to overstate what is being said when acting for the screen. I've always kept this in mind, except when we were shooting *The Miracle Worker* where I went overboard. The problem was that I'd already staged the play, and it ran for two years. I'd also made a televised version and had lost all objectivity. This is the reason why I'd never make another film based on a stage play.

Q: *Your movies are interwoven with the fabric of American society, its history and way of life. In* Four Friends *the characters are discovering a country and themselves.*

A: Yes, in the end they reunite. What I like about the United States is that young people don't think their lives have ended when they become adults. This isn't the case in every country. The possibility of change, the freedom of doing things, for me this is part of the democratic process. It's the final message to take from *Four Friends*.

The Path to Consciousness

ANDRÉ LEROUX / 1983

L: *Why did you decide to stage the play* Monday after the Miracle?

P: The quality of the writing and my longstanding friendship with William Gibson, though I should confess that when I started on the project I wasn't so passionate about it. The subject matter interested me, but I didn't care much for the producer. However Gibson gave me my first break when I directed his play *Two for the Seesaw* on Broadway, and I couldn't refuse when he asked me to direct *Monday after the Miracle.*

L: *Do you still feel close to the characters of* The Miracle Worker *after all these years?*

P: No. I don't think they've endured particularly well for either Gibson or me. About two years ago *The Miracle Worker* was produced for television after which Gibson was asked to write a sequel to his original play about these two characters, Annie Sullivan and Helen Keller. He began doing research and slowly this new play came together.

L: *How did you and Gibson originally work together on* The Miracle Worker?

P: He came up with the original idea, and I helped him develop it for television. We spent several days working to find an overall structure, which wasn't terribly difficult because we were able to draw on the remarkable letters of Annie Sullivan and reliable literary sources like Helen Keller's memoirs and a book about Annie.

L: *What interested you about the relationship between Annie and Helen?*

From *24 images* (June 1983). Translated by Paul Cronin and Remi Guillochon.

P: It was an extraordinary situation. The relationship between these two women represented the development of human intelligence, the progress from ignorance to knowledge. This gift of knowledge and its subsequent transmission are dramatic and moving.

L: *This passage from ignorance to knowledge, from shadow into light, can be seen in all your films. In* The Left Handed Gun, *for example, the main character of Billy the Kid is very much in the dark at the start but slowly and painfully comes of age as he is overcome by certain realizations that eventually lead to his self-destruction. Why are you so interested in such primitive characters who slowly become aware of their inner selves?*

P: It's difficult to say but probably because of my own life. I grew up amidst various families because my parents divorced when I was a child. Moving from one home to another meant I met people who helped me discover my true self and taught me the important things in life. I was really quite a rebellious and obstinate youngster, I always put up a fight. Over the years I met several extraordinary teachers who helped me discover that life could be something other than suffering, and thanks to them I was able to open my eyes and heart. I have tremendous respect for teachers. So one way or another you can probably find this theme in all my films.

L: *Even in* The Chase, *which is hardly your most personal film.*

P: In some way yes, but *The Chase* is unlike most of my other films. It's the only true Hollywood film I've made. The whole thing had been put in place before I even got involved. The script, which had been rewritten a number of times, had Lillian Hellman's name on it, and Marlon Brando was cast before they asked me to direct. Consequently I did no more than the unconscionable minimum as director of the film. The finished product was too polished for my taste.

The whole thing was shot on the studio lot, and for Columbia it was going to be their big film of the year. During the shoot tensions ran high. Studio people were everywhere, spying on what we were doing, and the production became an experience in itself, which it never should have been. It was totally disorientating for me. Up until that point I'd worked only on small films where I'd had complete control, but here I was thrown headfirst into a real circus. There were journalists running about asking for endless interviews, there were people just hanging around watching, and studio heads were there because they wanted to be in the middle of the action. It all made me crazy. The shooting of *The Chase* was certainly more of a cinematic event than the film itself.

L: *Which elements were out of your control?*

P: The script and the editing. Sam Spiegel, the producer, effectively edited the film himself. When I started on *The Chase*, I'd already signed a contract in New York to immediately direct a play once the shoot was over. Spiegel and I agreed that the film would be edited in New York, but once the filming was over he told me he wanted to edit in either Los Angeles or London. He completely ignored our initial agreement, and since I'd already signed the contract to direct *Wait until Dark* on Broadway, I had no choice. Spiegel edited the film in London while I was in New York, and once I'd finished work on the play I went over there—at my own expense—to see what was going on. He'd finished editing eight reels, and I was so disturbed by what I saw that I went straight back to New York.

L: *How would you have edited it differently, given the chance?*

P: The rhythm would have been different. I wanted to start telling the story very slowly, and then by the middle everything would be swirling around like a dizzying whirlwind with events crashing against one another. Unfortunately this isn't how Spiegel did it. The whole thing was too dizzying from beginning to end, and there was no real rhythmic progression of intensity. It became too frenetic too quickly. If the editing hadn't been so quick and had a different narrative energy, the film would have been saved.

L: *But wasn't the internal rhythm of the shots what you had in mind?*

P: Yes, but I would have used specific shots that didn't even make it into the film. Brando did some incredible things in some scenes, but those shots weren't used. Spiegel didn't always make the best decisions.

L: *This wasn't the first time you had no editorial control over a film. Did you edit* The Left Handed Gun?

P: No, I was hired to direct the film and didn't have final cut. I only saw the completed film in New York when it was commercially released.

L: *Were you surprised when you saw it?*

P: Literally stupefied. I just couldn't understand why they'd made certain choices over others. No one's ever explained to me why certain shots were chosen over much better ones. We shot a really beautiful sequence in which Billy the Kid is seen playfully teasing a salesman, but for some reason it didn't make it into the final version.

L: *How do you feel when you see the film today?*

P: I'm surprised at how good it is. While I was making it, I remember wondering if it was going to be worth watching. Everything was so carefully planned before we started shooting, but at the time I really didn't know anything about filmmaking. I was a theater man who'd never worked in an art form that doesn't demand continuity. I really didn't know what I was doing, so I invented a style that worked for the subject matter at hand. When I made *The Miracle Worker* I moved away from this to a more neutral way of working. There are certainly some sequences where the feel of *The Left Handed Gun* comes through, but too many sequences of *The Miracle Worker* are visually uninteresting. I suffer in silence when I look at those scenes in the film that don't seem to have anything like my imprint on them.

L: *Was there a great dissimilarity between your original intentions for* The Left Handed Gun *and the finished film?*
P: Not so much a great dissimilarity as a difference in taste when it came to specific shots. The studio kept in certain scenes that I would have cut. When I'm shooting, I often let a scene go on longer than normal so the actors can get used to the emotion and dramatic continuity. The rhythm I was looking for in *The Left Handed Gun* isn't there in the final version of the film thanks to the choices the studio heads made when they were editing.

L: *What was that rhythm?*
P: One that alternated between slowness and speediness. A fast scene would open onto a slower one. I used this in *Bonnie and Clyde*, but with *The Left Handed Gun* I wanted to surprise the audience. I didn't want them to be able to predict what was going to happen next, like the sequence where the young man in the wheelbarrow goes around the tree. This surprise effect works only if the rhythm of the preceding sequence is totally different. Unfortunately the difference in rhythm between scenes wasn't big enough to achieve this effect. This rhythmic monotony really is the biggest problem with the film.

L: *You are always trying to disconcert your audience through sudden changes in tone, genre, and rhythm.*
P: This is precisely how I feel cinema should function, and I'm only now beginning to realize how to achieve this. I'm still in the process of discovering the possibilities editing can offer. Changing rhythm instantaneously is one of those things you can do only when the rhythm itself becomes a way of telling the story, something that's inconceivable in theater.

L: *How do you maintain a balance between all these changes in rhythm?*
P: By making sure that during editing the story is connected by all the tonal changes.

L: *Are these changes worked out before filming begins?*

P: Yes. When working on a particular shot, I always consider the shot that will precede it in the finished film. In *Bonnie and Clyde*, for example, this prevented the film from becoming too tragic. The chase scene ends with various shots which lighten the story, and Charles Strouse's bouncy music also relieves the tension. By changing the tone and rhythm of the film I wanted it to begin as a comedy and then quickly change direction and become a tragedy.

L: *But weren't you afraid these rhythmic changes might turn the film into a big cartoon?*

P: I was aware of this problem and wanted to turn the whole thing into a ballad about these two legendary people who wanted to live intensely and have a good time, rather than a cartoon. The film needed to be bursting with life, and I think it succeeds in evoking this strong sense of vitality. Bonnie and Clyde are never aware of the moral implications of their actions until the moment when their lack of consciousness turns on them. The transition from the unconscious to the conscious was supposed to happen brutally through a violent rupture of tone and rhythm.

L: Bonnie and Clyde *gives the impression that the characters lived in the sixties. Of course we can't ignore the historical facts of the era, but it looks like your reconstruction of the thirties isn't absolutely accurate. The costumes, for example, wouldn't look out of place in the sixties.*

P: When we were working on the film, the studio asked if we wanted to shoot in black and white. The producer Warren Beatty, the screenwriters Robert Benton and David Newman, and I all discussed this possibility, but finally decided that color would be best. I felt color would give the film a contemporary feel. I also felt it was important that the film speaks more for the sixties than the thirties. The costumes we chose are a good example of this.

L: *I think that audiences instinctively understood this metaphoric aspect of the film. They sympathized with these two criminals who—just like the young people of the sixties—defied authority. Were you concerned that audiences identified with* Bonnie and Clyde?

P: Absolutely not. For me, Bonnie and Clyde weren't real killers. They were just children living in an era suffering from a severe socioeconomic crisis, one that fomented their frenzied urges and led to murder. I didn't want to make killing their main objective or even their primary mechanism for doing things. This is why Clyde is so angry with C. W. Moss after the first bank robbery. Out of sheer panic, rather than some kind of premeditated criminal act, Clyde shoots a bank employee hanging on to the car during their escape. Afterwards Bonnie, Clyde and C. W. hide out in a movie theater, and Clyde punches a seat because he's so angry at what's happened. He's furious at C. W. whose clumsiness and thoughtlessness led to the shooting. If only he'd parked the car closer to the entrance of the bank Clyde wouldn't have had to use his gun, and events would surely have unfolded very differently. It was important to convince the audience that Clyde became a killer unintentionally.

L: *Do you think the film would have been harsher and rougher in black and white? Color seems to give it a dreamlike quality and romantic softness.*
P: If we'd gone for black and white, it would have been a completely different film. Everything would've had to have been more historically accurate: the little details, the costumes, even the landscape. The film would have been more like a documentary and less romantic.

L: *Sex and love are brought together at the end of the film in an explosion of slow-motion violence. Their deaths have an incredible sensual and sexual energy to them as their bodies writhe about in a kind of orgasmic delirium. The lovers are united in death.*
P: It's at this moment when reality becomes legend, and Bonnie and Clyde are transformed into mythic heroes. On the brink of death they knowingly look at each other with loving tenderness. They know it's all over.

L: *Perhaps the transition from reality to legend happens earlier when the sheriff reads Bonnie's poem, which is then blown away in the wind after she and Clyde have made love in the field.*
P: Yes, this is where the legend takes hold in the story, but I wanted Bonnie and Clyde to become legends even beyond the reality of the film. Their deaths propel the legend beyond reality, and this is why I shot the scenes in slow motion. The rhythm of the death sequence was established by a combination of six different speeds of film. During editing we cut a piece of film shot at one speed with another piece shot at a different speed, for example from forty-eight frames per second to ninety-six frames per second. All these very short cuts created this effect of spasmodic violence and lent a romantic texture to their deaths. We spent three days filming the death scene. During the shoot in Texas people came from all over explaining that years ago their parents had met Bonnie and Clyde. One woman even brought a piece of cloth from a dress that allegedly belonged to Bonnie. She told me that her mother had even made the dress Bonnie wore at her wedding. That whole

part of the country is steeped in the legend of Clyde Barrow and Bonnie Parker. It's where Robert Benton and David Newman both grew up, and they knew everything there is to know about Bonnie and Clyde.

L: *Did Robert Towne help with the script?*
P: Not much. Warren Beatty and I are both friends with Towne, who was with us throughout most of the shoot, but he didn't really do much with Benton and Newman's script.

L: *You have made several films in color and others in black and white. What are the differences between the two?*
P: It's important to ensure that the color of a film doesn't bury it under a wave of prettiness and make it look too artificial. Color makes audiences feel detached, apathetic, and, in turn, uninvolved. Black and white is closer to reality, though I'm not exactly sure why. Maybe it's because of its chromatic characteristic, maybe it's just my personal view. For filmmakers of my generation black and white is connected to writing and printing, to newspapers and current events. It has a kind of aggressive quality and an almost documentary-like veracity. Color, on the other hand, inevitably softens reality by getting rid of brutality. It's really strange.

L: *So you use color not to establish greater realism but to create dramatic, symbolic, lyrical, and poetic effects?*
P: I'm always looking to integrate color into narrative strategies. It has to be part of the story. It's certainly as important as any other element of filmmaking.

L: *In* The Miracle Worker, *for example, the conflict between ignorance and knowledge is symbolically expressed by the use of black and white. Black is associated with ignorance, with inner darkness and prejudices, while white symbolizes the openness to life, access to knowledge, and the awakening of the senses.*
P: The film was conceived and made with these elements in mind. I wanted the flashbacks to stand out in the film, so we did all kinds of tests to find the right texture and gave them a grainy quality that suggests Annie's haunted past. They had to be engulfed in pain and suffering. They needed the same intensity as a terrible nightmare.

L: The Miracle Worker *moves progressively from shadow to light and strangely ends with the darkness of night. In the last sequence, where Annie rocks Helen on the steps, the two women are isolated in the darkness of a gentle summer night, while in the background, inside the house, a kerosene lamp can be seen burning. They are enveloped by the shadows but framed in a way that the light source subtly separates them from the darkness surrounding them. Through this image a superb feeling of peacefulness emerges, a sense of complete reconciliation with oneself and with the rest of the world. I find it's the most beautiful finale of any of your films.*

P: The last images of the film express tenderness and softness, in contrast with the explosive violence that emphasizes the different phases of evolution in Annie and Helen's relationship.

L: *Do you like* The Miracle Worker?

P: No, I don't think it's a very good film. We didn't take full advantage of the expressive means of cinema. The film moves me a great deal, but I felt limited by the stage play and regret having been too faithful to the dialogue. Instead of expressing things through the camera and editing, I let the words take precedence over the image, and the result was too theatrical. If I'd conceived the film in purely cinematic terms, it would have been much better. I would have cut a lot of the text and visualized Helen's difficulties instead of having her father explain things. There wouldn't have been any long sequences with characters talking endlessly.

L: *But you could hardly say the film is just a piece of on-screen theater.*

P: It's half and half. I wasn't thinking in purely cinematic terms. My way of thinking is rooted in the theater, and at the time I hadn't yet shed my theatrical conventions. It's fair to say that my love for film is filtered through my love for theater.

L: *It seems that the choice of angles and points of view, the use of light, of black and white, and the editing all intensify the text in a very cinematic way. The film highlights the theatricality of the story in order to transcend it.*

P: This is true, but there are still many sequences that really bother me, including almost all the scenes with Helen's father, which to me don't ring true. On stage we needed a character that could stop or provoke the dramatic action. Helen's problems needed their own voice, and it's thanks to the father's dialogue that the dramatic conflict is defined. We just needed a character to stimulate drama. When adapting the play to the screen, we should have gotten rid of the father's expository dialogue. A single shot of Helen would have explained to the audience how difficult it would be to penetrate the darkness inside her. After shooting and editing the film, I decided never again to film a play that I'd already directed in the theater, which is why I've no intention of filming *Monday after the Miracle.*

L: *Since you felt so strongly about Gibson's text, was there any improvisation in the film?*

P: It's my least improvised film. I like improvisation very much at all stages of the creative process, and of all my films *The Left Handed Gun* and *Bonnie and Clyde* have the most improvisation.

L: *How important is the script?*
P: During pre-production I work very hard on the script, but once shooting starts it's much less important. For me the script is simply a point of departure. By the time I begin filming I've already had my fights with the screenwriter. Every angle has been explored, and all the scenes have been polished to perfection. The script has become a kind of map that doesn't bear any similarity to the land it represents, and inevitably it evolves during filming. Actors bring their own ideas, the locations inspire everyone, creative technicians bring a whole new dimension, and if you're fortunate enough to work with an actor like Marlon Brando, the script can only be enriched by his creative input.

L: *Have you always been happy with the scripts you have worked with?*
P: Not always, no. *The Chase, The Missouri Breaks*, and *Night Moves* were rewritten several times. The scripts for *The Miracle Worker, The Left Handed Gun*, and *Mickey One*, on the other hand, didn't need any work at all.

L: *It has been said that during the editing of* The Missouri Breaks *you and your editors Stephen Rotter and Jerry Greenberg were overwhelmed by the sheer quantity of material, and that Dede Allen, your favorite editor, came to your rescue at the last minute and saved the film.*
P: No, that's not true at all. Dede started work on the film at a very early stage.

L: *She edited* Bonnie and Clyde, Alice's Restaurant, Little Big Man, Night Moves, *and* The Missouri Breaks. *What does she bring to your films?*
P: It's difficult to explain what Dede does because she's so much more than just an editor. She's an artist who's an absolutely essential part of the creative process. After filming I'm always completely exhausted and wonder whether what I have in my hands is any good. It's at this moment that Dede, solid as a rock, enters the scene. She looks at all the footage, sets about clearing the decks, and finds the best way to start editing. It's at this point that her help is most appreciated. She'll put together a very careful first assembly and unlike most other editors is able to give some real coherence to the footage. After filming ends, I always slip away for a couple of weeks to rest. The first thing I do when I get back is look at what Dede has done, by which point she's always given some shape to the film. Then we work together until it's finished. Unlike the people who edited *The Left Handed Gun* and *The Chase*, two films I

didn't edit, Dede always chooses the best takes. We share similar tastes in acting, we're always on the same wavelength. Occasionally I tell her she hasn't picked the best take but after looking at what she has discarded realize pretty quickly that her initial decision was the right one. Often I'd like the chosen take to be better, but this has no reflection whatsoever on Dede's work. She's someone who's completely committed to her job, jumping headlong into the material. Sometimes I'm satisfied with the editing on a sequence, but she isn't, so she sends me home and tells me to come back tomorrow. She'll work all night, and by the next day she's nailed it.

L: *How do you work with your scriptwriter?*
P: In the same relaxed way.

L: *Which element of the filmmaking process do you like most?*
P: It's difficult to say because each element brings its own pleasures, but if I had to choose, I'd say editing because up until the moment when I start editing, I don't believe that the film actually exists. Before editing the film exists only in my head. I never know if what I'll see on screen will be true to my imagination.

L: *Do you pay close attention to the distribution and marketing of your films?*
P: I try but it's not easy, unlike Warren Beatty who is very good at that kind of thing. I've never been very good at it.

L: Four Friends *was not widely released in the United States and was not a commercial success. Do you think the advertising campaign was the reason?*
P: Yes, but Filmways, the distribution company, went bankrupt just before the release, and Orion Pictures took over distribution without making any real effort to sell the film and lure audiences. They just wrote it off, but thankfully the film was a success in Europe, in France, French-speaking Canada, Spain, and Scandinavia.

L: Four Friends *seems to be a direct continuation of* Alice's Restaurant.
P: You're absolutely right. It's another viewpoint of the same era and generation. I've nothing more to say on the subject, and I'm not sure what I'm going to do next. All I can tell you is that I'd like to make a big budget action film.

L: *Do you feel your films are all part of one single body of work?*
P: No. I tackle each new film individually and don't see it as being connected to my other films. It's only afterwards that I realize it might be part of a coherent body of work. The more I try to make my films differ from one another, the more they resemble each other. Any similarities are completely unintentional.

America Has Changed

PAOLO MEREGHETTI / 1990

M: *In the ten years that have followed* Four Friends *you have not been very prolific. What happened?*

P: America changed a great deal in the eighties. Reagan and his individualistic philosophy rose to power and conquered the whole world. For filmmakers the biggest problem was finding money for their projects. Before looking for stories, characters, and actors—as we did in the past—now we have to look for money. It would be impossible to make a film like *Little Big Man* today. Producers invest only in the least unusual and most humdrum ideas. What characterized the eighties was the triumph of big business, especially in America, where film is dependent on big corporations. There's absolutely no government assistance, no public body to help with film production, so you either find the money or forget about it.

M: *What can a filmmaker like you do?*

P: Sometimes I'll try making a slightly offbeat film with the least amount of money possible. I also started working in theater again and directed a Polish play called *Hunting Cockroaches* by Janusz Glowacki in New York. I liked it a lot, as did the public. Then I directed *One of the Guys*, a play by Marylin Miller about a group of friends who help one of them get through an emotional crisis. It wasn't that great, but the author's a friend of mine, and I couldn't say no when she asked me to help get it staged. And of course I've been trying to make films, but more than once, after persuading an in-

From *Jeune Cinéma* (October-November 1990). Originally published in Italian, *Linea d'Ombra* #48 (April 1990). Translated from the Italian by Maurizio Borgese. Reprinted by permission of *Jeune Cinéma*. Translated from the French by Paul Cronin and Remi Guillochon.

dependent producer to help, his company was bought by a bigger one and the project was dropped because no one there was interested in it. Back to square one. This is what happened with *Four Friends*, *Target*, and *Penn & Teller Get Killed*.

M: *What about* Dead of Winter?
P: I can't take full credit for that film. I offered to direct it to help out Marc Shmuger and Mark Malone who wrote the script. It's a good story, but they couldn't find the money to make it, something that happens quite often with inexperienced writers. They were school friends of my son Mathew and came to see me. I promised to vouch for them when dealing with MGM, otherwise the producers wouldn't have moved forward with the project. To keep my promise I agreed to direct the film, although not because I was particularly drawn to it. It was a good script, but the shoot was problematic.

M: *It doesn't sound like a very good situation to be in.*
P: No indeed, though this kind of thing has happened to plenty of other directors. Altman, for example, even though he works more than I do, isn't doing the kind of work that we loved so much from him in the seventies.

M: *Does Altman have the same money problems as you?*
P: Of course, among other things. The problem is that America has changed, it's lost its direction. For us filmmakers there's barely anything left worth making films about.

M: *Aren't there any actors willing to take risks and push certain projects?*
P: There aren't any stars who'll take a role just because the character or the story interests them. Perhaps Nicholson or Brando, but all those actors who aren't as famous are only interested in one film after the next until they reach a certain level of stardom. They want a good script, one they're certain will be a hit, just like their previous films. They take the same roles they've already done.

M: *What was the overwhelming characteristic of the 1980s?*
P: Probably selfishness. In the United States there is no real social unrest. No one's truly interested in the poor. Anyone who can't afford a nice house is put to one side. This is the most overwhelming legacy of the Reagan years: to have left behind the rapport our country needs with its social conscience, to have severed the moral obligation that unites us all. We all believe everyone can achieve their dreams, and for a long time—basically throughout that decade—the facts showed this was possible. Not only that we can dream about what we hope for, we can actually make it happen. The whole country

agrees on this. Everyone just wants more and more, but I really don't know how much longer this can go on. How long can America continue to exploit Asia and the Far East without giving anything back? The message we're sending out as Americans in the last couple of years has been "I only care about myself." Personally I feel nostalgic for the messages we sent out in the sixties. Back then America really gave the impression of being alive. Today only Gorbachev seems alive.

M: *Do you feel powerless when confronted by this situation?*
P: Sometimes I really feel depressed and get very angry. I feel like I'm going crazy. We've remained professional and now can't make the films we want to make either because our ideas aren't as pleasing or because no one wants to finance them. This is the situation many filmmakers, including me, find themselves in.

M: *Do you think television is in some way responsible for this?*
P: Television is full of what people want to see. I don't think anything original will ever come out of television. Our revival will come through film, theater, even cabaret, but not television.

M: *Is this why your last film stars two magicians?*
P: If you're looking for new actors, go to the theater, not agents' offices.

M: Penn & Teller Get Killed *didn't do well in the United States. What kind of film is it?*
P: It tries to demolish certain rules in order to open things up to new ideas. Making allowances for this, the film pulls apart various clichés. In one scene Penn and Teller, who in the film are nightclub entertainers in Atlantic City, decide to go to a big casino. Teller, who never says anything, stands behind a gambler who is playing a slot machine. He begins to throw coins into the gambler's drop box. The gambler has no idea where the money is coming from. He continues to play, becoming more and more surprised before he realizes what Teller is doing. Penn, who is standing next to the gambler says, "Are you going to put up with that?" The gambler says, "No! I mean yeah! I mean I can't clock a guy for giving me money!" "Yes you can. I would!" Penn says, "Just another example of the pig power structure throwing worthless trinkets to the proletariat." At this point the situation becomes comical. Teller continues throwing money and Penn shouts, "Commie bastard! I'll show you distribution of wealth!" and throws some coins at Teller. It seems that a revolution is breaking out in the most unlikely of places, an Atlantic City casino.

M: *Is it difficult for you to think about whether a film is going to make money or not?*

P: I've no desire to direct a money-making film if I have to give up what I truly believe in. It really doesn't interest me in the slightest. I'd rather do something else, like work in theater. At least it would allow me to avoid begging Hollywood for work. I don't like living far from New York and wouldn't want to become a mere cog in the system. We have to believe in what we're doing, which isn't easy because the system is always forcing us to put our beliefs aside. Young filmmakers have a clichéd style that's unique to film school graduates. Sure, they're all technically skilled but there's nothing original in their work. All their films seem the same.

M: *I'm not that pessimistic, though I do feel that many new directors have one common characteristic: they seem to lack real passion.*

P: Perhaps that's the real problem. A film is no longer made just because the filmmaker feels passionately about it, which is why I defend Scorsese's *The Last Temptation of Christ*. The subject doesn't particularly interest me, but he's wanted to make this film for a very long time, and he did all he could to make his dream come true. This fact alone makes the film stand out from everything else.

M: *In what way is New York different from Los Angeles?*

P: You can lead a life outside of business and filmmaking in New York. Here in Manhattan I have friends outside of my work. Sometimes we talk politics. I often have dinner with Alger Hiss. If you remember, his case in the 1940s marked the beginning of the McCarthy era, and he was an important figure in the State Department. Due to a false accusation based on false testimony he was imprisoned for five years. You think I'd ever have dinners like that in Hollywood?

Arthur Penn

RICHARD SCHICKEL/1990

S: *Could you talk about your family background?*

P: It was a very disordered childhood. My parents were divorced when I was very young and, during the depths of the Depression, I was taken to live with my mother and brother. This sort of family dislocation meant a lot of movement and was pretty severe. Finally for me it involved being sent away from even that part of the family, which meant I was brought up in a little part of New Hampshire for a couple of years and in New Jersey by some relatives for a couple of years. It was a pretty fragmentary childhood, a dozen elementary schools in—whatever it was—six or seven years. More than a dozen. So there was constantly a new neighborhood, new friendships, severed friendships.

S: *Were you and your brother together or had you been separated?*

P: We were living with our mother, but my brother and I didn't get to be really good friends until we were both sent to live with my father in Philadelphia when I was fourteen and Irving was nineteen.

S: *Your father was a clockmaker?*

P: He was a watchmaker and an extraordinary engraver. In the last years of his life he began to paint. I wish I'd known him better. He was rather a mystery to me, not an emotionally available man at all. I know less about him than I should. But I do know about his work, which was extraordinary. He really was an extraordinarily capable man.

S: *That sense of craftsmanship and highly technical detail seem to me the two elements that go into making a movie. Movies are, at a certain point, extremely*

From an interview conducted 22 May 1990 for the documentary *Arthur Penn* (1995). Used by permission of Richard Schickel.

nitty-gritty in terms of their craftsmanship. It often comes down to, "Do we cut on this frame or that frame?" Yet on the other hand there's this gigantic emotional is-sue that is going on behind any serious film.

P: I think unquestionably. My father trained me to be a watchmaker for a brief time, and I tried but wasn't very good at it, though not because I didn't have the dexterity for it. As a matter of fact I do a lot of welding and con-struction, that sort of stuff. But what I couldn't do—given the fact that he became mortally ill very shortly after I started doing this—was maintain the kind of responsibility necessary to look after the business, something he was very skilled at. For me there was a kind of emotional collapse during the pe-riod when he was dying. I couldn't keep the business going and it fell apart.

S: *You must have been very young.*

P: I was high school age. I became a kind of free ranging spirit and drifted into theater groups in Europe after the war while I was in the army. It was clearly an attractive place for me. Then I came back to the States, went to college, and then went back to Italy for a couple of years on the GI Bill. Then I came back to the States and got into live television, and that's when I dis-covered that I needed to call on those sorts of physical skills and that kind of dexterity. In those days we had three cameras and four lenses, so we were working with twelve lenses while we were on the air live. We had to know what each camera could do and how they complemented each other.

S: *You came out of live television at a time when everybody else's background tended to be theater, or else they went into movies directly when they were nineteen or twenty. Live television existed for how long? Perhaps a decade, and then televi-sion went to tape and film. Some part of me romanticizes that period in television because it seems to me that people were creating their work under such enormous pressures.*

P: They called it the Golden Age of television, though it wasn't that golden when we were doing it. The tensions and pressures were enormous, and I can't begin to explain them all, but you can imagine going out live on the air and having to deal with all these cameras and microphones and booms and actors making changes and getting from one place to another. It was enormously complicated.

At the time Broadway was a place where people came to work and were signed to plays so these superb actors—Henry Fonda, Kim Stanley, Geraldine Page—were on Broadway. What would happen to them is after that during the year they would go stir-crazy, so they grabbed the opportunity to do even a one-hour television drama, in this case largely well written, because we had this wonderful group of writers like Paddy Chayevsky and Horton Foote. It was a wonderful opportunity for those of us who were young and new to the world of drama and theater to work with the most extraordinary people in the country. That was part of the privilege. What happened was that throughout the course of several years I became more and more involved with the acting process and less and less involved with the mechanics. I began to accept as a given that I could do the mechanics in my sleep, which in point of fact turned out to be relatively true, even when I moved over to film.

S: *Though you began in a kind of humble way in television.*
P: That's right, literally holding cards for Milton Berle. That was my first job at NBC. I think it was 1951.

S: *And one time you actually took over the direction of a show?*
P: Yes, that was on the *Colgate Comedy Hour.* By then I was an associate director. My job was to prepare the next shot that was coming up. At a certain point there I realized that the director wasn't doing his job. In point of fact he'd slumped over the console, so I started calling the shots for the rest of the show. Meantime people were coming in and out of the control room, and they took him away in an ambulance. It turned out that he'd had a massive internal hemorrhage from an ulcer.

S: *An excellent example of the pressures people operated under in live television.*
P: It's not possible to recount that kind of pressure. You needed the talent but also the physical stamina to survive it. The incidents of heart attacks in those control rooms during that era was extraordinary. Young guys would either crack up or have a heart attack or smoke themselves into oblivion. The pressures were that great.

S: *What attracted this rather extraordinary group of writers to television?*
P: I must lay this at the feet of one man, Fred Coe, who was the producer. He had the good sense to say, "Whatever this process is, it begins with writers." He had the most wonderful relationship that he developed with writers and subsequently with directors so that we became an extraordinarily close-knit group. The sense of mutual respect in that group was just terrific. It all emanated from Fred. He was a superb leader.

S: *Is it something you have encountered anywhere else, that sense of community you found in those days of television?*
P: No, not really. To a small degree it existed in the old Actors Studio but that was clearly not a professional environment.

S: *What was it about Coe that made him this way? What were his qualities?*

P: His essential quality was the great respect he had for writing. The idea that is often practiced in Hollywood of "We get another writer in to do this and another writer to do that" was just unimaginable to Fred. He would go to the mat and defend even the most eccentric writers. They were to be admired and defended, no matter what. If there were illogical aspects to the writing, so much the better. He also struck up wonderful relationships with the writers. He would ask, "How many plays are you going to write for me this year?" The guy would say, "Five." Fred would then give him money for the five shows. If he didn't write the five, Fred never went back and said, "Hey, you didn't fulfil your contract." It was all done on the understanding that the guy was writing as best he could.

S: *Does any of your television work particularly stick in your mind?*
P: Before *The Miracle Worker* I did a thing called *Man on the Mountaintop* that I think won a Peabody Award. Over those years I must have done sixty or seventy shows, many hours of TV. Finally I did *The State of the Union*, which was the first big color show that NBC did, with Margaret Sullavan and Joe Cotten.

S: *Your first films came out of your television experiences.* The Left Handed Gun *had been done as a television program.*
P: Not by me, but it had been done on *Philco*. Then Fred decided to do it as a film, and I think he went to Delbert Mann first who, having done *Marty*, was by then a very successful Hollywood director. He'd come out of live TV with us but I guess wasn't available or something, so Fred asked me if I would do it.

S: The Left Handed Gun *is often thought of as a psychological Western, the start of a trend of a more subjective, inward-looking view of Western archetypes. Had that been a characteristic of the television version? Was it something you brought into the film consciously?*
P: I wasn't particularly aware of this in the TV version, but Leslie Stevens changed the story quite considerably for the film. It had to be larger for the screen. It began to take on this kind of quirkiness that you are referring to, something that—as I say—I wasn't aware of. But I thought it was important to inject these kinds of personal things into it, so that in certain respects there are clear references to me and my father in the film. The relationship with Mr. Tunstall at the very beginning is based on a desire to engage more closely with a kind of father figure, one that's terminated rather quickly and vividly in a killing. It's conceivable that this is what launches Billy on to his career. He is trying to rectify this death and, of course, exceeds the boundaries

of propriety in doing so, eventually ending up an outlaw himself. That's basically the story from a psychological standpoint. It's about status. I think this reflects something of my own personality and my own personal views.

The film came out and was totally disregarded here. Then André Bazin and *Cahiers du Cinéma* began to write about it, and lo and behold I received a telegram one day that I was the recipient of the first annual Belgium Film Critics' Award for *The Left Handed Gun*. I simply couldn't believe it. But what I did discover was a level of serious film criticism I'd never anticipated. What was absolutely fascinating was how accurately Bazin had seen into that film, how accurately the other people who were writing at that period—who were his disciples—saw what I had intended with it, my most private and secret thoughts.

S: *It was an era when psychological metaphors were coming into play in television. Psychiatry and psychology were riding into popular culture with guns blazing.*
P: Absolutely, and in no small way because of Chayevsky and *Marty*. When that de-romanticized story went on air, it suddenly woke people who were making films and doing plays and television to the sense that there's a whole body of humanity that we're not dealing with. We're dealing with rather prototypical aspects of theater and movies. Let's get down underneath it, let's talk about the unattractive people. Let's talk about a butcher and a girl in the Bronx. I wouldn't lay it totally at the feet of Chayevsky, but I would say that he was responsive to what were clearly the postwar psychological perceptions of people, this body of humanity excluded from the world of drama. This separation had been enormous up through the war. Now, suddenly, we were talking about real people.

S: *There is a striking contrast between the atmosphere of* The Left Handed Gun *and* The Miracle Worker. *One has a sparseness to it, the other has this incredible compressed intensity. When I think about* The Miracle Worker, *I remember it as being composed almost entirely of close-ups.*
P: As a matter of act, if I had my way it would have been even more intense with even more close-ups. What happened with *The Miracle Worker* was interesting. It started out as a television show. Actually it was a narrative for a dance that Bill Gibson had written years previously to all of this, for a modern dancer friend of his. When he was writing *Two for the Seesaw*, there was a period when he needed some money and I said, "Listen, I'm doing TV. I can get you some money if we do something together." So he wrote the script of *The Miracle Worker*, and I tried to sell it to TV but no one would buy it.

Fortunately at that point Martin Manulis was starting *Playhouse 90*, and to those of us that he had contracts with he asked, "Do you have any material?

I've got to do an hour and a half every week." I said, "I have this thing I think is extraordinary." He thought it was wonderful, so we did it on television, and it was a big success. Then while we were out of town with *Two for the Seesaw*, Bill Gibson turned to me and said, "You know, I think I could turn *The Miracle Worker* into a play for Annie Bancroft." I said, "You're crazy. I don't know how you're going to get that onto the stage. You're talking about a play in which one of the two principal figures can neither see nor hear." Then *Two for the Seesaw* opened, and it was a great success. Bill Gibson went back up to Stockbridge and a few months later said, "Listen, I want to show you the script of *The Miracle Worker*." Lo and behold it was a brilliant adaptation for the stage.

This is a long-winded answer to why I wish I had been even more intense with the camera on *The Miracle Worker*. It should have been more fixed on the child, but I didn't know enough about cinema at that point. If you'll permit me one small anecdote about the scene when the water hits Helen's hand and she, after all of these associations that Annie has fed into her hand, finally understands. We had done that on Broadway for two years to standing ovations and screaming audiences. I thought, "I know how to do that scene on film. I'll do it in one basic shot." Well, I shot it that way and went to look at it in the dailies. It was terrible, absolutely terrible. It was something we had rehearsed and done for two solid years, and here we are repeating it on camera and it's dead. Absolutely dead. What I realized then for the first time was that I had to go in and fragment the event. Helen's hand. Helen's face. Annie's face. Annie's responses, seeing something in Helen's face. Water dripping into the child's hand. Essentially this was the film experience that really taught me something about movies. I was able to provide myself with the raw materials in the cutting room where I could expand and contract the moment and direct our attention to the most exquisite and exact place that I thought we had to be. Give me Helen's hand, then her face, then Annie's face.

S: *Do you feel with* Mickey One *that your understanding of film technique was increasing? It does have a wonderful liveliness to it.*
P: The film was based on an unhappy experience I'd had with another film that I started and then got fired from. I thought, "I don't want to mess with commercial Hollywood. I want to do what I want to do." Here I had my second film, I'd been nominated for the Academy Award, and I made a deal to make two small films for a million dollars each. This is now several years later, so the million dollars is about the equivalent of $700,000 that we started with on *The Left Handed Gun*. I thought, "I want to get in there

and do something utterly personal, utterly my own way." So what I did was to invade that area excessively. What's interesting is that it was the period of the French *nouvelle vague* so a lot of people think that *Mickey One* was influenced by that. And maybe in small part it was, but I suggest also that some of the French *nouvelle vague* were influenced by *Mickey One* and *The Left Handed Gun*.

S: *Perhaps I'm wrong, but it seems to me that you hit your stride stylistically with* Mickey One. *It seems a true Arthur Penn movie in the fullest sense.*

P: With all the youthful excesses. Yes, it is an Arthur Penn movie in that sense. I went ape. I decided, "Look, this is not going to be a popular film. I'm going to do the best I can with it. I want to tell everything I know and want to play with the camera and expand on certain ideas that I have been developing." Well, they're all there. I'm proud of the film because it was an attempt to claim a certain identity with the medium, something which then lapsed into a kind of period of getting caught in the commercialism of Hollywood when I did a film called *The Chase*. After that I did nothing where I was able to use any of my ideas until *Bonnie and Clyde*.

S: *Brando is legendary for being difficult to work with. Did you ever have any problems?*

P: None, absolutely none. I think he's probably the most maligned actor in the history of movies. I think what happened was that there was a social change that took place in America which had, of course, an aesthetic correlative, a certain sense of a different kind of postwar hero. *Marty*, Brando, *Streetcar* and, consequently, the development of an aesthetic that supported this, the Method. And who was the personification of that? Brando, clearly. People who made jokes about him scratching his underwear with a hole in it either were insensitive or they never saw him on stage. Brando in *Streetcar* was one of the most breathtaking performances that I've ever seen. He was speaking to my generation and my aesthetic, saying, "Wait a minute. This is a whole new way to act, a whole new way to behave, a whole new way to live on the stage."

He brought that with him to Hollywood, as well as a very rigorous sense of what is right and fair and what is not. When a studio crossed him or somebody broke their word to him or somebody lied to him, there was an enormous counter-reaction from Marlon. He is a counter-puncher of enormous proportions. He's an eminently fair guy, perfectly assessable and decent and available. To other actors he's as generous as anybody can be. He has an abundance of gifts and makes those prodigally available. If I'm shooting a close-up on an actor, Marlon is standing alongside the camera and working as hard as if he were in front of the camera. He's not just saying the lines, he's out there working. He doesn't like the economics and the environment. He doesn't like being the star, but he loves the work, he loves the process.

It was a delight to watch him hunker down on a set. He would arrive and slowly make it his own. This would be moved around here and that would be there, and pretty soon it was his place and his environment. It was just lovely to behold. The other actors, who were of no small accomplishment themselves, would literally watch him work. It was a privilege, like going to school with one of the greats.

S: *Do you think you are more open to actors improvising than other directors?*

P: I certainly hope so. I think the essence of really good acting emerges once an actor separates himself or herself from the language, from the obligation to just speak the words, and then begins to embed that language in a system of life which has all the little abhorrent things we all do constantly that somehow theater and film sort of edit out. I remember there's a famous story about Katherine Hepburn weeping in a scene. They showed the scene to one of the studio executives who said, "No way that goes on the screen. She's got snot running out of her nose." In a sense it's a sanitizing process. All the little things—the dandruff, the things that we all carry with us, our funny behavior—are taken out so that these people look like stick figures instead of full drawings. That's the quality I so admire in actors, when they can develop what Stanislavsky called "public solitude," which is behaving as if you're alone in public. It's a gift that the great actors have.

S: *How did* Bonnie and Clyde *come about?*

P: Benton and Newman had written it, and Beatty found it. The writers had been involved with Godard who was going to shoot it in two weeks in some interesting and bizarre way, but it never came to pass. Then Truffaut was interested. I didn't have any contact with either one of those guys at the time to discuss it. It was simply not anything I knew about until Beatty bought it and said to me, "C'mon, forget *The Chase.*" I had just come out of that film and was a really upset and desperate fellow. It was a bad experience for me. I had been humiliated by it, I felt that I'd sold out, that I had done something I should never have done, which was go to Hollywood, so I just said, "The hell with this, I've got another life. I work in the theater. Why don't I go back to New York and just do that." And that's what I did. But I was also more or less dysfunctional for a period there. For a couple of years I was really deeply disappointed in myself, and one of the things that Beatty did as a friend was persist. When he sent me the script I said, "Gee, I don't think so. I don't really want to do a film about a couple of bums essentially."

And he said, "Come on, you can do it and we can make it something better than that." He was a real friend. He kept at me until I finally said yes.

I really threw myself into it. I began to talk with Benton and Newman and realized that I had a lot of associations myself with Bonnie and Clyde. I remember as a kid seeing the photograph of them on the front page of the newspapers and more importantly I remembered the era, the depths of the Depression. So I was able to bring that aspect to the film. I said to Benton and Newman, "If this film isn't embedded in the economic Depression, if that era isn't presented in detail, it won't make sense." I put in that scene where the farmer's house has been foreclosed by the bank because it was part of the absurdity of the times that the banks kept foreclosing on these mortgages to the point where the banks were bankrupt themselves. It was kind of eating your own entrails.

Little did I know that *Bonnie and Clyde* was going to resonate so strongly to audiences in 1967. The story just happened to be appropriate to the sixties without anybody ever saying, "Hey, this is very analogous to what's happening out there in the streets right now or at the 1968 Democratic National Convention in Chicago." There was a sense of going along with society until a certain kind of anarchism began to be evident, which was on a much more primitive and bucolic and simplistic level during the period of *Bonnie and Clyde*. In 1967 it was resist the draft, resist the war in Vietnam, break out of these kinds of constrictive mores, have a sexual revolution. Back then you went along with the farms being foreclosed and people being destitute, and then at a certain point thought, "Wait a minute. The money's in the bank. Let's go to the bank and get it." And a very simplistic solution ensues.

S: *The final sequence with its excessive firepower was not unlike what was going on in Southeast Asia at the time.*

P: They used literally a thousand rounds to kill them. In those early discussions with Bob Newman we talked about the ending and I said, "I know how to do this ending. I can see it now." And I literally could see it, just as it showed up on the screen. It's one of those interesting experiences, because after we finished shooting the movie, we were cutting the film in New York with a very good editor who said, "I don't know how to put this scene together." I knew that it had to have these changes in tempo, that it had to have this balletic quality. We composed it in such a way as to have four cameras all ganged together, running at different speeds, because it's all varying degrees of slow motion. When you shoot in slow motion, it means a lot more film is going through the camera, so we used special cameras that would eat up the film in enormous quantities. Each component of these shots had to be done just for a brief time. What it amounted to was four days of getting one shot in the morning and one shot in the afternoon. We had to load these two actors up with all these body hits with a piece coming off of Warren's head and all of that relating to the JFK assassination. It was all carefully constructed.

But those four days were sublime. I said, "Oh, I wish I could live like this forever." I was in a state of absolute revelation. I knew just how to do it. I knew what the mechanics had to be and just prevailed and it came out that way. When you change the audience's relationship to the medium for a moment, it throws them off their sedentary stride, as it were. They are sitting there watching the frames go by and then suddenly they're not sitting there. They are included in the film.

S: *Were you prepared for the controversy that arose out of the movie?*
P: No, but then I didn't think it was excessively violent. I knew it had to be vivid, but I kept thinking, "Look, what are we seeing on the news at six o'clock, for Christ's sake?" What's coming out of Vietnam at this point?" We were seeing bodies, kids with transfusions being rushed into helicopters and flown out of Vietnam. How could a fictional movie with somebody getting shot possibly generate such controversy? Well, it did. Bosley Crowther [of the *New York Times*] happened to be on a campaign against violence in movies. I don't know what world he was living in at that point because clearly we were trembling in the streets with this potential violence. We were seeing it. The Democratic National Convention was a fact of life, folks. What the hell did Crowther want movies to be? He wanted them to hark back to that sanitized, immaculate, romantic period.

S: *With* Alice's Restaurant *you dealt directly with the moment, but in a much sweeter way. It also has a very naïve quality to it after the technical sophistication of* Bonnie and Clyde. *It's a very simple seeming movie.*
P: It focused on a simple event. After the violence of that period certain kids went and carved out another kind of world, one they hoped was going to be much more benign, a world in which they said, "Wait a minute, you have your violence and you have your actions. We're going to go out and just close it all out. We're going to live the way we like to want." It literally happened in the town in which I lived, Stockbridge, up in Massachusetts. They moved into a church and set up a pseudo-society. Unfortunately, as with such dreams, it's impossible, it seems to me, to contain them. Things begin to encroach on them, and the certain childish, naïve, sweet quality was tested again and again, and eventually was ruptured. That's the story.

I had a lot of sympathy for the life these kids had created, but I also had a certain sense that it wasn't going to endure as well as a nostalgia for it that would remain. That's what the last shot of the movie is, when Arlo leaves. There is a shot where we see Alice standing in the door of the church where she's just remarried Ray, the wind is blowing her veil, and this whole wedding has gone awry and Arlo leaves. The camera dollies back and is pulling away at the same time that it's zooming in, so the intent there is to say, "I'm separating, but I cannot lose that memory." It was an enormously complicated shot. It took four days to do it but I loved the challenge of it because, once again, I knew what I wanted. I could see it. It was a kind of Proustian reference to the nature of memory, to the tenacity of memory at the same time as you try and separate yourself from it.

S: *You said that* Night Moves *was the darkest of your films.*
P: It's dark because it was during a time of great despair. It was after the Kennedy assassinations. I'd been one of the people advising Jack's staff on techniques to be used on the debates with Nixon, and I was literally with Bobby just before he went to California because we were starting to do some commercials. When they were killed, the bottom just sort of dropped out. I was looking for a film to deal with this despairing aspect, the loss of confidence and optimism that I associate with the American temperament. Then along came a script called *The Dark Tower*, written by Alan Sharp, a very fine screenwriter. It was a detective story in which the solution wasn't there for the guy who has to find it because he himself is embedded in the plot, in the problem. That's what I'm attempting to characterize in the very last shot of the film where Gene Hackman is wounded out on a boat in the waters off of Florida and he can barely steer. All he can do is touch the throttle of one engine on a twin-engine boat which sets him going in motion, round and round.

S: *You say the film comes out of the aftermath of the sixties but it was made in 1975. It was a long-term gestation.*
P: Right. As with *Mickey One*, which was made ten years after McCarthy, maybe I'm not astute enough to catch the moment clearly as it's happening or just after it's happened. I think there's a residual aspect to all of this, so that when you finally come to make a film about a time you need some distance to be able to talk about it. I didn't want to talk about these eras in a documentary fashion, but instead concentrate on the spirit and lives of these people.

S: *Gene Hackman is an actor whose career seems linked to your own.*

P: Yes, we're hooked together, we've done three films together. He's just absolutely wonderful. He brings to them what I was saying Brando brings, that quality of living outside the role. There can be no sense of anybody else ever playing that role. There's a large dark streak in Hackman's personality, a despairing aspect to him that sometimes verges almost on the tragic. There are constant efforts on his part to find a way to live, and he doesn't succeed at it. He's a man very much damaged by life and who wears the damage. He doesn't deny this. You see it with the camera.

S: *I have a feeling that* Four Friends *is an important film for you.*
P: It's hard to think of a film and try to estimate it. It was a film for which I had a lot of sympathy, about adolescence and a kid who was an immigrant to the United States and his inability to function with his father. In that sense there are lots of personal details that correlate with my own life. I think one of the things about the film is that there is an inherent forgiveness to it, and I guess that's what my unconscious connection to it was. Somehow we finally forgive each other and figure out a way to go on. If there's a meaning for me, that's it. I don't know if it's exemplified enough for it to convey itself to others, but that was certainly the meaning of the film for me.

S: *I like* Target *as a chase movie as well as the element of the ungrateful child, but Hackman's character is also a man trying to break out of the system.*
P: It's a simple-minded movie on those terms. It was done as a wildly physical, adventurous movie about the relationship between him and his son. It's a melodrama. I just like to flex my muscles every once in a while and do something relatively mindless, though any association with Hackman is never entirely mindless. He brings to all his films a certain specific gravity that you just can't circumvent. *Target* is a film about somebody who has tried to detach himself from the kind of absurdity of his time and just wants to tend his garden, but the circumstances of our lives won't let him. In this sense it's existential. You cannot detach yourself from the system of actions that define you. You commit those actions and that's who you are. Hackman's character starts out trying to deny this and is driven back into his other identity.

S: *The thing that was immediately attractive to me about the movie is that you have made at least one film that overtly celebrates adolescence, namely* Alice's Restaurant, *and in* Target *you have a sultry boy who thinks his father amounts to very little because he works in a lumberyard. He has no sense that this was a man of some parts. I think this is an issue that all of us who are parents of adolescents and post-adolescents deal with.*

P: I think one of the things that I was really trying to say about my life is that we are all the sons of fathers, and then we are the fathers of sons and daughters. And my gosh, how the perspective changes! I never knew much about my father. He was a withdrawn man, and I was a withdrawn adolescent. We didn't make enough contact to amount to a hill of beans. I regret that deeply, and I wish I'd known more about the man. Today I have a son and daughter who have genuine curiosity about my childhood and my wife's childhood and how the things were back then, about the war and what that was like. So often there's the pleasure of having children who have a genuine curiosity. I think, "Oh, what a blessing that is, to be able to talk to my children and have them be curious about me, and me be curious about them, and be able to exchange openly with each other." But when *Target* came along it harked back to my own relationship with my father where I thought, "This man is a rather dull and ordinary man." Except when I watched him work on a watch, except when I saw his painting, except on a dozen other levels. I realized, "Wow! How an adolescent can so underestimate his parent." That's the fantastic aspect of the film, and in that respect it's a fantasy.

D: *How did* Dead of Winter *come about?*
P: A couple of guys who'd been at the same school as my son, Wesleyan University, had written a script. They were trying to put it together with independent financing and weren't having any success. Somehow they crossed my path, and I said, "Look, if you don't succeed in getting independent financing, maybe I can help you." Finally they didn't succeed, and I said, "Okay, I'll call a studio." I called Alan Ladd at MGM and he said yes to it. I told him these guys were very clever, very talented. The film started, but the young man who was directing was caught in something so many bright young film people are caught in, which is the embarrassment of riches that is the historical residue of all these brilliant geniuses who have made films. He was caught asking, "Do I use a Welles shot here or a Hitchcock shot or an Eisenstein?" It's paralyzing and intimidating. It was just too much for him, and MGM wasn't satisfied. I had faith in him and said, "He's going to get better." I think he will one day be a fine director, but he came at it really as a film aficionado, without the hands-on experience of how to work with actors and where to place the camera, and it just got away from him. At that point MGM was just simply going to close down the film, and I felt terrible because I had gotten them to put up this money. Mary Steenbergen and Roddy McDowell and all these fine actors were working on it so I said, "Well, I got you into this, I gotta get you out of it." So I took over the film, and I made a film I would never have made in a million years, which is a kind of

Hitchcockian suspense film. It was really just a friendly, paternalistic thing I did for a couple of young kids.

S: *I can see how your Penn and Teller film links up to your theater life. It is no surprise you appreciate them.*
P: Yes, we just hit it off. They're rather extraordinary in the sense that they're de-mythifiers for one thing. One of the things they can't stand is any bullshit. They don't believe in UFOs, they don't have anything to do with the extraterrestrial aspect of things. People who bend spoons naturally stay away from these guys because they're superb magicians. Did you ever see their act? There is an easel with a pad of white paper on it. In front of that there's a little table on which there's a vase and a rose, and the light shines on the vase and the rose, throwing its shadow onto this white piece of paper. Teller comes out, looks at it, and very adroitly goes to the shadow on the paper and cuts a leaf off the shadow and the leaf falls off the rose. And he cuts another leaf off the shadow and another leaf and another. Now how in the world do you do that? It's an exquisite skill. That's a kind of wizardry that these people are capable of. Join that with two personalities of great irreverence and we're soulmates. We just became buddies, and are to this day. I just adore them.

S: *Another aspect to them, and the movie, is that they act out all our worst fears of magic acts. The guy gets himself tied up, and you think he could get himself killed doing something like that.*
P: That's a great send-up on their part of the other magicians who cut women in half and that sort of thing. In their case they do these elaborate constructs, and it gets away from them with Teller getting killed or chewed up or drilled, in this case, by a dozen industrial-sized drills that he's supposed to extricate himself from. Then you've got another play on that experiment with college students who are told to inflict pain on somebody else, and to the best of their knowledge they find themselves hurting other people. Against their own better sense of identification with the person who is being hurt, they were responding to authority.

S: *There is certainly some logic to the fact that Penn and Teller, who are subversive in that they try to upset all kinds of conventions, seem to be linked to the rest of your work.*
P: Definitely, yes. There's an absolute logic to it. They are irreverent, audacious, in your face. That's their attitude, and they make it stick. Where this connects with me is that I have that same attitude. "Don't you see how you're living? Don't you see what you're doing? Is it any good? Is that how

we want to live? Is that who we want to be?" I do it in a quite subversive way by endowing the counterculture outsiders with a certain kind of hero-ism. I'm saying, "Wait a minute. Have respect for and learn from these fringe inhibitors, these people who are pushing out the limits of our consciousness, our morals, our values. Let's have some sense of inclusion because there's something to be learned from these freaks on the outside." Penn and Teller are the truth-tellers in a subversive society, and they use the medium of magic to ask, "You think you know what you're talking about? It's an illu-sion. *This* is reality." That's where we are joined at the hip.

S: *I was reading an interview with you from 1969 or 1970 where you said that "The movies are a director's event." What did you mean by that, and do you still think it?*

P: I'm talking today as somebody who works about an equal amount of time and with, I think, equal success, in both theater and film. Theater is clearly the writer's medium. It belongs to the author, the text is everything, and properly so. It has to be treated with reverence and respect because it's a fixed form. It's a one-shot movie, in a sense. What you see up there is what the author's ingenuity has been able to accomplish in placing the characters in interde-pendent associations and contexts. The personalities are elucidated and made vivid through what they articulate. That's a gift given to very few people in any given generation. There's an Arthur Miller and a Tennessee Williams, a Lillian Hellman and a Eugene O'Neill, but you can count them on the fingers of one hand at a given time. The movies are different. They are not really so much about what people say as about the contradictions between what they say and what they do. The camera is so illuminating and informative because it's telling us, "Wait a minute, that's not so. What he's saying is only part of it. What he's doing is a whole other part of it." With relatively simple people like Bonnie and Clyde their story would be the most boring play ever done, but on film it's lively, contradictory, both knowing and unknowing, wise and dumb. It's all of those things because there is a disparity between the spoken word and the action.

We touch here on that ancient argument about the *auteur* theory which seems to me an ungainly theory at best. It was used at *Cahiers du Cinéma* to say, "You can see continuity in a director's work, and there is value to this." But it has been carried to an extent that I think is perhaps ludicrous in that it doesn't represent the collaborative aspects of film which have to be re-spected. A film is made up of Brando and Redford and Beatty and Bancroft and me and Lillian Hellman and Horton Foote and Alan Sharp. It's that kind of mixture, though one person can legislate it. Only one person stays with it from the beginning to the end. There's only one parent. It's a one-parent family. The director takes it from the beginning and carries it through and edits it and scores it and closes it out. If it's not a director's medium and a director's event, then I don't know whose it is because there's nobody else there all that time.

S: *Of course certain movies of the thirties, for example, were corporate events. If you were an MGM director there was a specific corporate sensibility, and you made your film according to that sensibility or you went elsewhere.*
P: Yes, and one of the things they did very cleverly was say, "If I'm not going to be able to edit this film and I'm going to be consulted in the most cursory way, I'm not going to shoot a lot of material that they could edit differently." So guys like John Ford would give them no alternatives. He clearly wanted certain things done in certain ways. They developed a whole kind of irreverent body of film technique. There's a thing called "crossing the line." Ford didn't give a hoot in hell about the line or the axis because he knew what he was doing and that he was going to shoot it a particular way. Directors like Ford developed their own survival skills.

S: *I have the feeling that saying, "Gosh, if I do it this way, I'm going to violate one of these rules" is not high on your list of priorities.*
P: No, it's not. One of the places I learned that was on live television. When I first started in live TV as a director, you took home a floor plan and had these sort of plastic overlays that showed you what a 75mm lens would look like and a 50mm lens and a 100mm. You literally had to come in with a shot list for each of the operators of each of the cameras, and you followed that shot list meticulously. That's the way I was trained, and I followed it for a while before I became more audacious. What we did was come in with this meticulously prepared shot list and detailed plan of how we were going to photograph it. Everything was totally rehearsed. But what became clear to me was that the actors are acting on live TV with a certain kind of wonderful inconsistency. It was not a meticulously laid-out performance. They began to have different emotions, and I thought, "Gee, my shot list doesn't include that, and yet it's happening right here before my eyes, and I can't photograph it because I happen to be on the wrong camera at this point because that's what I thought we were going to be on." So I began to change and said, "We're going to work from the actors and make it up as we go along. Eventually we're going to be audacious enough to do this on the air."

I thought there was going to be a public burning at NBC. They were panicked, understandably so, but slowly they began to work to this, and we would eventually go on air with just a general sense of what we were doing. The specifics were dictated by what was happening in front of the camera instead of the camera forcing the actor to get into position to be photographed. I brought that sense of audacity with me to film. I don't care too much about the orthodoxy. I want to know it, I want to understand it, but I don't happen to love it. If there's something that is symptomatic about my personality, it's that I work best when I am irreverent, audacious, breaking the rules and jumping the line.

S: *I take it you are not a big fan of storyboarding?*
P: Not at all. I hate it. So many directors use these beautifully drawn details of the sequences of photographs that they're going to take. They adhere to them meticulously. I come on the set without a shot in my head, and then we start working with the actors and with the life and then finally, when the life is visible, I begin to perceive how to photograph it. But I photograph it after the fact rather than having life adapt itself to the photograph.

S: *Do you think your theatrical background sets you apart from most other directors? Elia Kazan said that Hollywood directors are scared of actors, but not him. As a director, you seem to stress the role of the actor.*
P: If I had to develop a credo it would be "From the actor." It all comes from the actor. There's nothing like it when the actor feels the role and you're genuinely interested in what he or she does, rather than having them conform to a system that you have already developed and where they're simply a cog. This comes out of a respect for the actor and creates an environment for the actors where they flourish. Kazan and I are both from the Actors Studio. We have developed this technique over years out of respect for what we have seen actors do, and consequently no actor terrifies me.

S: *Finally, can you characterize what a director is, what he does?*
P: There are so many layers to being a director. There is the simple cohesive force that holds together the idea of the film and sees that it is represented in all its parts, so that finally it becomes an ideational whole. That's one level. There are other levels, one of which is to be an instigator of certain trouble. You set one actor against the other in a benign environment, but you say, "Act out in an infantile way. Give voice to those rather primitive forces and I will maintain the atmosphere." You need to fend off conventional behavior and any orthodoxies. You suggest and invite and elicit and solicit every kind of behavior you possibly can that doesn't follow conventional forms. Finally, there is a personal aesthetic that goes with all good directors. There is a consistency of thought and approach, of visualization. There is no question about it. It's a rather mystical

area, one that while I'm doing it I'm not aware of. It's only after I have conversations like this or I see a body of my work or somebody else's work where I can say, "I know that's a Kazan film, that's a Fred Zinnemann film, I can tell a John Ford or Orson Welles film." It's clear that there's an abiding sensibility. It goes back to our discussion about that apparently contradictory sensibility of being able to organize accidental, irreverent, disparate and fragmented behavior in a highly technical sense.

Is There Anything Film Can't Do?

LARS-OLAV BEIER AND ROBERT MÜLLER/1994

Q: *There are several changes of rhythm in* The Miracle Worker. *When Annie Sullivan is trying to teach something to Helen, the scenes are shot in very long takes, but other scenes are very fast-paced. Did you have this contrast in mind when you were developing the subject?*

A: Yes, I felt we needed to have a change of pace. After all, it's not a very active film. What we have is a long scene where Annie is unpacking and teaching Helen things, like what the word for doll is. It's a scene about how laborious her job is, about how many times she has to explain things. I have three young grandsons, and I watch how their parents talk to them. Over and over they say, "Do you want some egg? Do you want some toast?" That's how we teach our children. They learn through repetition. So imagine trying to teach these things to a child who can neither hear nor see what the object is. That was the task at hand. In order to make the end of the film as exciting as it is I had to make the beginning as slow and boring as it is. We slowly begin to pick up the rhythm, and then in the middle of the film there is a scene where Helen has had enough of Annie teaching her things. She doesn't want to eat with a spoon, and Annie says, "She's got to eat with a spoon. She's got to learn this." Helen's family spoils her and says, "Leave the child alone." Annie throws them out, and we have a long scene—about nine minutes—with a hand-held camera. The child won't use the spoon, but Annie insists, and the child throws away the spoon. Annie picks up one spoon after

Previously unpublished interview conducted 19 October 1994. Originally published in German in *Arthur Penn* (Dieter Bertz Verlag), see page xvii. Printed by permission of Lars-Olav Beier.

another and Helen throws them all away. It's a very kinetic scene, and finally she folds her napkin and eats with a spoon. I can't take credit for these very distinct changes of rhythm. Bill Gibson wrote that for the stage version.

Film, after all, is rhythm. That's what bothered me about someone re-cutting *The Left Handed Gun*. There's nothing really terrible about the recut. When directors complain about someone else recutting their film, it's not as if someone totally desecrated it. But a director has a rhythm in mind, a certain way he wants to tell the story. The film might start slowly and then pick up velocity. A film is made up of a series of pieces, events and experiences. If you change an event here, you also change it there.

The great thing about United Artists during the days we made *The Miracle Worker* is that they never suggested changes inside the film. They looked at it, sometimes they didn't like it, but they left it alone. They said, "The filmmaker knows what he is doing." I only wish Hollywood would learn that lesson. They don't know what they're doing, and they're damaging the medium. Not that it won't recover. Every medium goes through a period of fools, which is where we are at now.

Q: The Miracle Worker *has some elaborate stream of consciousness scenes, with double exposure, rather strange sound, and grainy picture.*
A: It's a historical fact that Annie herself had very bad eyesight. She was medically blind and had attended a school for the blind. I wondered how to convey that experience to an audience. One part of this is that Annie lost her little brother in the orphanage to tuberculosis, so in a sense one of the things she is doing is redeeming a life. She's calling back to life in Helen the life she feels guilty of having lost in her brother. All of this is experienced through eyes that barely see. We experimented with the camera by putting a plate between the lens and the film. We discovered that if we had a tiny hole in the plate the light would come through and get onto the film emulsion. We then blew it up to the point where the emulsion could barely hold the image. We stopped at the point where the image started to abstract and had become dots and wiggly lines. I think it was something like sixty-four times the size of the original image, so what we had on film was just this little dot of light enlarged to fill the screen to give the hint of an image. We also changed the speed of the sound. It's about highlighting the differences between so-called "objective" film and so-called "subjective" film. In this scene, the two eventually become one.

Q: *You spend a lot of time in the editing room. Do you think your interest in editing is related to your work in live television, when the director was also an editor?*
A: I think it does. I was very fortunate back then. Not only were we directing and editing the shows but, when we were on the air, the directors

were also acting them out. Though you might plan to cut on a particular line, when the actors were live in the middle of a performance, something changed. You had to be in emotional synchronicity with them. I think that everybody who went through that period of live television became very respectful of what actors do. We would sit right beside the camera playing a scene with the actors. Now, I'm a terrible actor, but it's about knowing where the actor is emotionally. Is the actor there yet? Is he or she going to be there in a moment? I can't do that if I'm back here. I have to be involved. Warren Beatty made me sit under the camera. He wanted to be able to see what I was doing.

Q: *Being so interested in editing, do you think you shoot film differently than other directors?*
A: Yes, I think so. I shoot film based on this concept of rhythm. I want to be able to control it. If you cut into a dolly shot, it feels like someone just slammed a door in your face. If you cut out of a dolly shot before the dolly has stopped moving, you feel like somebody has pulled you out of your chair. There is a subconscious rhythm when you are shooting. When I have one of those dolly shots, like at the end of *The Miracle Worker*, I'll do it fifty times until I get it right, knowing I won't have any other material to cover this scene. You don't shoot a film in sequence. Because you shoot based on locations, you might start on a scene that's in the middle of film. In one go you shoot all the sequences in a particular location regardless of where they'll end up in the film. The day of shooting might be hot, cold, the crew might be angry, things might not be going well. Regardless, you have to go out and shoot. Sometimes if you shoot the scene based simply on how you're feeling that day, when you come into the editing room and put the scene in its proper place, you want to die. You discover it's terrible because it was played in a different way and at a different rhythm from the rest of the film. I like to have control of that rhythmic aspect in the cutting room, so I cover scenes in a lot of different ways. It's not that I don't know what to do with the scene, it's just that if I'm standing out in the middle of Montana in 120-degree heat, what I'm able to perceive then and there might not be what I want in the film that's going to be shown next winter.

Q: *The elliptical storytelling of* Mickey One *relies heavily on the editing.*
A: Yes, it is elliptical. The story goes in one direction and then back again, although the second time you have different information because you have already gone through that loop once before. The film is about a man who feels trapped. Personal entrapment is really the theme of the film, how we can get locked in by our own fear and terror and humiliation. It's a film

about not being a complete person. That humiliation is what gives it that elliptical turn, so I thought we should tell the story that way too. We start out and see things happen once. Along the way, we pick up knowledge about the main character. Then we see it all happen again, and eventually it comes down to a scene where he's standing alone in the middle of a bright light, trying to figure out who he is, who those people are behind the light, what they want of him and what he wants of himself. That's the beginning of the film's denouement.

Q: *When you edited the film were you influenced by European cinema?*
A: Yes. Godard had sent out a message to everybody with *Breathless*. He said, "You don't have to worry about visual continuity. Go where it's interesting." Hollywood had spent thirty years developing this narrative continuum that had to be without seams. Get rid of all the seams so it flows. Then along comes Godard and says, "It doesn't have to flow. Life doesn't flow. In fact, it moves in a different rhythm." It's easy not to notice this because when you start working in a medium, you inherit all the prejudices of that medium. It's true in painting. The big moments of change in art happen when someone does something crazy. Cubism? Are you crazy? We look at Impressionism now and say, "That's the way it looks." But the early Impressionists had such scorn heaped on their heads. People hated them.

Q: *Can you say something about your relationship with Dede Allen, who has edited many of your films?*
A: Dede is a wonderful editor and collaborator. First and foremost she understands actors. The whole Meyerhold theory of rhythm is one we share, so we work very quickly and closely together. We see things in a similar way. Dede has characteristics that I don't have. She's very dogged and will stay with something until it's right. I'll say, "Come on, that's enough. Let's leave that alone." I'll come back the next day, she'll show it to me, and it'll be totally different. "When did you do that?" I'll ask. And she'll say, "Oh, I stayed here all night working on it." She's crazy but wonderful and gets things better than I ever imagine they could be.

Q: *You have always tried to find new and unusual ways to portray violence in your films. One example is Brando's death scene in* The Missouri Breaks.
A: I think that was in the script where Jack Nicholson says, "You've just had your throat cut." It's a pity that scene isn't as good as it should be. We had Marlon propped up against a board. I'd ask him to do one more take and to give me something more. I don't know how many takes we did. Finally, at a moment when we didn't have the camera rolling, he said, "Is this what you

want?" and did this death paroxysm that was just wonderful. Unfortunately, we never got it on film. We've all seen chickens with their heads cut off. I felt we should be seeing someone on screen whose body is fighting for air, but it didn't happen. That's life.

Q: *The audience probably expects his death to be much more spectacular after having seen him kill all of Nicholson's friends. Were you playing with the audience's expectations?*

A: You can develop expectations in the audience and then change those expectations, but if you don't have something of what they want and expect, you've failed the narrative. With *Missouri Breaks* I think I failed the narrative. A lot of people wanted a real shoot-out between the two of them, but I said, "We've seen that a million times." Only I didn't come up with something better. I felt it needed a whole scene before that, one of the two of them really stalking each other. The way it turned out it's only Jack stalking Marlon.

Q: *Scenes of violence in your films last a long time, for example the beating of Marlon Brando in* The Chase *and Warren Beatty in* Mickey One.

A: I guess it's just my way of reacting to when John Wayne punches someone once that's the end of the fight. Maybe that's the end for John Wayne, but when you look at two guys in a bar fight, it's the dumbest, most awkward thing imaginable. They fall over, they bump each other, it goes on interminably. Marlon said to me, "If we're going to do this scene, let's really do it until the brutality is boring." The idea was his. Instead of throwing movie punches he said, "How about if we really hit each other but we shoot it at twenty frames instead of twenty-four?" They really are punching him. They action was filmed slow, but then projected at regular speed. You see the fists land and the distortion of flesh, just like in real fights. It worked like a dream.

Q: *In some films you connect violence with humor. For instance,* Bonnie and Clyde *becomes more and more violent which is unexpected since the earlier part of the film is comic. At the start of* The Missouri Breaks *Nicholson's friends are like little boys, but it gets darker and darker, and in* Little Big Man *there are clashes between very violent and humorous scenes.*

A: In *Bonnie and Clyde*, until they rob the bank with C. W. Moss outside, they haven't killed anyone yet. C. W. is outside the bank in the car and keeps it running. Bonnie and Clyde get out of the car and go into the bank. C. W. sees somebody pull out and sees a parking place and thinks, "Well, I'll park the car." It's dumb, but then he's a naïve little country boy who's robbing a bank for the first time. The bells go off in the bank and Warren and Faye come running out. Where's the car! Oh my God, there's the car parked between two other cars! They have to get into the car but C. W. has to back it up. All the while the bell is ringing and Warren is getting more and more frantic. It's funny. Finally he gets the car running, and out of the bank comes somebody who jumps on the running board. Without thinking Warren turns and fires and kills him. It's about moving from comedy to violence in one sequence. From that point on it's irreversible. They can never go back. Life is over for them at that moment. They change from being kids and bank robbers to killers. Then comes that scene in the movie theater when they are watching the girls dance to "We're in the Money" and Warren is furious with C. W. Moss. Faye is simply loving the movie. For her it's OK. She just wants to watch the movie. I wanted three different levels of perception about that existential moment when their lives have changed irrevocably, and for me humor is the best way to do this. It disarms the characters, it disarms the audience. You get there and only afterwards realize, "My God, we killed somebody. We'll never be able to go back to where we were two minutes ago. We'll never be those same people again." For this reason, I think it's one of the best sequences in any of my films.

Q: *Do you see any connection between* The Miracle Worker *and* Night Moves? *In both films lots of scenes are staged around windows. In a way Harry Moseby is blind and searching for his own identity.*

A: That's actually the point of the story. This was a period when we'd had all those assassinations in America. It was a terrible period, and I felt we were wandering around in a kind of blindness unaware of what we were doing to ourselves. It was a crazy period, and I thought we should tell this detective story in a way that could only be understood by what we see, not by what we are told. That's the way the film ends. We learn who has been doing these things at the exact same moment Harry Moseby learns it: by looking through the glass-bottomed boat. We worked backwards from that moment in the film. Since that was going to be one of the film's key images, I decided to go back and start the film with allusions to that image. Similarly, in *Bonnie and Clyde*, during the family reunion scene when Faye meets up with her mother, there's one shot of a kid rolling down a hill in slow motion. It's part of my game with the audience. I'm saying, "When that comes up again, pay special attention to it. It doesn't mean anything now, but it's like a piece of music. When you hear that sound again, things are going to change."

A Summing Up

MICHAEL CHAIKEN AND PAUL CRONIN/2007

Q: *What are your first thoughts upon reading the interviews in this book?*

A: That interviewers really do ask such silly questions. For example back in the day so many interviewers asked me about Billy the Kid being gay. I never thought of Billy as being gay. *The Left Handed Gun* is about adolescence, and for me Billy was just a confused young man. To have answered questions like that seems absurd to me today. In most interviews, especially the press junket ones I would do, I'd never get a chance to elucidate my answers to these often ridiculous questions. Most of the time I've also been edited into the ground and consequently the portrait of me that some of the early pieces paint isn't accurate. Unlike some of the later interviews in this book, the early interviews read so insubstantially that I wonder if readers will get anything from them. I suppose it's because while some interviewers are genuinely searching for ideas, others are there to validate positions they have brought to the table.

Q: *The format of the University Press of Mississippi books is to establish a historical chronology, which means it's useful to include pieces from all stages of your career, however awful.*

A: Sure, but I don't believe some of the earlier pieces have any weight historically speaking. The quality of the questioning is very poor. You're much too generous to the interviewers. They're dopes.

Previously unpublished interview, conducted in summer 2007.

Q: *We'll look into cutting a few of the interviews.*[1]
A: I would appreciate that.

Q: *We have a few questions based on our editing of everything that precedes this interview.*
A: Sure.

Q: *As a child you acted in high school?*
A: I was mainly backstage actually. I had a deep voice back then and would shout from off-stage in a series of rather terrible plays.

Q: *And then you worked at your local radio station?*
A: In those days they would dramatize the news and needed, for example, Stalin to make a declaration of some kind. They would employ someone to do a Russian accent, so some of us who were still at school did this. The job paid rather well. This was at the time when my father was dying.

Q: *You were at the Battle of the Bulge?*
A: Yes, but I wasn't front line. Ours was more a defense action. We were in the King's Hunting Lodge before turning tail and running. We got the hell out of there, and they chased us to Liège. I'd been in the 106th infantry, and just before the Ardennes I was transferred to something called 15th Army Headquarters. I was with them all the way across the Rhine into Germany, which is where we were when the war ended.

Q: *Did you see* Band of Brothers?
A: I did, and it rang quite true to me.

Q: *Many influential American directors of that era fought in the Second World War.*
A: Having emerged from the war alive was a kind of license to be unrestricted in our filmmaking and ideas.

Q: *You taught acting at Black Mountain College?*
A: Well, kind of. I had just arrived from Germany where I'd spent time running the Soldiers Show Program, which was originally headed by Captain

---

1. *We looked into it and decided to cut three short superfluous pieces, though we did leave most of the early interviews Arthur is referring to. To cut anything for the reasons the subject of this volume suggested seems contrary to the overall strength of this book's format. The point of a collection like this is to witness the evolution not just of a particular film director's ideas but also the way he is handled by interviewers.*

Josh Logan, but I never really did much beyond taking on an organizational role. It wasn't as if I was directing the show. The whole thing was designed to entertain the incoming army of occupation. I think the idea was to divert the soldiers from the German women. I worked as a stage manager while we toured around Germany, and when the war ended in Europe, I decided to stay and make some money, so I went to Heidelberg and got demobbed, and they left me in charge of the show. This was where I got my first experiences of working with professional actors. When I got to Black Mountain, I told various faculty members about this, and they said I should teach an acting class. I told them I really didn't know much about acting, but they insisted. When they announced the course, I explained I would get a book about Stanislavsky, and we would start together on page one. Out of a student and faculty population of maybe 120 people, sixty showed up. I thought, "My God, you're all terribly misguided. I don't know anything about what I'm about to teach."

Black Mountain was structured around the idea of trust. The people who taught there never imposed particular ideas or classes on students, instead they trusted the students and their need for knowledge about certain things. The whole thing grew out of individual encounters between students and teachers. There were no courses of study as such. You were just there, you studied whatever you wanted. If you wanted to study philosophy, somebody would say, "Bill was the head of the department of philosophy at Chicago." Scholars would come through for months at a time. They wanted to write a book, so Black Mountain gave them a place to live and food, and they wrote a book. In was a wonderful place. We had all these fine intellectuals there, including people from the Bauhaus in Germany. They were allowed into the country because they were artists but weren't allowed to teach in the universities because they weren't American. It was crazy. For about ten years they were stuck between being refugees and not being able to do what they wanted to do, then suddenly the universities woke up to the fact that Walter Gropius was there. Then Charles Olson and a group of poets came to Black Mountain, and it became a center for poetry with critics like Alfred Keyes and Isaac Rosenfeld, but by that time I had left to go to Italy. At Black Mountain I was reading a lot of T. S. Eliot, and he kept speaking about the Italian Renaissance poets. I became interested in the country and thought, "I have two more years on the G.I. Bill, where do I want to go?" I wanted to look at paintings, try to read a little bit of Italian, and that's what I did. Italy was very poor at that time, so I could live on the little bit of money I had from the G.I Bill. I would just travel around and read.

Q: *And you studied acting with Michael Chekhov?*
A: I took some classes—maybe eight sessions—with him when I was out in Los Angeles training floor managers and working as an assistant director on the *Colgate Comedy Hour*. I had been sent out there by NBC in New York because it was the beginning of national programming. Previously live shows from the East stopped around Colorado, I think it was. More and more programming started to come out of California, and so more and more people needed to be trained as floor managers.

Q: *What do you think of the state of theater today?*
A: Theater is much weaker in New York now than it was when I started out. I think one problem is that the writers are working for Hollywood studios. Many talented young writers come right out of film school or university and head over there to make a fortune. That's their dream. Nobody is writing for the theater, even though it's one of the best places to train to be a good screenwriter. This is why I started a theater on 42nd Street, the Actors Studio Free Theater. I took the money from our program *Inside the Actors Studio*. We get a royalty from that which I put into a theater where we would do new plays with very good actors. We didn't charge for it. It's an interesting audience that comes to free theater. Some are very well-to-do, and some can't afford to go to the theater at all.

Q: *Throughout the book you rail against the studio system even while you worked within it for so many years. Did you ever think about making your films outside that production model?*
A: Not really. There was no real way to break out of it, even though I started making films at a time when the studios were on their knees. If you wanted to make a little film, you had to do what Cassavetes did, which was get out there with a bunch of buddies, stay drunk, and do it. But with my reputation I couldn't get a 16mm film distributed. The unions would never have touched it. Today it's all been relaxed, but it just wasn't possible for me to work that kind of way back then. In a way I see myself as the middle ground between Cassavetes and those who totally capitulated to the studio system and bought right into it with those gorgeous homes out in Los Angeles.

Q: *You started making films at a point when the studio system was fragmenting, bringing your personal sensibilities to that structure. A few years later* Bonnie and Clyde *was at the vanguard of what is now called the "New American Cinema."*
A: The studio system—and the way it works today—was not designed for unusual films or working practices that deviated from the way everyone was

used to. I remember starting out on *The Left Handed Gun*. I had heard that John Ford, who was well aware that a studio editor would end up cutting his film, would shoot only what he needed, nothing more. Very little coverage. That was my plan on *The Left Handed Gun*, though actually I had no alternative because we had such a tiny budget. I went out to the location beforehand and nailed markers to the ground with details of which lenses needed to be used. All I was asking for was two cameras where they usually used one, but the studio cameraman felt terribly insulted. It just wasn't something these people were used to. Directors were expected to come in and throw themselves at the mercy of the studio technicians. These guys had come up through the apprentice system in Hollywood. You can imagine how upset they were with me.

Of course it took a few years for the studio system to fragment. The span was probably 1957 to 1967, from *The Left Handed Gun* to *Bonnie and Clyde*. Between those dates the orthodoxy of Hollywood drove me out of the business. Someone telling me "I'm going to edit your film" just about knocked me over, so working in the theater was much more appealing to me at the time.

Q: *Over the years you've had two production companies. The first was Florin, established in 1958, the year of your first film.*
A: That was just me. I had just done five shows on Broadway, they were all hits, and I needed a company to cover myself. It was for tax reasons. Like many others I incorporated myself and lent my services out for a fee, which meant I was working for my own company.

Q: *The second is Tatira-Hiller that you established with Warren Beatty. Where did those names come from?*
A: Tat is the nickname of Warren's mother, and Ira was his father's name. Hiller is my middle name. Simple really. We actually set that up around the time of *Mickey One*. In the fifties lots of people, including lots of actors, were setting up companies. It was the beginning of the destabilization of the studios. Up until this period the studio had the whole game, they owned everything. After television struck a blow in the early fifties, they were obliged to make more and more deals with the stars, who wanted more control. From the studios' perspective it was a kind of anarchy, but it was really only individuals carving out ownership of their own work.

Q: *There is very little talk of documentary film in this book. You seem to have an intrinsic distrust of the form.*
A: I do. Up until recently it was unacknowledged that documentaries were essentially half-fictional. For years the old documentarians were really de-

fensive. "There's nothing invented here," they would say. "I was there and just shot what I saw." But of course the preselection that goes into making a documentary, just deciding on a subject matter, means the whole thing is built on a constructed narrative. Today it's acknowledged that this way of working is the product of invention and the filmmaker's perception of reality.

Q: *You've taken a writing credit on only one of your films.*
A: Yes, but like many directors I worked closely with the writers of the scripts. I co-wrote *The Left Handed Gun* with Leslie Stevens. The character Hurd Hatfield played was my idea, but I didn't want a credit. It just wasn't appropriate. I was very punctilious in those days. The writer is the writer, the director is the director. Of course there was interaction, but you don't invade anyone else's territory. That's how we worked. It's something I learned in the theater: the writer's words are sacrosanct. The tradition in television was to work with the writers on the script, and these guys were excellent writers who knew more than I did. I certainly wasn't teaching them anything, but at times it was good for me to ask certain questions and have them elucidate certain things. When it came to *Alice's Restaurant*, I knew Ray and Alice from Stockbridge, Massachusetts, and the original idea was mine, so I took a writing credit for the film.

Q: *Back in the early fifties you wrote some television plays?*
A: I can barely remember that, but yes I did. They were crappy little scripts, but I was trying to get started. Ezio Pinza had a show on the network, and the guy who was producing it asked me for something, anything. I wrote a script and gave it to them, but the director of the show said, "I don't know how to direct this. You direct it." So I did direct at least one of them, perhaps two. It was actually the first thing I worked on there, so in point of fact I started out as a writer/director.

Q: *What are your feelings today about what happened to you with* The Train?
A: In a sense I look back at what happened and feel quite fortunate. If I'd made that film, I believe I would have gone the wrong way. I would be rich and in Hollywood, deep in the system. Of course there were some really good people in that world, but fortunately I got fired. At the time I was upset because I had brought that film into existence, but the whole thing was a startlingly clear demonstration of the way the industry works. With the perspective of forty years I can sit here and say I'm glad it happened. I don't know if I'd have had enough resistance to the Hollywood life that was opening up to me.

Q: *And the following year you made* Mickey One, *which is so radically different from most studio films. There are clear influences from the French New Wave, but were you also aware of the tradition of New American Cinema? Did you know people like Shirley Clarke and Amos Vogel?*

A: I knew Shirley but hadn't really seen many of those kinds of films. I was just too busy. I did five Broadway shows and two movies back to back. It was nonstop. And I have to confess: I just wasn't that interested in movies.

Q: *Not many directors have juggled both theater and film in the way you have done.*

A: True. When I think about it, theater is probably more exciting than film. A good script of two hours and a heavy hitter like Anne Bancroft can really take you a long way.

Q: *When it comes to directing actors, is there a difference between film and theater? Is there a difference between acting for film and theater?*

A: What I can say is that there's certainly an important quality of throughness you learn as a theater actor, and as an actor if you spend all your time in film—which is a much more fragmented process—you'll never really learn this.

Q: *Does a good film director also need to be able to work in theater?*

A: I think that's being unfair. Take Howard Hawks, for example, a director I admire and who—to my knowledge—never worked in theater. Interestingly live television was a lot like theater, but with cameras.

Q: *One thing that comes through from the very start of this book is your appreciation of French cinema of the era. At the same time you mention that it was the French critics who first publicly appreciated your films. You worked with the cinematographer Ghislain Cloquet on* Mickey One *at a time when not many American directors made films in America with foreign cameramen.*

A: I knew I wanted to shoot *Mickey One* in black and white, but by then most of the American cameramen were shooting in color. I screened one of Ghislain's films, it might have been Becker's *The Hole* or Louis Malle's *Le Feu follet*, and invited him over. He spoke halting English, and I spoke halting French. I was very fond of him, such a wonderful cameraman. Just after *Mickey One* he shot two films for Robert Bresson. I worked with him again on his last film, *Four Friends*.

About the influence of the New Wave on my work, and maybe American cinema of the time, I don't think there's such a direct cause and effect. It was more about the possibilities of film that were emerging here just as much as in France. With directors like Nick Ray, Anthony Mann, and Sam Fuller it was in the air, showing up in little spots, begging to come to the surface.

Q: *A lot of directors talk about their collaborations with cinematographers, devising color palates, things like that.*
A: Not me, I leave it pretty much to the cinematographer. I never talked about things like color, except with *The Missouri Breaks*, where I had an image in my mind of the West a having striated light, with light hitting everything through cracks. Of course I always went out of my way to establish a good relationship with the camera operator because I had to trust him to shoot in exactly the way we'd rehearsed. When I was working as a TV director, I had a good sense of what lenses I wanted for specific shots. There were so many new developments coming in every month, like zoom lenses. Before this the entire structure of filming was based on turret lenses, which meant that if you were on camera A you had to make a cut to another camera B so you could rack the turret on camera A over and change the lens. These spinning lenses were the kind of thing we constantly thought about when live on air. But even a few years later, in Hollywood, the number of lenses available to us had increased tenfold, and film stock was much faster, so it was all very different from the relatively primitive world of television in the fifties. The technical aspects of film never intimidated me, I just took it for granted that when working with a crew I would be able to work out what we needed. The real skill I learned working on live television was being able to walk into a room or onto a set and immediately see the interesting angles. The placement of the camera certainly never intimidated me.

Q: *Was the impact of* Bonnie and Clyde *really as earth-shattering as they say?*
A: From our perspective, yes. We were flabbergasted. But for the head of distribution of Warner Bros. and Jack Warner himself it was a nightmare. "What the hell is this?" they said. When the film was first released, they had no idea what to do with it and threw it into drive-ins down South. They figured the redneck kids would like the guns, and for the executives it was an exploitation film, a B-movie. Naturally it died a quick death, even though in the few places it was released in the North the film had a real synchronicity with how the young people were feeling politically. They were looking for some identification and validation, and *Bonnie and Clyde* really seemed to speak to them. Warren heard that message and went to Jack Warner and begged him to re-release the film, which they did, and it was a great success. That's when the line "They're young . . . they're in love . . . and they kill people" came about. It got a lot of people into the movie theaters.

It was fascinating to see how people in Europe responded to the film. The studio wondered if it would play anywhere outside of America, but in Scandinavia and London and Paris they were dressing up like Bonnie and Clyde. They stood up and screamed. What was strange was when the critics retracted their original reviews. Pauline Kael convinced Joe Morgenstern to retract his *Newsweek* review, after which the critical blocks began to tumble. I remember Bosley Crowther of the *New York Times* reviewed *The Miracle Worker* and basically said I was the destiny of American film. Then he saw *Mickey One* and blasted it. We were at a discussion group at Lincoln Center, and I said to him, "What the hell was that? If you don't like the film that's fine, but don't attack the whole impulse to try and do something new." He reviewed *Bonnie and Clyde* when it screened in Montreal and was just furious. The more he hated it the more the letters poured into the *Times* telling him how wrong he was. He would retaliate, so week after week there were battles on the pages of the newspaper. Eventually he boxed himself into a corner and was fired.

Q: *The sound in* Bonnie and Clyde *is quite brutal.*
A: The gunshots at the end of the film are actually Jack Palance's explosive gunshot when he kills Elisha Cook Jr. in *Shane*. We used the same sound effect. We screened *Bonnie and Clyde* to the press for the first time before it was absolutely finished, and Warren had his hand on the volume levels. When it came to the end sequence, he looked at me and I gestured that he should make it louder. Joe Morgernstern saw this, and as a result of that I think he developed his idea that the film was purely exploitative.

Q: *Many interviewers over the years have asked you about the violence in your films.*
A: To my mind, the Second World War really cut violence loose in every imaginable and terrible way. It's no longer the world of Renoir's *La Grande Illusion*. I saw enough violence during the war to make me think it wasn't something we could ignore or sanitize. In those days there were rules from the Hays office that said you couldn't have someone shoot a gun and someone else get hit in the same shot. There had to be a cut in between. I thought the hell with that. Remember, this was during the war we were watching on television. We were seeing young men in body bags with their chests open. I always felt that in *Bonnie and Clyde* the violence grew out of what was happening to these people. The violence was never a central part of the story, unlike the work of people like Tarantino.

Q: *Just after* Bonnie and Clyde *you spent time doing theater in Stockbridge.*

A: I first went to Stockbridge in the early fifties. Bill Gibson and his wife introduced me to the place. I had met Bill in 1948, and we corresponded during the time I was in Italy. When I got back, I would stay with them in Stockbridge, and I just fell in love with the place. Peggy and I got married up there. Anyway, there was a summer theater program there, but summer stock was failing by this point. I don't know why, but it just wasn't working. Viveca Lindfors and George Tabori, her husband who was a very good playwright, had the idea of starting a theater festival where we would do work of more substance than regular summer stock. We would have a longer substantial rehearsal period, for example. I got some money from David Picker at United Artists, and we got started. The first year was extraordinary. We had Dustin Hoffman, Gene Hackman, Estelle Parsons, and Frank Langella, and did quite ambitious plays. They were primarily classics though we did do a new play by Elaine May. There was community involvement, but they didn't really respond. They wanted their conventional little summer stock theater. What we were doing was too heavyweight and it lasted only a couple of years. Bill Gibson took over the running of it. I always considered it a success. I believe the phrase is a *succès d'estime*.

Q: *Were any of the productions filmed?*
A: No, because the Equity rule was that you couldn't photograph a stage play. Throughout my earlier career it was absolutely forbidden. Equity was terrible about it, and everyone was fighting for jurisdiction. The kinescopes they made of my television shows were all wiped. They had copies at one point but destroyed them all. Neither union—SAG and AFTRA—would bend.

Q: *We're curious about the things that have inspired you in the early years. Poetry? Fine art? Literature?*
A: It's difficult to say with any exactness. I hadn't ready any serious literature until I went to Black Mountain where I read a lot of the Russian and French canons, for example. It was an intense period of reading and reading. In Italy too, where I studied art too. Where better to do that? Remember there is a lot of drama in the Renaissance paintings, for example Masaccio. There is a vibrant tale inside each of those images. It was a ball to be able to wander around Italy for no money tracking down a specific painting.

Q: *You mention Freud in one of the interviews.*
A: That was more of a personal thing. I really wanted some information about my relationship with my father.

Q: *And what about your political education and interest in social justice? When did that start?*

A: It was just always there, certainly during and after the war. When I was at Black Mountain, we were in the South and there was a small civil rights group that I was involved with. My army training had been down there too, so I had a pretty clear view of just how dreadful it was. Years later, when I was living in Sammy Davis Jr.'s house in California while I was making *The Chase*, during the Watts riots, a lot of guys from SNCC [Student Non-Violent Coordinating Committee] would come to the house and hang out and raise money. And of course Marlon was very active.

Q: *Several of the interviews talk of the time between* Little Big Man *and* Night Moves *when you did not make any films.*
A: *Little Big Man* was physically a killer production, and I just ran out of gas. I was also rather depressed about the whole nature of where we were, politically and culturally. I taught at Yale for about a year, a small postgraduate class in the School of Art and Architecture, not the drama school. I can't begin to tell you the scripts I turned down, projects that went on to become great films. The break I took was really only me wanting to take a step back and evaluate where I was, and also the desire to spend time with my children. I just wanted some time at home, that's all.

Q: *You worked with the Kennedys in the sixties. What exactly did you do?*
A: I first worked on John's campaign. I taught him how to debate with Richard Nixon because that was the first ever major television debate, which is why they came to Fred Coe. Fred and I were these veterans of live television. The very simple thing we said was, "Go to the close up." John Kennedy in a closeup is going to be very much more appealing than Richard Nixon. Each candidate had each hired a sort of advertising agency to advise them, and they made certain rules. "If you go to a closeup of your candidate, we're going to do the same thing for ours, and for the same amount of time too." They had stopwatches and every time we went in, they did too. Of course this is what wrecked Nixon. When Bobby started to run, the people from the Jack Kennedy campaign called me and asked for help. We made the first sort of political campaign commercial for Bobby in Washington. Then he went to California and never came back. I was going to stay on and do the whole campaign.

Q: *Many of your films—notably* Alice's Restaurant *and* Four Friends—*are about what went on during the sixties in the United States and, importantly, the disappointments many people felt once the decade was over.*
A: Here's the thing: I didn't actually take the sixties very seriously. I thought there was an awful lot of theater going on. Of course issues like Vietnam and

civil rights were very real, and the opposition to the war and racism was, I thought, splendid. Progress was certainly made. But in certain areas this opposition was elevated to a level of insubstantiality. It was more show than substance.

Q: *What does your Jewish background mean to you?*
A: Nothing. I explored it personally around the time of the Holocaust, but it never ended up in my work. Both my parents were born in Lithuania, but I don't know when they came over. By the time I was conscious, they were in the midst of a divorce, and vituperation and ugly talk was dominant. I was never inclined to say, "So tell me about yourselves." My mother worked as a nurse at the Good Samaritan Dispensary on the Lower East Side and spoke Yiddish, but never to me and my brother.

I was always more interested in being a human being than being a Jew. I have no religion. What offends me about religion is the sectarian tribalism involved. I don't find any pleasure in all that huddling.

Q: *There is hardly any talk in the book about music.*
A: When it comes to films like *The Left Handed Gun* and *The Chase*, I had no control over the music whatsoever. Of course some of my films, like *Mickey One* and *Night Moves*, have very interesting scores, but to me music is just supportive. For some directors music is absolutely central to their vision, but not for me. It's not primary. The action is primary.

Q: Inside *is a good film. Terrifying and powerful.*
A: It came from the manager of Louis Gossett, who owned the script. A very strong piece of writing. The story is set at that moment in history when it was possible to perceive the end of the apartheid regime. We all know that the last throes of a regime that's going down in flames are its most savage. I did it for Showtime, a cable TV station, down in South Africa. They were worried about how old I was, so they sent some executive over to check me out. The first day I shot twenty pages, and she didn't bother to show up the next day. I had a very good cameraman, and we used two cameras, which sped things up. Of course I learned to work that way during my television years. In the fifties we would block the film out in the studio, rehearse for six or seven days, and prepare shot lists for each camera. That was the worst part of it for me, this mechanical planning at the beginning. After a while I resisted it and pretty soon was able to do the whole thing without preparing all the shots beforehand.

Q: *What is* Fiorello?

A: Fred Coe and I were talking about doing a TV show called *Biography* which, of course, now exists. I started doing research about Fiorello La Guardia who was New York's mayor of my youth. I felt the story would make a hell of a musical, so I took the idea to Hal Prince and his partner who eventually bought and produced it. It was never my intention to direct the show.

Q: *And* My Mother, My Father and Me*?*
A: I had done *Toys in the Attic* with Lillian Hellman which had been a success. Then she had this bizarre idea to adapt a novel into a stage play and hinted that she wanted me to direct it. I didn't want anything to do with it, so a well-respected musical comedy director did it instead. Apparently it was a total disaster, even though Ruth Gordon and Walter Matthau were in it. It flopped in Boston, and in total despair Lillian called me in Paris where I was and said, "Come to New York and help." I said, "You're a few days from opening, what can I do?" I remember she said, "Are you my friend?" So I got on a plane and came back, but there was really nothing to do. I just sat there and gave a few minor notes, but the backlash from the actors was tremendous. I remember Ruth Gordon, in total histrionics, saying, "I won't do what you ask unless you restore the lines they cut in Boston!" I really had very little exposure to the play. My working relationship with Hellman eventually came unstuck because Spiegel hired several writers for *The Chase* and Lillian assumed I was part of that conspiracy.

Q: *Kazan's name comes up a few times in the book. Did you know him personally?*
A: Sure. I remember seeing Brando in the original production of *A Streetcar Named Desire*. He was so brilliant, but despite the visual ability of the cinematographers Kazan worked with, I never felt that the visual structure of his films was commensurate with the internal power of the stories.

Q: *Is there a film you would like to make today?*
A: I'd love to make a film about the nature and consequences of youthful sexuality and what emerges from that. There needs to be a wonderfully romantic story made about this. It's something that's tickling in the back of my head.

Q: *What does "independence" mean to you?*
A: It's a very flexible concept in the world of film and theater, but it's really about the minimalization of the amount of obstacles that other people can put in your way. There's always someone who thinks they can do it better.

Q: *What do you consider your primary job to be?*
A: Story is the key. I don't aspire to be a philosopher.

Q: *What advice do you have for aspiring directors?*
A: I don't really know what film schools do. They obviously turn out some good people, but when people ask me, "My son wants to be a film director. Where should I send him?" I always say, "Get him into a theater company." It's pretty fundamental: learn about acting. Whatever you feel about their narcissistic tendencies, actors are your basic material as a director. You have to know how read them and know when things aren't quite right, and when the actor isn't comfortable. This comes from spending time with them and observing their process. I learned a lot about directing from working with actors. You can always get help with the technical aspects of film, but with actors it's just you and them. Beyond that, good luck.

INDEX